Unlocking the Secrets of Successful Women

*Minnesota Women Share Tips and Strategies
for Achieving Your Goals and Living Your Dreams*

Joan Kennedy

Unlocking the Secrets of Successful Women
Copyright 2013 by Joan Kennedy
First edition

All rights reserved. No part of this book may be reproduced or transmitted in any form or by any means, electronic or mechanical, including photocopying, recording, or by any information storage and retrieval system, without permission from the author, except for the inclusion of brief quotations in a review.

Throughout the pages of this book, you will witness 40 women succeed by working through their fears, and overcoming obstacles to achieve their dreams.

ISBN 0-9601920-6-9

Publisher: Younique Press, St. Paul, MN

Book design by Alan Pranke

PRINTED IN THE UNITED STATES OF AMERICA

Dedication

I dedicate this book to all the wonderful women who were very generous in sharing their personal stories of how they accomplished their goals—and are now living their dreams.

Table of Contents

Foreword 1

Acknowledgments 3

Introduction 4

Our Stories

1   Never, Ever Quit 5
Kristen Brown – Entrepreneur/Author/Certified Coach/Speaker 11

2   Keys to Success 11
Barbara Hunn – Keys Restaurants

3   Getting Paid for What You Love to do 15
Colleen Szot – Wonderful Writer, LLC

4   A Knack for Thrift Leads to a Career Shift 21
Michelle Dustin – Personal Shopper/Stylist

5   Dancing to Your Heartbeat 25
Deb Lysholm – Dancer

6   Finding Your Own Path 31
Jill Johnson – Business Woman/Management Consultant

7   Success Starts with a Dream 39
JoAnne Funch – Entrepreneur/Dreamer

8   Reinventing New Chapters in Your Life at any Age 43
Nadia Giordana – Author/Speaker

9   You Have to Believe You Can Do It 47
    Tara O'Brien – Real Estate Business

10 One Day at a Time 53
    Marilyn Sellars – Singer/Entertainer

11 A Love of Art Drew Me into Living My Dream 61
    Pat Lindquist – Writer/Consultant for Special Events & PR

12 How Five Became Eighty 67
    Connie Anderson – Author/Editor/Writer

13 Yes, Please 71
    Molly Cox Ziton – Speaker/Humorist/Author

14 H20 For Life – Youth Changing the World 75
    Patty Hall – Co-Founder of H20 For Life

15 Making Hay: The Journey to Entrepreneurship 81
    Linda Hachfeld – Publisher

16 Success: A Daily Journey 85
    Roxanne Zoet – Military/Teacher

17 From Survival to Joy 91
    Gloria VanDemmeltraadt – Writer/Author

18 Attitude is Everything 95
    Julie Kay – Interior Decorator

19 If You Feel Scared; Do it Afraid 99
    Victoria Kriz – Hair Salon Owner

20 Roaming With Ellajane 109
    Ellajane Knott – Columnist, Reporter/PR

21 Fit 2b Well 115
    Julie Lother – Business Owner/Physical Trainer

22 Find Meaning in a Midlife Career Move 119
    Mary Treacy O'Keefe – Co-Founder & President of Well Within

23 God Always Has a Plan; I Just Forgot to Listen 123
    Devie Hagen – Elan Speakers Agency

24 The Russian Express 129
    Zhenya Melnick – Business Woman

25 The Artist in Me Finds Her Wings 135
    Sharon Wagner – Artist

26 From Adversity to Success 139
    Nancy Chakrin – Entrepreneur/Health Care Advocate/Business Mentor

27 The Career Path of a Creative Woman 147
    Melissa Carpenter McGath – Business Owner/Graphic Designer

28 A Life Focused on Health and Wellness 151
    Janice Novak – Director of Improve Your Posture

29 Healing on the Mountain 155
    Meg Blaine Corrigan – Counselor/Speaker/Author

30 An Unwilling Expert 159
    Becky Henry CPCC – Speaker/Coach/Award Winning Author

31 From Barely Surviving—to Really Thriving 163
    Susan St. James – Business Woman

32 A Voice For My Mother 167
    Jaclynn Herron – Teacher/Author

33 Choosing Wisely 171
    Irene Kelly – Coach and Mentor

34 Carving Out a Future…The Old Fashion Way 179
    Kristen Tombers – Butcher/Business Woman

35 How Feng Shui Changed My Life 185
    Carol Seiler – Consultant

36 What I Was Born To Do 189
    Gloria Perez – President/CEO Jeremiah Program

37 Making Her Mark 195
    Kathy Heiland – Author

38 Overcoming Personal Challenges to Help Children in Need. . . . 201
    Andrea Miller – Painter/Writer/Inspirational Speaker

39 Nike Has the Answer: Just Do It! 205
    Diane Keyes – Home Stager and Author

40 The Past Is Not Your Future 213
    Joan Kennedy – Speaker/Author

Additional Tips and Strategies. 223

Biographies—More About These Successful Women. 227

About Joan Kennedy, Story Collector 241

Joan Kennedy

Foreword

In 2013, I was inducted into the Minnesota Women Business Owners Hall of Fame with twenty-five other amazing Minnesota businesswomen. This was an extraordinary honor to be included with these other remarkable women. As the youngest of this inaugural group of inductees, it is humbling to reflect on the 150 years of Minnesota business history represented by this esteemed company. Many of the women selected for this Hall of Fame were role models and an inspiration to me in my early career. They shaped my views of how to become a successful woman entrepreneur and be a leader within our business community.

As a business consultant, I have worked with a lot of business owners, and met a great many more during the years I was president of the Minnesota Chapter of the National Association of Women Business Owners (NAWBO) and served on NAWBO's national board. I have been on the board of directors of the Minnesota Chamber of Commerce and the Greater Minneapolis Chamber of Commerce. Currently, I serve on my second federal board for the U.S. Small Business Administration. I am also chair of the Minnesota Department of Employment & Economic Development's State Small Business Development Center Advisory Board.

All this listing of achievements is to show you that I have seen women achieve—and I've seen them fail. Success comes on many levels, as you will read in the forty stories shared with you in this book. These amazing women pull back the curtain to reveal what it is like to be self-employed—as a consultant, writer, speaker, butcher, baker, decorator, woman in the military, personal shopper, restaurateur, artist, etc.

I hate to admit it, but I still have those days when I worry I'm never going to have another client. I have to work hard to self-talk my way out of it. As human beings, we do not operate at the same level of confidence everyday. It ebbs and flows, depending on the situation. I am like every woman in this book.

I think a lot of women don't believe in themselves. Such crisis of confidence is a success killer, and it is poison to achieving success. It becomes the crutch we use, "Because if I don't try, I can't fail." And therefore, "It didn't happen for me." Well, if you didn't even try, it becomes a self-fulfilling prophecy.

The women I've seen who have had a wide range of success put themselves out there. They ask for more responsibility. They learn from their mistakes, and they never make the same mistake more than once—they simply make different ones. The key difference is they learn.

Many people are just afraid to put themselves in the light because they worry too much about what others will think if they don't succeed. Personally, I admire the women who try, who are willing to ask for help, and who are coachable and implement the sage advice they are given. Frankly, a lot of times, this is my test for young women. If I give her a piece of advice or suggestion, I can tell whether she has implemented it. If she doesn't, I move on because if she's not going to listen to the advice I shared with her when she asked before, why then should I spend any more time with her?

I think for women in general, you have to aspire to more and allow yourself to be in rooms where your voice can be heard. Then trust that people will listen—even if it is only one person. But that means you need to prepare. Lots of women don't put in the work needed to move up into the next level, and it's because we are pulled in too many directions. We've got kids, we've got spouses, and we've got aging parents, and all these things are pulling at us. Sometimes it becomes easy to have an excuse for why you dropped the ball. Staying put is fine, but what if your skills and talents are what the world needs?

Most people aspire to being a great success, but they are not willing to do the necessary hard work. It does not happen without effort. People will say, "Jill, how on earth did you do it?" Trust me, it's not a secret. Yes, I was bold enough to put myself in the position to be acknowledged, but I also did the work at an exceptional level. Success with one client gives you confidence, so then you work to achieve a bigger one.

Take each opportunity as a learning experience and always be learning. This book is a gift to yourself. It's an opportunity to listen with an open heart and to understand that your life can be as wonderful as you dream for it to be.

– Jill Johnson, Johnson Consulting Services

Acknowledgments

First, I must thank the forty women who allowed me to share their wonderful story of living their dreams. Each one is a successful example of doing what she loves.

I would also like to extend my deepest thanks and appreciation to a number of people who made a special contribution with their ideas and thoughts.

My special thanks to Connie Anderson of Words and Deeds, Inc. for her sharp editorial skills, her constant support and handholding, and for keeping everything running smoothly. I could not have completed this book without her, and appreciate her stepping in to help—when help was really needed.

I am very grateful to my dear friend, Laurie Hansen, who contributed many stories of successful women to this book. I will always hold valuable her input, insights and close attention to this work.

Special thanks to Patty Kennedy Bronstien, who continued proofreading the stories through her marriage, honeymoon, and the birth of her new grandson, Sebastian.

I much appreciate the second effort by Gloria VanDemmeltraadt to make this book the best possible. Her keen eye is much appreciated.

My thanks also to Rick Mancuso for his encouragement and much-needed help in making some of the stories immeasurably sharper, to Pam Lund, for her initial editing and personal involvement in this book, and Beverly Lambrecht for helping with the stories in the beginning of this project.

My thanks to the rest of my family and friends, for their continued love and support.

– Joan Kennedy, **Story Collector**

Introduction

Everybody builds a dream in their lifetime. You're either going to build your dream, or somebody else's. So build your own!
—Christopher LaBrec

I am delighted to bring to these pages the stories of so many successful women who work in all fields of endeavor.

I spent a year interviewing and getting to know these successful, talented and passionate women. I was honored that they wanted to be a part of this book and tell their stories of what life demanded of them in order to go beyond their fears, self-doubt and failures and to finally reach the success they work so hard to accomplish.

And my hope is as you read these stories they will inspire, motivate and energize you to pursue your innermost dreams and visions.

So start now by creating a new life for yourself, one that meets your deepest dreams and desires. As Elana Lindquist put it, *Success means fulfilling your own dreams, singing your own song, dancing your own dance, creating from your heart and enjoying the journey, trusting that whatever happens, it will be OK.*

It's a great day in your life when you discover all of your latent abilities, many of which are greater than you realize. So, begin now to create your own wonderful and exciting adventure

*– **Joan Kennedy**, **Story Collector***

CHAPTER 1

Never, Ever Quit

PEACE ... it does not mean to be in a place where there is no noise, trouble or hard work. It means to be in the midst of those things and still be calm in your heart.

– Unknown

Kristen Brown

When I was younger, I thought I wanted to be a doctor, and initially even took pre-med courses in college. However, after a big fat F in my second year of Chemistry (my first-ever grade below a B), I ended up changing my path and getting a business degree. I landed a job in corporate America, however it never felt like it was "enough."

Then in 2007, my healthy young husband Todd died of a heart attack in his sleep—at the age of 30. He had no risk issues, was a tall skinny former college athlete. After he died, I was in a pit of self-pity, anger, regret, sadness and grief—all wrapped together. At the same time, I was raising our daughter, who was ten months old when her dad died.

A couple weeks after Todd died, I got a new boss who made my life very challenging. She wanted me to work long hours, travel, and would be contacting me about work issues late into the evening. All of this on top of my grief prompted me to begin looking at life in a new way. I immersed myself in self-help books on grief, happiness, personal development and work happiness. This made me realize, I needed to do something more with my life, in order to move forward.

After Todd died, one of my biggest challenges was money. I now had a single income, so I had to make enough money to feed us and make house payments. I had always worked full-time. I love to work hard and play hard, and being a stay-at-home parent was never for me. But I always liked having the security net of our dual-income household, so I would have options.

Suddenly having only a single income took away the flexibility, and it was tough to make ends meet sometimes.

I also discovered working for someone else wasn't my dream. I slowly came to realize my dream is to be writing and inspiring others to go after their own dreams to make them a reality. If it were just me, I could live off ramen noodles and water and be perfectly fine living on people's couches. I know money isn't everything, but it is essential when you have a child. I must be a role model and provide her with opportunities for happy growth—a stable home, a well-rounded life of fun activities and exposure to other cultures and ways of living, many of which require money.

In addition to the financial and job challenges after Todd died, I was stressed beyond imagination. I was sick all the time. My brain was foggy, and I couldn't sleep. My hair was falling out. I lost over twenty pounds without even trying. I was a mess, but couldn't figure out how to dig myself out of the deep depression holding me. I was not willing to go down the prescription anti-depressant road. I didn't want to make this choice and then get stuck relying on a pill to feel good or mute my feelings.

I wanted to *feel* what I was feeling emotionally, because I knew how important it was to the healing process. However, I didn't want to feel what I was feeling physically, with the constant illness, weight loss, and hair loss. I tried therapy and always left feeling worse than when I walked into the session. I knew I needed some extra help, so I turned to natural herbal supplements to support my body and brain. I experimented with everything short of illegal that had been shown to improve stress and depression. Still I couldn't find the right thing to help protect and support multiple body systems from the damage stress chemicals can cause when they build up and circulate over time.

So, I created one: Happy Hour Effect, which was a completely unplanned and crazy development in my career and life plans. I'm not a chemist or pharmaceutical expert, or herbalist, but through all of the experimentation, I had also done a lot of research on natural remedies. I put together a formula of ingredients I thought would be effective in targeting the many symptoms stress was causing for me: sleeplessness, moodiness, heart palpitations, hair loss, low energy, and many more. I did more research and found an FDA-approved lab to help me determine the right ratios of the ingredients to ensure your head wouldn't explode from the wrong combination and ratios.

Once I had the formula down, I knew I was onto something. I had done so much research on stress while researching the ingredients that Happy Hour Effect evolved from just a health supplement into a full lifestyle philosophy.

Plus my years of working in retail merchandising put me in perfect position to sell my product to retailers. I took a chance and flew out to GNC for their New Vendor Day. They accepted the product and placed a big order. I took the health supplement to events and even met some celebrities when I showcased it at several events in Hollywood. It was a wild and fun ride, and it exposed me to so many new opportunities. Unfortunately, the cost of selling a health supplement is huge: product liability insurance, product storage fees, shipping, and EDI expenses. It was too much for me to manage on my own, so when the product neared its expiration date in 2012, I made the hard decision to let that part of my business go, and to focus on work/life harmony and entrepreneurship speaking, coaching and media.

This career change began in 2009 when I officially left a well-paid job in corporate America to start living my dream. I started my business, Happy Hour Effect, and also wrote, self-published and promoted my first book, *The Best Worst Thing*, detailing my life after my husband died suddenly. Much to my surprise, it became an Amazon bestseller which helped me secure an agent and multiple offers from traditional publishers for my second book, *The Happy Hour Effect: 12 Secrets to Minimize Stress and Maximize Life*. It shares my stress-reducing secrets and strategies—and it also hit the Amazon bestseller list. My third book, *The Entrepreneur Promise*, is in progress, and helps other aspiring entrepreneurs and authors commit to their goals so the inevitable stresses of life don't sidetrack them.

Now I am living, breathing and growing Happy Hour Effect, which I like to call my "empire in progress." My whole life, ever since I could hold a pencil, I had always been a closet writer. I realized I had always wanted to write, and everything I did supported my goal. I rediscovered folders full of stories and silly childhood poems. Writing became my therapy after Todd died, and I started on my journey to becoming a published author.

My motivation is that it inspires me to inspire others. My daughter motivates me every single day. I never want her to look back and remember a mom who was sad, depressed, or cranky—but to see an amazing mom who survived and thrived, even during the tough stuff in life. I want her to be inspired to do the same thing with her life—whatever she dreams of doing—and to go after her dreams even when times get hard.

It took an army to help me become successful. I have used many coaches and mentors over the years. I attend a writers group called WOW (Women of Words), take different writing workshops and classes, and attend conferences. I also read lots and lots of books. All these things and people helped me reach where I am today—a successful author, speaker and coach.

No one should try to go it alone. You need partners, friends, and family members who are willing to come along on your journey. It's a lonely road if you try to do it by yourself.

It feels amazing, scary and exciting, but most of all, it feels very fulfilling. I never feel like I am going to work; rather this is a natural part of what I need to do every day. My work never feels like a ball and chain or a burden like so many people describe their 40-hour workweek.

In order to get publicity for my book and my company, I read every book available on public relations (PR), exposure and pitching, and took many, many classes and conferences on learning how to position yourself for PR success. The key to getting publicity is to create a strong platform positioning yourself as a credible expert who can keep the audience tuned in, and prevent them from turning the channel. When you step back and remember a producer's job is to engage viewers, you can more easily pitch yourself and what the segment should look like to be interesting and visual.

I now have over a hundred national and local appearances under my belt, and I'm a blogger for The Huffington Post. I started small, did the work and put myself in the shoes of the producers and editors. I do the work for them in creating engaging content that will keep viewers tuned in.

When I got "that call" from a big TV show, I was ready. Through research and experience, I knew the most important thing to remember about media and PR is that it won't make you an overnight success, or bring in instant millions. A media appearance is a *tool* you can use to elevate your credibility, create buzz about your business or book, and give you that X-factor to set you apart from the competition. When I got the call saying "Live with Kelly & Michael" wanted me on the show, I literally screamed. I had been preparing for this opportunity for a couple of years, honing my skills on-air, on local media, and via videos I post on YouTube. And, in fact, it is those YouTube videos the producer found online that prompted them to book me on the show.

When I appeared on this national TV show, they were getting 4.5 million viewers every day and recently had jumped above Ellen to #1 in the daytime talk-show category. I thought I would most definitely see a spike in book sales. But guess what: not even a tiny uptick in sales. I was disappointed, but when it came to booking my next speaking gig, and I mentioned my appearance, the event planner was impressed. I took a chance and quoted *double* what I had been charging. She didn't blink an eye and signed the contract on the spot. This kind of media appearance can be a game changer when you use it the right way. I use it to secure speaking gigs with less effort, charge more for my services, and more easily book other media appearances. But as a freestanding thing, it's only as valuable as how you position it.

I teach a lot of classes and coach clients on how to position and elevate yourself above the competition. This work is gratifying because I did so much research and experimentation figuring out how to do things—and if I can save someone the time and money of recreating the wheel, I'm happy to do it.

Being successful feels and looks different for every person. It depends on how you measure it. For me, success isn't about money, but being able to live a happy, peaceful life with my daughter. A stressful job in corporate America would be secondary to what I especially love to do, which is speaking and helping others.

For other people, success is about money; for others it is about sales quotas, or relationships with family, friends and loved ones.

I think what it takes to be successful is knowing what and how you measure success—and then focusing hard on reaching those goals. Having stick-to-it-ness is essential, and winners never quit, even when the going gets tough. A lot of people have asked me: How did you make this work—being a widow and a single mom—and sometimes having to take a day job? It's because I never ever, ever quit—even when money was tight, even when people were telling me I was crazy, and even when people were criticizing me for making different choices.

At times, I wondered if I was doing what I needed to do for myself and my daughter and our future. It is a struggle every day because it's lots of work being an author, entrepreneur—and single parent. It's a constant juggling and harmonizing act. You have to figure out how to move past difficult things, and not let them drag you down. The past is the past, and we've all got loads of crap in our past; let it go, keep moving forward. Tomorrow is a new day, and every moment is a new chance to start over and keep on going with a fresh attitude.

Success to me means:
Commitment – when you set out to achieve a dream or goal, you must commit 10,000 percent, and not get sidetracked when things get tough.
Harmony – a big dream shouldn't overtake your whole life. You should commit to your goal, but also commit to knowing when to step away for a while and get back to your family, health and relationships.

Fun – if something isn't enjoyable, then why do it? Make every task a joy, even the ones that aren't so much fun.

Connect; don't try to go it alone. Find partners and supporters who can motivate you along the way.

Stay grounded. Remember what motivated you to undertake a change or goal in the first place. Keep this motivation front and center as you make progress so you don't stray or get demoralized or do things for the wrong reasons.

www.HappyHourEffect.com

You have to figure out how to move past difficult things, and not let them drag you down. The past is the past, and we've all got loads of crap in our past, let it go, keep moving forward.

CHAPTER 2

The Keys to Success

Don't let the bastards grind you down.
—Beverly Oien

Barbara Hunn

When I was a little girl, I dreamed of *me—The Superstar Pop Singer*. Without realizing how the process works, the dream kicked in. Shortly after, I won a prize on Ted Mack's Amateur Hour radio show singing "Old Man River" and Patsy Cline's "Crazy."

Just like that.

In those idealistic younger days, I just "jumped right in"—with *dreams* and *dreaming*. I loved the thought of being a star, and participated in an Irish Theater Group, even playing Yenta in "Fiddler on the Roof."

I dreamed.

I've always prided myself in staying active and fit. I love swimming. I'd see myself as a swimmer, thinking, "I am a swimmer." Then during the Aquatennial, I came in first for my age group swimming *five miles* across Lake Minnetonka. I actually never thought of myself as being competitive, but as I think back, I always *wanted* to win, no matter what type of race.

Even though I had a good start in developing success factors by simply dreaming and doing—*stuff happened*. Unfortunate events can obstruct clear, established, and projected pathways. First, my baby brother died. It started an avalanche of sad events in a developing child's life.

My four siblings and I grew up on St. Paul's West Side. My mother was Irish-Lutheran; my father, a stiff-upper-lipped Brit. I was ten when my three-and-a-half-year-old brother died. From then on, my remaining two siblings and I were pretty much on our own—left to our own devices.

The loss took its toll on my entire family. My mother had a major nervous breakdown. Our dad was very sad when his son died, but he never showed any emotions. It was a chaotic time for a while, culminating two years later in my parents' divorce.

We wouldn't forget Billy, and on Sunday, we'd head out to Sunset Memorial Park to visit his grave. Out of the tragedy of losing my brother came the return of visualization and projection because, along the way, I saw my first dazzling blue sparkle of a private swimming pool. So, this positive glow developed from the sad Sunday pilgrimage.

In retrospect, I see successful people have a way of transforming tragedy into hope. Every week, I would look for that pool on the way to the grave, imagining one day I would have my own.

Following in my mother's footsteps, I became a psychiatric nurse. But this career goal was also jinxed almost because immediately after getting a new job, I had to resign. Married with three children and about to deliver Roy, my fourth child, I suddenly was unable to walk because I was so pregnant—and nursing requires a lot of walking. *Go figure.* Right then and there, a chance for a new career was averted.

Raising four children was a challenge, but I'd always been a frugal saver, budgeting everything. I just knew we had to "make do," and we did. Through all this, I kept the picture of a swimming pool in my head. I knew it was what I wanted, and didn't have a clue if I would ever be able to own my own pool.

Back then, a dear friend, Beverly Oien, had great belief in me. I had always been used to hard work. I also knew I had to stay focused to be good at whatever I was doing. Beverly and her business partner bought the Dairy Queen in St. Anthony Park, and I started working for Beverly. It was part-time work making Dairy Queen ice cream *things,* and hot dogs. My kids worked there, too. Beverly had a bad hip and, as it progressed, she asked me to help manage the Dairy Queen, along with her partner.

One day, Beverly took me down to Mr. D's restaurant on Raymond Avenue where we sat in the very last booth. Beverly said, "If I buy this place, would you run it?" I said, "Why not, I could do that." For someone to trust me that much was a true gift. I was thirty-seven at the time, married with four young children—Carol, 14; Jean, 13; Celine, 12; and Roy, 10.

If Beverly thought I could do it, I wasn't about to disappoint her. This became the *first* Key's Restaurant, and I had a hand in naming it. As we were going down to the bank, she said, "We've done everything but name this place." Since Beverly was about to head down to her favorite vacation haunt, the Florida Keys, I thought, "Let's call it *Keys*." I was also thinking I'll probably never get down to the *real* Florida Keys." Many years later Beverly told me that "keys" was her mantra, an image she would focus upon whenever she projected her dreams.

Beverly had faith in me, and to this day, she remains my trusted savior. I treasure her indulgence during those difficult times.

The year was 1973 when the first Key's Café opened with me at the helm. It took a lot of hard work. Then, Keys Restaurant opened at 5 a.m. and closed at 3 p.m., Monday to Friday. We were closed on weekends.

Somehow I just did it. "I worked hard, handled the kids and the house." During the first five or six years I was still married. I was working from four in the morning until four in the afternoon. Then I'd go home and take care of my children. In the morning, before school, the kids would come to the restaurant with me and have breakfast. Then I'd have them make caramel rolls. I'd put together a little "lunch to go," and the school bus would pick them up right outside the restaurant.

The restaurant was my baby. I liked being in the restaurant alone; late at night I'd look around, sense the energy there, and I'd feel very powerful.

That's how it all started. It was like a moving snowball going downhill. I had all the kids working for me. Cooking came naturally for me. To this day, I'm still most comfortable and have the most fun cooking "on the line." There is a community—a kind of dedicated camaraderie that happens when you work alongside the folks who help generate your livelihood: togetherness, common bond, and love.

I was always a partner, but not on paper. When we incorporated in 1980, I then became a legal partner on paper, now owning 50 percent of the stock. Because of health reasons, in 2001 Beverly decided to sell me her stock option for the other 50 percent. She wanted to make sure I was 100 percent owner. At the time, we had seven Keys Restaurants. Beverly was only part owner of the first Keys restaurant on Raymond—and none of the others.

Today, I own the name—and my children now in their fifties, own the restaurants. Forty years later, and nine total Keys Restaurants in the Twin Cities, and I'm still going strong. I still have my name on the Keys on Raymond Avenue and the one at the Foshay Bar and Grill. My philosophy is the same today as it was when Key's first opened. "I give nothing but the best!" It is all about the food and the service; both must be top-notch. The food is all made from scratch, and we use *no* frozen or pre-cooked processed food. Portion control never has been nor ever will be in my vocabulary. I err on the side of *all you can eat!* The cakes, for instance, are big enough to sink a battleship.

Key's is a family business. All my children and several in-laws and grandchildren work with me. It's kind of my job to keep all the balls in the air.

In order to keep up my energy—juggling all those balls, being on my feet at least eight hours a day—I exercise regularly. I love to walk, lift weights, stretch, do sit-ups and, yes, *swim*. I also love to ride my motorcycle; it exercises not only my body, but also my brain. I race through space, trying to honor the speed limit because I earn my escape every day facing the joyous reality of serving both the hungry community of Minnesota and my trusted workers. When I was younger, I thought success meant being able to have a swimming pool. I have since changed my feelings on that subject.

Success to me is getting to wake up every morning, feeling blessed and thankful to get to do the work I love. Success means that I'm passionate about my job. I follow my bliss. I simply pop into the kitchen and create beautiful, scrumptious food every day with my helpers. We make lots of people happy. I've often felt seeking the happiness of others before oneself is the best plan for being truly the happiest.

Hard work, staying focused, and visualizing has been the key to Keys' success. I strongly believe "visualization is a preview of things to come." See the successful person you want to be later. See it in your mind ... now. *Be it now.*

Hard work, staying focused and visualizing has been the key to success. I strongly believe visualization is a preview of things to come.

CHAPTER 3

First, Love What You Do; Second, Get Paid Doing It

If you do not breathe through writing, if you do not cry out in writing, or sing in writing, then don't write, because our culture has no use for it.

—Anais Nin

Colleen Szot

I knew I would be a writer from an early age, and I sold my first article for a dollar at the age of nine. What I didn't know, and what I found nearly impossible to believe, was the idea I could earn a living doing it. Writing was always something I had to do, like reading or eating—it was essential to my life. The idea someone would pay me to do what I love was a pipe dream to me.

My mother always believed in me and gave me my first typewriter. Throughout my adolescence and well into my twenties, I wrote articles for a host of well-known publications: *Scholastic, Highlights, 16, Teen,* and later *Redbook, Esquire,* and *Ladies Home Journal.* I also wrote for local radio stations at a time when they all had their own newsletters: *KRLA* was one in Los Angeles, and *KFWB,* was another, well known as the home of Wolfman Jack. I didn't actually get paid for the radio stints, but received free records and albums. At just fourteen, I earned a spot on Saturday morning radio by interviewing the big rock bands coming to my hometown on tour.

I have always loved fan letters. I would find out who was on tour, when they were landing in my city, and then write their manager, their promo director, even the stars themselves (call it blissful ignorance) and ask for an interview. My theory at the time is—and it still holds true today—these big name people are interviewed by newspaper writers, radio honchos, and record promoters all the time, but how often do they get interviewed by a kid? The response was amazing, and from the ages of 11 to 14, I interviewed Buffalo

Springfield, the Animals, Smokey Robinson and the Miracles, Roy Orbison, the Turtles, and many, many more.

My interviews did triple duty back then. I would write an article for the radio station's newsletter, send in a recorded interview, and then write an article for my local newspaper, or *16* magazine, even *Rolling Stone* on occasion. Finally I got paid. This was the 1960s, when the Beatles, Rolling Stones and Dave Clark 5 were big. It was a great platform for a burgeoning writer.

By the time I went to college, I had managed to save $10,000 to put myself through college. By then, my writing repertoire had expanded to include greeting cards ($25 a card!), and newspapers across the country. I discovered if I researched and wrote an article with no timeframe attached to it, any newspaper would jump on it, rather than have a reporter do all the legwork. Plus, by selling to newspapers around the country, I kept the copyright and the byline and could sell the same article several times over.

For instance, I wrote an article on the infamous St. Valentine's Day Massacre in Chicago. Around the first of the year, I might send it to a hundred newspapers in every state. Then they would file it, and come Valentine's Day, they would resurrect it, and send me a tear sheet and a check. Those checks ran the gamut from $25 to $250, depending on the newspaper and the placement. Every year, for maybe ten years, I would send out the same article to different newspapers, and with one specific story, I probably made close to $10,000. Of course, I was dependent on the honor system of the fine newspaper, but rarely, if ever, did someone stiff me, because they wanted more of the same.

And I obliged, by writing the story of the first Christmas tree, the tradition on Christmas cards, the history of St. Patrick's Day, why fireworks and the Fourth of July are so closely related, and many, many more. The subjects didn't always revolve around holidays, although I personally liked the genre. I would write about historic people (Benjamin Franklin was a favorite), and one little-known aspect of their life (Franklin wrote under the pseudonym of Mrs. Silence Dogood, and the mysterious woman became a popular correspondent); unusual pets; and anything and everything of interest to me. By the time I graduated from college I had quite the writing portfolio.

But another genre of writing appealed to me while in college: TV writing. As a child, I loved *The Dick Van Dyke Show* and fancied myself Sally Rogers. Riding the train into the city (any city, it didn't matter), working with other writers all day, pitching ideas to a TV star…sounded like my idea of heaven. At the time, I hosted a college TV show called *Backstage*, where I would interview people I found interesting, among them: Jonathan Winters, June

Foray (the voice of *Rocky the Squirrel*, *Natasha* and other iconic animated figures), Tom Snyder, and Edward Asner. I had dug into my old bag of tricks to use the fan letter ploy again, and as before, the response was phenomenal. For some reason, these larger-than-life stars jumped at the chance to be interviewed by an unknown host of a little college show. Who knew?

Edward Asner actually became a good friend at the time, and I knew his whole family. They sent me a graduation gift, and stayed in touch for quite awhile. Ed encouraged me to write a spec script for *The Mary Tyler Moore Show (MTM)*, and he even submitted it for me. The MTM Script Consultant, Treva Silverman, took a shine to me, and even used my suggestion of casting Ted Bessell as Mary's boyfriend. To this day, Treva is a Facebook friend.

I went on to write thirty to forty TV scripts for *The Bob Newhart Show, All in the Family, One Day at a Time,* and *Rhoda*. But of those thirty plus TV scripts, I only sold seven or eight. I was told there was basically nothing wrong with the scripts; they were just going a different direction, or losing an actor, or had a different story arc in place, or were developing a spin-off. And TV scripts were very, very different from article writing. If *Redbook* rejected an article I had submitted, dozens of other publications would accept my story. But with TV, you simply can't take a script for *All in the Family* and re-write it for *MASH*. Once it was rejected, for whatever reason, it went into the bottomless desk drawer marked "Unsold."

You can't survive very long writing spec scripts, so luckily I discovered advertising—or, rather, it discovered me. I was freelancing at a radio station when they asked me to do a Public Service Announcement (PSA) for an anti-drug campaign, which meant I wouldn't get paid. I said sure, but I had to write in my off time. I did, and coined the phrase, "Don't be a dope about dope," which became, "Why do you think they call it dope?" It was parodied on Saturday Night Live, and LL Cool J wrote a song titled, "Why Do You Think They Call It Dope?" You never know where an opportunity can lead.

With this as my only experience in advertising, I had to start somewhere, and for me, it was as a receptionist at Benton & Bowles in Los Angeles. The creative director knew I wanted to be a writer, so he would often ask me for a headline for this product, or a tagline, or maybe write an ad for this service. I loved it, and he was so gracious. About nine months later, when I decided to interview for a writing job at another ad agency, he gave me a portfolio full of all the ads, tagline, and headlines on which I had worked. I could go into this interview and say I was responsible for this or that. It was the kindest, most generous gesture anyone has ever shown me in this industry.

I went on to work for some top agencies in Chicago, J. Walter Thompson and Foote, Cone & Belding among them. I worked my way up from copywriter to Senior Creative Director, and in 1994, I decided to open my own freelance company. I returned to my love for television, and decided to specialize in Direct Response, creating one- or two-minute TV spots featuring an 800# or website, and half-hour infomercials. I was blessed to cut my teeth with the iconic NordicTrack brand, then considered the gold standard in fitness, and in infomercials. I often joke about how I did not renew my non-compete with NordicTrack in 1995, and shortly afterwards they went under, which was just timing. I specialized in fitness and counted Tony Little and Jane Fonda among my first clients.

I have to laugh when someone asks if I have experience in a specialized market. Believe it or not, I have been asked if I have "frozen pizza" experience. I honestly believe if you are a good writer, you can write almost anything, with the possible exception of technical or medical writing. I have written four George Foreman Grill shows (I even wrote a show for his daughter, Freeda), eight for Tony Little, and countless more for the Sleep Number bed (Select Comfort), Oreck, AARP, Sharper Image, Tony Robbins, Sony Pictures and many, many more. In the late 1990s, I earned a reputation as the "Golf Writer," and penned award-winning shows for Orlimar Golf, Gary Player, and more. I wrote the first-ever infomercial for Deepak Chopra, and other shows for Olivia Newton John, Joan Lunden, Kathy Lee Gifford, Maria Menounos, Susan Lucci (a longtime hero*)*, Mark Victor Hansen (*Chicken Soup for the Soul*), and a dozen more celebrities. My work has appeared in Japan, Germany, Italy, the UK, Australia and even Dubai.

The lesson here is to never pass up an opportunity. If you're an up-and-comer, take on occasional spec work, ask for copies of the published or broadcast work, and always, always ask for a written testimonial. I have dozens on my website and even some on my client reel.

Think of writing as something to help you earn a living? Research what free-lance writers are charging on an hourly or per-project basis, and build your professional portfolio to showcase your (paid) talents.

Let's say you love decorating or touring open houses. Did you know you can get paid for writing up creative house descriptions—for real estate companies? Are you a foodie or just someone who enjoys gourmet food? Get paid for writing restaurant menus or reviews—and enjoy some of the best meals in your town. Are you spiritual? Many ministers and pastors pay for someone to write their sermons, or a column in the church newspaper. There's also a growing market in writing blogs. Many CEOs, artists, speakers, and other people, simply don't have the time to write their own blog, so they give a free-lance writer a list of topics and pay to have them penned. My good friend Guy Kawasaki, noted author and speaker, was one of the Apple employees originally responsible for marketing the Macintosh in 1984. Today, his schedule is so jam-packed he hires people to research interesting articles for him to post on Facebook. Many, many others hire free-lance bloggers, as well.

Success to me was, and still is, something I love to do and get paid. I found success in an unusual niche—TV commercials and infomercials—and parlayed it into a comfortable income. What are you passionate about? Find it, follow it and do it, and you'll never regret it.

www.wonderfulwriter.com

Success to me was, and still is doing something I love to do and get paid. What are you passionate about? Find it, follow it, and do it, and you'll never regret it.

CHAPTER 4

A Knack for Thrift Leads to a Career Shift

Choose a job you love, and you will never have to work a day in your life.
—Confucius

MICHELLE DUSTIN

One night in March of 2011, when I was lying in bed, this idea just came to me. Excited, I jumped out of bed and ran to grab my laptop. I hurriedly typed an e-mail to Laurel Hansen, the business director at Arc's Value Village Thrift Stores. I told her about my idea, and asked if she would meet with me.

Laurel agreed to meet for coffee. Before our meeting, I did some research and put together a PowerPoint presentation explaining my idea, and why I was certain it would be a success. I felt such confidence and excitement, I didn't even think about being nervous.

As we sat across the table from one another sipping piping-hot coffee, I said to her, "High-end department stores offer free personal shopping services. Why can't Arc's Value Village offer this same type of VIP experience to its customers?"

I told her about the reaction I often received when I'd tell people about my thrift-store finds. The response was always the same, "I wish I could find things like that at the thrift store; I just don't have the eye for it," or "I get so overwhelmed at the thrift store, I just don't have the patience to sift through all those racks."

I described my vision in detail. Customers would schedule their free personal shopping appointment and fill out a brief profile form describing their sizes and style. Then I would do all the legwork, shopping every nook and cranny of the store to find them clothing and accessories matched to their needs. I would coordinate whole outfits for them to try on, and would offer feedback on fit, color, shape, and style.

I explained to Laurel that the completed outfits would be of significant value to customers, saying, "It's relatively easy to compile a collection of great thrifted *pieces*, but the real challenge is creating outfits around those great pieces."

The PowerPoint presentation outlined how a personal shopping service could increase sales, drive brand loyalty, cultivate new customers, and set Value Village apart from other thrift stores. On the final slide, I listed several reasons why I, Michelle Dustin, an avid thrift store shopper, was the one for the job. The last bullet point said simply, "She's got the Gift of Thrift!"

The economy was tanking; people were very interested in saving money while still getting a great value. The green movement was gaining in popularity, and more and more people were opening up to the world of secondhand goods. I told her I was confident it was the right time for this service, saying, "In business, timing is everything."

Laurel, who is now my boss, has a great poker face. Whether she was convinced at the time this it was a fantastic idea—or I had lost my marbles—she didn't let on. I left the coffee shop unsure what would come of it, if anything. Later I learned my innovative thinking and my ambition to make it happen had impressed Laurel.

Initially I was offered a six-month contract to test out the viability of the service. Value Village sent out a press release promoting their complementary new offering. Esme Murphy of WCCO was one of the first to report on this novel thrift service. She scheduled an appointment, and it was evident how amazed she was by the head-to-toe outfits hand-selected just for her, the designer labels, and the rock-bottom prices. Her overwhelming enthusiasm was worth its weight in gold. Moments after her story aired on WCCO, my email inbox quickly filled up, and my appointment schedule was booked up for months.

The service was not only proving to be popular, but also profitable. In a thrift store, where average sales are $15-$20, seldom did you see sales averaging $100 or more. One of my first customer sales reached an impressive $300.

I was beginning to see my own success story unfold before my eyes. During the six-month trial period, I was doing part-time personal shopping services while balancing a full-time career as a quality assurance (QA) editor. QA wasn't my dream job by any means, but I enjoyed it, I was good at it, and it provided a steady income. But as the trial period was coming to an end, I knew I couldn't continue the juggling act. Although the personal shopping service was thriving, I wondered 1) how long could it last, 2) was there potential for me to grow in the position, and 3) am I ready to take a leap of faith?

I was faced with a decision—pursue thrills, risk and adventure, or play it safe. Although I thoughtfully pondered both options, and at times let my fears and doubts sway me, I knew deep down, I'd always regret it if I didn't take a risk and follow my true passion. I told the execs at Arc's Value Village I needed to either make the personal shopping service my full-time career, or walk away. I asked them to make me an offer, and they did.

Lucky me! I now have a full-time career in which I am inspired, excited, and challenged every day. When I reflect on the path that's gotten me here, I am reminded of a quote by the fierce clothing designer, Diane Von Furstenberg, "I didn't know what I wanted to do, but I always knew the woman I wanted to be."

Before that night in March of 2011, when this idea surfaced, I had never considered a career as a thrift store personal shopper, because it didn't exist. So, inspired by Ms. Von Furstenberg, I can say I didn't know what I wanted to do, but I always knew the woman I wanted to be. The woman I wanted to be is one who will follow her instincts, take risks, and blaze trails where there are none.

All the things now your reality were once simply ideas in your consciousness.

CHAPTER 5

Dancing to Your Heartbeat

To get through the hardest journey we need take only one step at a time, but we must keep on stepping.

—Ancient Chinese proverb

Deborah Lysholm

Dance has been an integral part of my life since childhood, and with each passing year, became increasingly instrumental in defining who I am. Striving for a career in dance, more specifically building a performing arts center, was my main focus. Like a freight train heading down the tracks, my passion never derailed.

Since things from the heart speak the loudest to me, I wanted and needed a career that would summon absolute zeal. For this reason, I named my performing arts center *Heartbeat* because all genres of the performing arts must come from the heart to be real.

My introduction to dance was when my mother enrolled me in lessons at a local neighborhood dance studio at age four. Luckily, I had a gifted teacher who was passionate about the art form and teaching. My dance teacher saw something in me at a young age, and continually encouraged my parents to keep me involved in dance. By the time I was in fifth grade, I was literally at the studio five days a week. Soon, people referred to me as, "The girl who loves to dance."

After high school and college, I continued my training in dance with noted professionals in New York City, Chicago, and Los Angeles. My teaching/performing/choreography gigs became more frequent, creating a clear line of vision to my future career. Master teachers and mentors like Dianne Walker, the late Gregory Hines, Jimmy Payne, Savion Glover, and Jason Samuels Smith, to name a few, furthered my education in dance and increased my motivation to open my own performing arts center. However, the biggest motivator was my ever-increasing student base because it reflected my ability as a teacher and dance artist.

A fusion of people, experiences, and dogged determination helped forge my path to success at this stage. My family, friends, dance instructors, and my dance students, gave me confidence I was on the right path. Various jobs in the business world groomed me for managing Heartbeat. The person helping me the most, however—was me. I knew from the onset any rise or fall of success fell *only* on my shoulders, therefore I had to be tenacious and come to grips with a true understanding of the work involved. It required I be married to it. My loveliest cheerleader and co-passenger on this journey was my daughter, Kristin.

Riding in tandem with my desire to build my performing arts center, was my desire to start a new life for Kristin and me. Kristen also began dance training in her childhood and eventually received a BFA in Dance at the University of Minnesota. When Heartbeat opened for business, I had actually reached two goals, a new life for both of us directing the performing arts center we had built.

Of my instructors/mentors, two stand out the most to me. Dianne Walker, a world-renowned tap dance artist, counseled me on many decisions I had to make, connected me with many other dance professionals, and constantly encouraged me to keep moving forward. Gregory Hines took time out of his busy schedule to come to Minnesota to teach a master class for my students and to show support of my desire to build Heartbeat. This master class led to several other classes with Gregory over an eight-year period, and chances to perform with him in Chicago and New York City. He referred to me as "a rose ready to bloom."

I recently published a memoir in which the challenges I faced to fulfill my dream are presented in great detail. Below is a brief summary of my book, *Dancing to My Heartbeat* detailing those challenges:

> "Deborah Lysholm, a professional dancer, prayed she could outrun the bullets as her husband chased her outside on a blustery April night in 1992, aiming a rifle at her. After 23 years of a terror-filled marriage, she knew she had to leave him—no matter how much she feared him and believed his threats that he would find her and kill her. Instead of becoming another statistic, she summoned unbelievable courage to start a new life for herself and her college-aged daughter, Kristin. A cosmic slingshot propelled Deborah and Kristin into an unknown universe, traversing discriminatory court battles including the first-ever domestic violence lawsuit filed in civil court. They staked their place in the performing arts by building

a celebrated performing arts center, capturing the attention of entertainment luminaries, and embarking on exhilarating and often humorous world travels, discovering the women they were meant to be. Their journey "from victim to victorious" is an inspiring odyssey.

"Deborah's story begins with a glimpse of her Norwegian ancestors' explorer spirit and familial mantra: Keep a family together at all costs. Sandwiched between her parents on a motorcycle, Deborah arrives in Minneapolis at the age of four and begins what will be her career and future salvation, dance lessons. In college, Deborah meets Richard, her future husband, and a year into their marriage, her dream of a loving and blissful life with Richard ends abruptly when he violently kicks her in the back during her eighth month of pregnancy. Thus begins a life of fear and pain until the night Richard threatens her with a gun. Fierce survival instincts roar as Deborah bravely seeks a new life for herself and Kristin, enduring the gut-wrenching depths of a first-ever domestic violence lawsuit in civil court, where she faced shocking statements from a reluctant judge. Selling her house, she risks everything she owns to pursue her dream of building an unparalleled performing arts center, Heartbeat Studios. Deborah and Kristin call on their daring ancestral DNA and set out on solo trips to Europe, Asia, Egypt and the forbidden island of Cuba, reaching out to the international dance community and inspiring partnerships and endearing friendships in a world they thought for so long did not care about them. Deborah and Kristin's journey is a hero's journey as they flee the centrifuge of domestic violence to follow a path from darkness to light."

Also detailed in the book are the "red flags" of domestic violence. Not being aware of these warning signs during the violent years, served as additional obstacles, making it impossible to pursue my goal, my dream.

Following are a few lines from reviews on Amazon for my book. I am honored to share them here:

The abuse is enough of an emotional pull, but the indifference by the police, the courts and just people in general is infuriating ... esp for the 1990's. I would have assumed this had not been the case. Bravo Deb for pushing on and making a better life for you and your daughter as well as many other abused woman who came behind you. Not only should every woman read this, but every young man should as well, so as a society we don't repeat history any more.

Who would have believed after 23 years of abuse she would shine so brightly.

Dancing to My Heartbeat is a celebration of triumph over tragedy. Awesome. You likely won't be able to put down this book. Be inspired; be educated, and be thankful for their safety, and for the lessons this book will teach others about life after violence. Deb deftly inserted the red flags of domestic violence into her story so her readers would understand how pervasive it is—and hopefully prevent another young woman from becoming a victim.

My dream flourished when my daughter and I opened our own performing arts center, Heartbeat Studios January 1998. I came alive at that moment because a new life was truly beginning for both of us. Making a living doing what I love to do is simply exhilarating! The performing arts, by nature, nurture creativity, so dreaming big is a daily occurrence. There is inherent vitality in generating ideas and then finding solutions.

Teaching dance places one in a position to nourish the children's talent as well as their self-esteem and self-confidence. Each day, with each student, in each class, many mini-goals are reached as we see the fruits of our labor contribute to the development of genuinely good people. Helping others realize their dreams or reach their goals is a magnificent feeling.

In January 2013, Heartbeat celebrated its fifteenth anniversary. Milestones in those years include:

- Establishing travel study/cultural exchange programs with partner studios in Barcelona and Tokyo. Students and teachers from Spain and Japan have visited Heartbeat, and Heartbeat's students and teachers have traveled overseas to their studios to study and perform.
- Producing two annual musical theater productions each year. Most noted is the permission Heartbeat received from Lucas Films Ltd. to present a stage version of the classis film, **Star Wars**, in June 2011. In June 2014, courtesy of Middle Earth Enterprises, Heartbeat will present a stage version of, **Lord of the Rings: Fellowship of the Ring.**
- Being selected as the only dance studio to travel to London to represent the United States at the 400th anniversary celebration of settlers sailing from Kent, England to Jamestown, Virginia.
- Developing a successful dance/movement program for students with Autism Spectrum Disorder (ASD).
- Maturing to a full-fledged performing arts center offering classes to 300-plus students each year in dance (ballet, tap, jazz, hip hop, modern, break dance, flamenco, dance line), acting and singing.
- Establishing several dance and vocal performance groups, bringing entertainment to organizations such as the Children's Hospital, large

- corporation gala events, NBA games, Orchestra Hall Hot Summer Jazz Festival, numerous benefit and charity fund raisers, community festivals, and productions in Barcelona and Tokyo, to name a few.
- Traveling on a State Treasury Department licensed trip to Havana, Cuba, and to the American University Cairo, Egypt where Kristin taught a month-long residency.

I have had the good fortune to have studied with professionals in ballet and jazz dance, and with luminaries in the tap dance community such as Dianne Walker, the late Gregory Hines, Jason Samuels-Smith, Savion Glover, Guillem Alonso, Roxane Butterfly, and Yukiko Misumi, to name a few. I have also been a featured dancer in productions such as Orchestra Hall Hot Summer Jazz Festival, O'Shaughnessy Auditorium, and several jazz clubs, and internationally in Tokyo, London, and Barcelona. Deborah's choreography is highly original, appearing in a range of productions from dance recitals, musical theater such as *West Side Story, Anything Goes, The Boyfriend, Oklahoma!, Grease,* and *The Wiz,* to public service announcements and major sports events.

If a woman asked me for advice about achieving success, I'd say:
- Define what success is to you. Pull the curtain back to see what success will look like. Not only must you have a clear vision of where you are headed, but also the humility to acknowledge that there is no end to the "achieving-success" process because the journey might take you in directions you never thought possible. Always do your homework to ensure every step or decision you make is done with eyes wide open. Embrace what you do, not only with pride, but with undying passion. Love the ride.
- Do not be afraid to ask questions or seek a mentor. Talk to many people and filter out what you know will be useful to your endeavor.
- When making decisions, always consider, "Who will benefit from my success? How will this make me stand out from my competitors? How will this benefit/define me?'
- It is sometimes said that reaching a goal is anticlimactic. It can leave you wanting because at first glance, it means your growth has stopped. Instead of a "goal plan" have a "growth plan" and make it a life-long process. Reaching a goal may seem you have "arrived." Rather, look at it like you have approached your potential at this time ... but be excited there is always more to learn and discover.

- Once you have reached your goal at this point in time, realize new responsibilities and expectations may come forth, so be prepared and embrace them, for they will, no doubt, lead to new goals.
- What does it take to be successful?
- True skill in your craft and belief in yourself can take you far.
- Being fearless and having the ability to dream big will set things in motion.
- Knowing what to do with your skills and possessing clear definition and purpose of your dream, is essential.
- Solid leadership and management expertise are required to establish respectful reputation in your field.
- The knack to adapt and redefine yourself/business, when necessary to stay ahead of the pack, is of utmost importance.
- Never forget from whence you came, and always be fair. Be steadfast and not afraid to dust off your boots and start over.
- The ability to see the big picture and understanding all the steps to get from A to B are required.
- Learn from each setback, even though they are discouraging, time-consuming, and many other unsavory names. They are part of your education.
- Be a good listener, even more than a good talker because the more information you take in, the more you will be prepared to pursue your goal.

My sixth-grade teacher once told me, "Deb, in life, no one is going to serve you anything on a silver platter. You, instead, must make the platter yourself." Her comment has always stuck with me.

www.heartbeat-studios.com
Facebook Author Page: Deborah Lysholm

Not only must you have a clear vision of where you are headed, but also the humility to acknowledge there is no end to the "achieving success" process because the journey might take you in directions you never thought possible.

CHAPTER 6

Finding Your Own Path

If you're going through hell, keep going.
—Winston Churchill

JILL JOHNSON

My mother and father owned a small auto body shop in a small town in western Wisconsin. I grew up in a family-owned business environment.

My first paid job was teaching dance for the Stillwater school system, and by the time I was thirteen, I was teaching for three or four schools.

During high school, I worked at a hair salon called Casa de Pelo, which in Spanish meant House of Hair. They called me "The Tornado" because as their Saturday receptionist, I always tried to grab the phone after the second ring, no matter where I was in the salon. I even earned the responsibility of making deposits, which was a big deal for a sixteen-year-old to drive to the bank with the moneybag.

The studio where I took gymnastics expanded, and I was accountable for developing their business plan. But more importantly, while in high school, I was very active in the Junior Achievement (JA) program. Then in JA, you started an actual business. You sold stock, you built a product, you sold the product, and you liquidated the company at the end of the year. I had enormous opportunity in Junior Achievement to learn about business, and I loved every moment of it.

Junior Achievement also had a variety of competitions. I took my competitive spirit from being a gymnast, and now I was competing in Junior Achievement competitions for President of the Year, Vice President of Sales of the Year, Speaker of the Year, Salesman of the Year, and Outstanding Young Business Woman of the Year. By my senior year, I had won all of these awards and was named the Achiever of the Year from St. Paul Junior Achievement—

their highest honor. I was working on *Harvard Business Review* case studies for fun.

A friend from the Chicago area, with whom I had co-chaired a conference for fifteen hundred people, was giving me ideas on how to prepare for our national competition. One day he called and said, "I have a lunch meeting scheduled, and I think you need to come to Chicago for it." I said, "Mom, I've got to go to Chicago." And she let me go. The lunch meeting was with Robert Cardinal, the senior vice president for Lester B. Knight & Associates, an international management-consulting firm, and then one of the nation's largest consulting firms. Walking out of the luncheon, I said, "That's what I want to do." I was seventeen years old at the time.

I did very well at Nationals. I was the only girl in the finals for National President of the Year, and placed third. I was also runner-up for the National Outstanding Young Businesswomen of the Year. These awards earned me some scholarship money. I also had received some scholarship money from St. Paul Junior Achievement, and I used it to help pay for my business degree at Drake University.

My focus and goal setting continued in college in the late 1970s and early 1980s. I had a little sign on my wall, "Get an A for your MBA," because I knew I needed a master's degree in business administration in order to have any chance in becoming a consultant. I was one of few young women in those business classes.

Trying to find my way, I ended up getting my first job in consulting. One of my MBA program professors had said, "The U.S. Small Business Administration, in their Small Business Development Centers (SBDC), is looking for MBA students to work as consultants with distressed businesses in central Iowa." I think I knocked three people over trying to get upstairs after the class to apply for the job. I was hired ten minutes into my interview, because Lou Woods, the director of the program, said, "It's obvious you have a real business background, and you are not going to spew theory to all these people."

My first consulting client was a pharmacist who had a cash-flow problem. He was a rough old bugger who didn't think he was going to like working with a girl (I was twenty-two). He had an inventory control problem, which was solved after I came up with an idea wherein fourteen thousand dollars of cash flow was released for him.

In similar communities in Iowa, the savings and loans were collapsing. The farmers were in crisis, and it was feeding all sorts of economic distress all around the state. I knew when I was going into those first consulting engagements, if I did not do it right, these people would lose everything. I thrived on the pressure and responsibility—I loved it.

My connections within the SBDC led to my working for an international consulting firm. This experience gave me the credentials I needed to be hired by one of the nation's largest public accounting firms, providing me with even more experience in the business of consulting. I stayed focused and found the way to make the idea of becoming a management consultant real. I worked hard to gain the experience and the credentials at each step of my path.

Starting in the consultant business, many people offered me help. For me, the word mentor had meant I could learn from everybody. Robert Cardinal was very influential, but I never spent more than two hours with him. He was that cardinal who sang a song, and it resonated deep in my heart. Then he went away. His words ignited a fire deep within me still burning today.

I have had bosses who gave me chances, and I grabbed those opportunities. I had people who advised me, when I was having those days of panic and terror, and talked me off the ledge, so to speak. I wish I would have had one person who could have magically opened the doors for me. But I came from a blue-collar family with no connections to the future I wanted to have. When my parents set me free, it was my responsibility to build my own path—and so I have.

I think my major challenges in fact revolved around my age and gender because I was focused on a high-level in business. In the mid 1980's, women were just starting to come into their own in the executive ranks. I had no women ahead of me to pave the path for me in corporate consulting. One of the reasons I became an entrepreneur was it was easier to control my destiny by being on my own.

It was hard to be taken seriously as a young adult because I wanted to give business advice, and most people my age did not have any business experience. But I learned from everyone. I used to bus tables for a woman restaurant owner across the street from my dad's business. I'd listen to these older adults talking about their business problems. Soon I gained credibility because people realized the environment I had grown up in, and the business savvy I had developed.

When I got the consulting job in Des Moines, the firm I worked for didn't have a formal training program. I created my own self-study curriculum. At night, instead of going home or going out partying, I studied old case files and thought, "What would I have done?"

Unlocking the Secrets of Successful Women

I made my own path. I was able to overcome the disadvantage of being young and female by the level of discipline and hard work I put into my preparation, as well as the quality of my work product.

Whenever I reached out for an opportunity, I was extremely well-prepared and then over-delivered. Even if I have a CEO of a two billion-dollar company in a meeting, I don't fall apart if I'm challenged for my ideas, because I am extraordinarily prepared when I go in a room. I know people at this level expect a high degree of preparation. Plus it gives me a hidden layer of confidence on which I can rely.

When I look back full circle at what Robert Cardinal talked about in our two-hour lunch in Chicago when I was seventeen, he talked about making a difference as a management consultant, and learning from each client experience. He talked about bringing your best to the situation. All those things, all these years later still resonate with me. I knew myself well enough even then to know I want to travel. I need diversity because I get bored very easily. I like a lot of challenge and want to learn new things. I crave responsibility and want to be accountable for making things happen. The profession of consulting provides these things for me.

Industry studies report less than ten percent of people who go into consulting ever survive ten years. Most people last as consultants for only twelve to eighteen months because they are not prepared for the reality of being an entrepreneur. They are not prepared to sell and manage the work. They finish a project or two; then find out being a consultant is not as easy as they thought. Then they go out and look for a real job.

For young women, my message to you is to network—work hard at building relationships. Many younger women have opportunities to be in settings with mature, successful women. As a young woman, you can approach these women and say, "Hi, I'm so and so. I appreciated your comments today. Would you mind if I gave you a call sometime, if I have questions about something?"

I find most young women ask if they can talk to me. They get my business card, but they never follow up, or they follow up with an e-mail, and I ever hear from them again.

Don't expect me to do your life plan for you. I likely don't have time to give you three hours in an afternoon, but I am approachable by phone. If I'm nearby, and you can swing by and have a cup of coffee, you might be able to get fifteen to thirty minutes. That may be all it takes for me to be *your cardinal.* Women like me also have access to other people who might be extremely helpful for you. But you have to earn that access. You have to follow through, and truly connect with me so I care about your future. Then I will support your dreams.

I think young women just assume it is going to be easy for them to network because of the availability of social media. To begin to build a relationship, follow the people you admire or respect on Facebook and LinkedIn. If you know something positive is going on with them, reach out and congratulate them. And don't unsubscribe if they put you on Constant Contact mailing list.

Not long ago, a young woman, who I had spent quite a bit of time with while she was in college, did something to change our relationship. She unsubscribed after receiving my email containing the press release about my induction into the Hall of Fame. I have no idea why, but it sure changed the dynamic about how much time I'm going to spend with her again.

The women I find who successfully navigate a professional and personal life are very creative about how they get it all done. A dear friend was a big-time partner in one of the major law firms. She was a trial attorney. When her kids were little, going to the grocery store was considered family time. It didn't matter what they were doing; they were together. It was about connecting and not wasting all their energy thinking: I should be doing something else.

I think one of the other things people find very hard to deal with is the feast-or-famine syndrome we all experience. I don't have a steady paycheck. I do not have clients lined up one after another. When I'm working with you, I'm working on your project, which means I'm not aggressively marketing. If I have four hundred hours involved in a client, I'm not focused on marketing to find the next one during those hours. It's being able to handle feast or famine.

In my line of work, it's about when the client needs me, not when I need the client. I'm very careful about money so I can weather those storms. It's why I am still in business twenty-six years later. It's because I didn't spend all my cash. Have I actually had dry spells? Absolutely. Have I had times when I was convinced no one would ever call me again? Absolutely.

When I do presentations on Confidence, I'm often asked, "Jill, do you ever get scared?" The answer is, "Of course." Every successful person I've worked with, or the biographies of very successful people I've read, all have had their dark period—the periods when they were totally uncertain as to what to do next. They didn't know if the big success they were aspiring to was ever going to happen, but they kept pushing forward. They didn't get stuck in their fears, and they didn't quit.

After thirty years of consulting, I still have those days when I get in my head that perhaps I'm never going to have another client again—ever. It's how you self-talk your way out of it. The truth is, as human beings, we are not at the same level of confidence every day. It ebbs and flows, depending on the situation.

Prior to being fully present at the death of my parents, I was totally on the success path. I was all about business, and I had a handful of friends. But what I found as I was midwifing the death of my mother and kneeling at her bed at the moment of her death, she did not say to me, "Jill, I wish I had another mutual fund." It was a life-changing realization, because she had raised me to have a big business career. I learned from her final gift to me that life is truly about relationships, not money or acclaim.

Now I make time, maybe not six days, but I make time. When I'm in the moment with someone, I'm truly in the moment with them. And I'm trying to give the gift of my *best self*.

I have been making my living for over three decades now, working as a management consultant. There were always periods when work was not coming in, or the money wasn't big enough, or I had to discount my rates in order to get the work. It was by no means a certainty. I had clients offer me jobs. I said, "no" to all of them, because as I told one client, "What makes me most valuable to you is I can tell you the truth, if I'm working on your staff, I have to worry about offending all these people. It's better for you if I'm external." I can make a difference in an organization, because I can help them through those periods of their transition.

I have been through four recessionary periods. Trust me, clients don't spend money on consultants during those difficult periods. I use the time to learn something new, for example, learning about the Internet. E-mail didn't exist when I first started my career. Fax machines were a new technology. I learned to use software and to leverage resources. I've continued to grow and expand as a consultant, because I always looked ahead at learning something new. I have to be on the leading edge. So when I walk into whatever is going on in my client's setting, I'm not just playing catch-up, I already have insight and understanding.

My reading program is very eclectic. I read all sides of the political aisle. I don't focus on a singular ideology. I may not agree with all the ideology, but I want to understand the undercurrent driving a point of view. I am interested in world history. I read a lot of biographies and non-fiction books to broaden my thinking and help me when my own confidence in low. Experience has taught me this constant awareness helps me move through panic and terror. I have people who know when I'm on the ledge, and sometimes they'll laugh at me. One of the things I've also learned is you may be scared, but don't spill it out for the whole world to see. Keep this private. Find a way to reconcile your fear, and then you pick yourself up and dust yourself off. You don't have to stay with fear, and let fear hold you down.

Another important responsibility for successful people is to give back, and to pass the hand of leadership insight onto the next generation of leaders. My involvement in the community and mentorship include mentoring a number of young professionals in the Twin Cities, helping them with informational interviews, resume critiques and connections. I have spoken at numerous youth leadership conferences and student events in conjunction with the University of Minnesota, the University of St. Thomas, St. Catherine University and my alma mater, Drake University.

My community outreach also extends around the world, even if I am not traveling there. I work with the Minnesota International Center, U.S. Department of Commerce and NAWBO to promote international trade and relationships among women. I have shared business information with women business owners from France, Denmark, Russia, Canada, and numerous countries in Africa and the Middle East.

People will ask, "What is your biggest success?" Honestly, I have to say I haven't had my biggest success yet. I don't know where the ultimate end is, but I know I'm not there yet. I've had days when I'm just bored with doing the same thing, but that's when I start to look for new ways to transform what I do into something bigger, more powerful and more impactful.

The most important thing in life is to learn how to trust yourself. Be authentic and be fully present. Have amazing people in your intimate circle who tell you the truth. Each of us has talent the world needs – so bring your talents forward and share them with us. Find your own path and don't be afraid to follow it! It will take you on an amazing journey you create.

Jill@jcs-usa.com
www.jcs-usa.com
Facebook: www.facebook.com/Jill.Johnson.USA
Twitter: @JillJohnsonUSA
Linkedin: www.linkedin.com/in/johnsonconsultingservices

Don't wait for the phone to ring. Get out and connect with people. Go take a class to learn a new skill. Read a book. Do something. Make something happen.

CHAPTER 7

Success Starts With a Dream

Let the beauty of what you love, be what you do.
—Rumi

JoAnne Funch

I'm not sure I ever grew up with an idea of what success was, but I did grow up learning to discover what brought me joy and what lit the fire of enthusiasm deep within me. My parents both had started businesses while I was in high school, and I suspect observing their choices helped me to become an independent thinker. Their road was not an easy one as I observed the long hours and many financial challenges.

I didn't venture out in life to be or do anything specific; rather I was on a journey of self-discovery throughout my twenties. My independence and creativity, both artistically and as a visionary, directed me to think outside the box of choices that many of my friends were making in their twenties.

I started following a dream of self-discovery and adventure at the age of twenty-eight. I took a job in California and moved across the country simply to have the experience, and to expand my view of what might be possible somewhere else. Having made several trips to California prior to the move, I felt exhilarated and had no fear of making such a big move alone, knowing there were such new and different opportunities I wanted to explore.

After working for several different companies the first ten years after I moved, each was a small business, and I observed both the good and bad of how they ran their businesses. It became on-the-job training for my future as a business owner. My first entrepreneurial venture began following a job lay off. I took a hobby and turned it into a moneymaking activity. This was a symbolic moment when something clicked for me. I discovered what I wanted to be in life was independent, and uncover my creative talents and skills. I remember reading issues of *Entrepreneur Magazine* and becoming inspired by the stories of success about people who were creative and now calling their own shots. I kept a clipping from the September 1990 issue of *Entrepreneur Magazine* because it impacted my life. The editor wrote in part, "Dreams are the stuff entrepreneurs are made of. They're what push us to succeed, beyond the realm of possibility." All these years, this article has inspired me to keep going even when I became discouraged or failed.

My parents encouraged and supported me along the way but ultimately my success came from my own self-determination. When an opportunity came, I seized it. I was and am still very self-motivated, coupled with a good amount of tenacity mixed in.

The challenges I faced along the way through my business success have been many—from lack of financial capital to becoming partners with my spouse. Early on, I was challenged with a girlfriend who had become a business partner, and this ended in bad feelings and a dissolved partnership. This was a great lesson in the importance of having all your legal ducks in a row regardless of the friendship—which we did.

After the dissolution of our partnership, in 1996 I started working with my husband in the business he had started a year prior called GIR Graphic Art. He began by developing marketing materials for small business, expanding over the years to provide a variety of marketing, promotion and design services. We changed our company name to GIR-Graphics & Innovative Resources with a tagline *"We Make You Look Good,"* which reflected a more diverse brand.

In 2005, my husband/business partner died from an accident. Suddenly I realized we didn't have a plan in place in the event of the death of either partner. This topic was one of those life-planning events we did not address.

From my experience, here are some things husband/wife business partners should talk about, put in writing and update as needed:

- Have trusted advisors established both of you know (attorney, CPA, financial advisor, insurance agent, banker, etc.).
- Have your legal documents in order: A will, trusts, powers of attorney and medical directives. Update as needed.
- Have access to each other's contact information of friends, family members and business associates.
- Have open and honest discussions about your wishes, especially if you have children from previous marriages.
- Talk about the "if's in life" while everyone is well and strong, if necessary, with an attorney or financial planner present. Discuss how you want assets to be distributed (especially if there are "yours," "mine" and "our"

kids), and any philanthropic legacy desires. This becomes extremely important if the surviving spouse gets remarried and more children are brought into the family.
- Think of your spouse as a key employee. If he or she dies prematurely, what impact would it have on your income, business, and your lifestyle. Protect your loved ones and obtain life insurance to help him/her survive in your absence.
- Know what each other is working on so the transition is easier.
- Keep personal and business expenses separate.
- Have *all* passwords, PIN numbers and other security info written down so the spouse can easily locate them.
- Business resources/vendors: both spouses should know where to locate contracts and contact information.
- Make sure both know the banking relationships.
- Depending on progression of inheritance, consider having the family home in joint tenancy with rights of survivorship.
- Know where to locate the safe deposit key and make sure you are on the signature card allowing you to access it.
- Double-check ALL investment and insurance policy beneficiary designations, including primary and contingent beneficiaries.

After my husband/partner's unexpected death, I was forced to make changes to the business, which included selling off the screen-printing business and retaining the marketing clients and services. In 2007-2008, I learned and implemented online marketing strategies and social media into the company, recognizing this was the future trend of marketing, and I knew with certainty this was the direction the business needed to go. Today, I help small business owners gain more exposure for their business through proven marketing strategies. I also teach social media strategies and implementation to individuals and companies.

Looking back, working with my spouse was the most challenging because it required balance and diplomacy to make both the marriage and the partnership work. When your partner is your spouse, you never get away from work. I had to learn to engage in other conversations with my husband, and to find outside interests to offer the needed balance.

Two years following his death, I decided to move from California where I had made my home for nearly twenty-five years, back to my hometown of Minneapolis where I had support of family and friends. My stepdaughter was finishing up school in California, and was making her way in the world, and

I simply had financial decisions to make about the business and home—and moving was my solution.

Not only was I starting my business again, but I was starting life again.

I believe success is defined individually and not universally. You can only measure what you achieve for yourself by your own yardstick. Perhaps you measure success in meeting your goals, or by your happiness or wealth. Success can also be measured by those in whose lives we may have made a difference, or by lending a hand up to another, by a kind word, by being a mentor, a leader or a friend.

Success in business and life takes vision, determination, resilience and a dash of courage from time to time. Success requires us to set some goals, be as prepared as we can, and then be willing to adjust the sails.

My real success came when I knew I was able to inspire others to their own greatness. This is my *why*—the why I get up every day.

Remember the *Entrepreneur Magazine* article I quoted earlier? The last paragraph had the most impact on my success; it is what kept me going all these years later, and perhaps it will inspire your own success.

Don't let anyone discourage your dreams. For without dreamers there'd be no computers, no automobiles, no airplanes, phone or electric lighting. Without dreams, there'd be no point.

www.girpromotions.com and *www.marketingdish.com*

Success in business and life takes vision, determination, resilience—and a dash of courage from time to time.

CHAPTER 8

Reinventing New Chapters in Your Life at Any Age

*Think of your life as a book; then ask yourself...
what chapters are yet to be written?*

—Nadia

Nadia Giordana

Growing up in rural Minnesota in the '60s and, later with a family in the '70s and '80s, I hadn't formulated a very clear idea about the true meaning of personal success and what "success" particularly entailed for a self-actualized and esteemed female enjoying life in the evolved, latter fourth of the 20th century.

"Back in the day," I was studious and had good grades, but any ideas I had about success were glamorous and fanciful—not at all steeped in goal-oriented reality. True...it's a good idea to dream, but the practical aspects of earning a living ought to have a place within attainable fantasy. Reality bites. The glimpse of bliss toward which I might have aspired somehow got sidetracked.

I always had a desire to be creative, and initially hoped to become a commercial artist, but art school entry then was not feasible. I had written poetry and short prose in high school, enjoyed English class, and was an avid reader. I loved the musty smell of old books from the library, right alongside the scintillating smell and feel of new books. Even so, it didn't occur to me that I could become a writer. I was a late bloomer.

I experienced a number of false starts and restarts in life (re-inventions I call them) until 2006 when I was laid off from a corporate position. Like most folks born in the middle of the last century, one aspired to lifetime career positions where you worked with one company, promotions included, until you comfortably retired with vacation and benefits. Not so in today's economy. Needless to say, I was shocked and surprised. At 58, losing this position was particularly scary. I wondered if being older and overweight had hastened my demise. I spent the following year nursing my wounded pride and feeling old and useless.

Eventually, I pulled myself together and began to work on my health—losing more than 80 pounds, and then writing *Thinking Skinny,* a book about the experience. Funny, I hadn't realized that imagining myself in the future *right here, right now* was maybe what I ought to have been doing back in the high school library.

Next, beginning to blog and write articles, I became a mentor to women in my age group. I found these new endeavors immensely satisfying. Additionally, the successful weight loss inspired me to tackle another stumbling block in my life, a deep-seated fear of public speaking. It wasn't long before I wrote a second book, *Reinventing New Chapters in Your Life at Any Age.*

It's true what they say: if you want to be successful, find and do the things you enjoy and especially love to do, and the rest will fall into place. Renowned scholar and author Joseph Campbell called it "following your bliss." These days I am enjoying the sense of freedom that comes with being an author; without a doubt, I'm finally using my creativity—my bliss.

In retrospect, I must say before my enlightenment about present-moment visualization, I encountered a lot of obstacles, without much access to help from others. But, one ought to be open to assistance of any kind when help is there for the taking. It never hurts to ask. My parents were there for me, offering help in the form of inspiration. I watched them during their lives trying and failing, doing and achieving, yet still being set back, sometimes, by disappointment.

I watched their exemplary way of facing challenge. Farmers have their share of major and complex ambiguity, what with the indeterminate fluctuations in weather and marketplace greed and indiscretion. They kept on persevering and adapting.

In 1979, around the age of 50, after raising four children to adulthood, they sold their dairy farm in Motley, Minnesota, loaded a semi-tractor and trailer with 37 tons of gear and equipment, said good-bye to family and friends, and set out to carve a new life for themselves on the frozen tundra of Alaska.

They built a log cabin, and they lived there for 27 years, living off the land and what little income they had. For the first several years, they had no electricity, running water, or indoor plumbing. My father trapped, hunted, and prospected for gold, while my mother built a large garden in a forbidding and very short growing climate. She picked berries, made preserves, sewed and repaired clothing by hand and with a treadle machine, and cleaned and canned salmon. Together, they dressed out, prepared and packaged moose, bear, caribou and other game.

All through those years, my father chronicled their adventure in his daily journal entries. Recently, I transcribed those journals and compiled and published them as a three-volume documentary journal entitled *10,000 Days in Alaska* by Norman Wilkins.

I cannot be more proud than I am today to claim them as mine. I never tire of hearing them tell their stories, and I've never lost my sense of amazement at what they have done. I'm making an effort to be as unique and as full of adventure as they are. I guess that means I have some surprises yet ahead of me. I wonder what they will be?

Just as Mom and Dad did, I faced a lot of obstacles getting to where I am today. I had to get out of my own way in order to move forward. Here's how: First, I had always believed I needed to be utterly perfect at what I did, or I would never be successful. For example, the reason I didn't begin writing at an earlier age, was I believed one's grammar and spelling must be flawless to be a writer. The reality is most discerning authors have their important manuscripts professionally edited. I also had to get over the mistaken idea that I had waited too long to become a writer, and it was already too late. It was important to get over this kind of thinking, and to embrace the idea it was not too late to resurrect my sidelined dreams and *do the things I've always wanted to do.*

To me, being successful requires these things:
- A willingness to risk failure, and to have the insight to realize failures are not necessarily bad. They move you closer to where you need to be in life.
- A love of learning new things—especially if you are an entrepreneur.
- Start thinking of yourself as a success long before it happens. *Right here... right now* visually see yourself doing and being what you love to do and be. This is very important.

My final advice:
- Don't worry about what others are thinking about you and what you do.
- Don't wait for their approval or permission for *it rarely comes.*
- Don't forget it is never too late to shake off negative self-talk and reinvent new chapters in your life.

"Think of your life as a book; then ask yourself...what chapters are yet to be written?"

Start thinking of yourself as a success long before it happens. Right here...right now. Visualize seeing yourself doing and being what you love to do and be.

CHAPTER 9

You Have to Believe You Can Do It

Everybody builds a dream in their lifetime. You're either going to build your dream, or somebody else's. So build your own.
—Christopher LaBree

Tara O'Brien

It seems successful people don't always fit into some formulaic mold. I certainly don't. I figure stuff out as I go along. In retrospect, I'm quite a survivor.

A wise man named Jiddu Krishnamurti once said, "Truth is a pathless land." I guess I never had to read or learn that. I don't necessarily have a path; I just keep going. I never felt I had a career path when I got out of high school. I thought, "You go to high school. You graduate. Get into college. Find a job. Raise a family. Then, make as much money as you can."

Both of my parents worked full time once my mom became a career woman. Even though I got a degree in Mortuary Science, without any serious aforethought, it only became a stepping-stone to Forensic Pathology. It sounded nice. "Let's just keep going!"

It may sound crazy but, in the middle of "keeping going," I suddenly decided, upon receiving my Bachelor's degree, "I'm tired of school and studying." There I was, a licensed mortician and sort of enjoying a trade, and I didn't want to continue. Maybe it was the excitement of ... romantic passion.

Maybe you can see the pattern here. I'm suddenly all excited about "tying the knot." I've slowed down momentarily, and my high school sweetheart and I decided to get married, start a life together. Then I couldn't do it.

I discovered at the very last second perhaps my guy and I were not on the same wavelength. He seemed too content in his life, living paycheck to paycheck. I don't know what got into me, but I knew I wanted more than day-to-day contentment. I wanted more excitement, without all the study and commitment to a question mark.

I was recalling the fact that, well, maybe my parents didn't have such a great marriage, after all. I mean, in retrospect, it was a battleground growing up. My parents made it work with them both having careers. So I decided, "What's love got to do with it?" It (love) certainly wasn't enough back home. Then my guy and I sat down, talked about getting married—and ended it.

My parents were gracious enough to allow me to return home for a while. Also, I did not give up my day job, but investigated the prospect of insurance sales without yet leaving the funeral business. I started the insurance classes.

When a friend called, saying, "I am opening up a real estate company. Would you be interested in coming to work for me? I thought, "I have nothing better to do; I might as well work for him."

Once I started my real estate classes, most days I didn't feel like I was going to work. I did some sort of work every day, but it simply didn't feel like work. I used to dread getting up in the middle of the night and driving to pick up a newly deceased person for transportation to the funeral home, or, on my way to a funeral, I would groan and think, "I don't want to do this. How do I get out of it?

Today, I get excited about real estate. I love it. It affords me the kind of lifestyle I like. I had told my ex-boyfriend I didn't want to be complacent, or struggling—and I wanted to make six figures. In my second year of real estate, I did make six figures, and I've never looked back. Switching careers into Real Estate was the best decision I ever made. My former boyfriend did choose the «kids and wife» future, and is working the same job he did thirteen years ago. He is complacent enough to be satisfied. I made the choice to give up the «kids and marriage thing,» in order to follow my career path.

When I started selling real estate, the market was just heating up. I certainly got in at the right time. I took my last $2000 and started a direct mail campaign to renters—and it was a great success. About this time, the Internet made a huge change in our industry. I jumped on the technology wave and rode it to my advantage. I started my own web page, www.taraobrien.com, and have had a great deal of success in growing my business through this avenue. I sell an average of 30-46 homes a year, and love the hustle of finding new clients. I have found a sort of competitiveness in myself I never knew was there. My first five years in real estate, I was among the top three sales people in my office every year, I have been featured as a "Top Real Estate Agent" by *Mpls St. Paul Magazine,* and have made Presidents Circle Honor six years in a row (top ten percent of agents nationally). Several real estate companies recruited me until I landed where I am today. To stay on top of the market, I keep up with the latest trends in real estate, and work hard at continuing to grow my company on a daily basis. When the market took a crash in 2008, life became very difficult, very fast. Overnight I went from being on top of my game to receiving no paycheck for several months—and was humbled in many ways.

I felt very sorry for myself and did a lot of complaining, kept myself up at night worrying about how I would make it through this, fearful I was going to lose everything. I decided to stick it out, and in January of 2009 put my negative attitude in check. I picked myself up, stopped applying for meaningless jobs and got back to work on my real estate career, making 2009 my best year ever. It still shows me every day you get out of your life what you put into it, and what you put into the universe, it will give it back.

My mom is in her sixties, and my dad has passed away. He had old-fashion values when it came to women in the workplace. But I think he knew my mom had to work. My mom tried to be "gracefully submissive," but modern economic trends in America are not in accord with the old fifties' "housewife and mommy thing." I learned from my mother's example. It didn't work for her—and won't ever work for me. They stayed married for thirty-two years before deciding, "Our kids are grown; it's time to go our separate ways." They divorced after eight years of being legally separated but remained friends until my dad's passing in April 2013.

When I was in the fifth grade I wrote a paper about where I thought I'd be when I was twenty-five. I wrote, "... living in a loft in New York City, no husband and no kids."

Yes, I said it. And up until two years ago, I had a townhouse, but it was in Minneapolis. No husband. No kids. I had a dog and the boyfriend. In this I believe: "What your mind's eye can see, your body will achieve." I'm very driven in my own head. If I think I'm going to be somewhere, I say it (and see it); then somehow, my path gets me there. I just keep going. It's so important to believe in yourself and what you want to do.

A couple of years into my real estate career, I thought, "Here I am; I've done it. I've got my own house. I have two cars. I don't have any bills. I have a great career. I'm self-employed. I'm my own boss. I have these great friends. I have this wonderful lifestyle. Interruptions and obstacles do happen, however.

I was partying all the time. It was 2005, when I realized the partying was actually beginning to take me over. I headed down a different path, one threatening my forward motion. I became what I thought I wanted to be: a well-known face in the downtown social scene. I had a lot of very well-known friends, most of whom were self-employed. We spent a lot of time on boats, in the bars, and running around the country having a great time. I thought

I had "made it." I put so much time into my partying it started to reflect in my work. I was missing appointments, not sleeping very much, and making my social life my priority. I didn't like the person looking back at me in the mirror anymore—and decided to make a life change. Fortunately, I got help. I quit drinking eight years ago.

Now it's a better path, a stronger path. I know what I'm actually doing, what each "next step" is going to be. I'm clearer about this process of planning in the moment.

It was fun, back then. I was young. I remember going to my tenth high school reunion. I met a female classmate who said, "I'm so jealous of your life. You have everything."

I said, "Yes, but I gave up kids and a family. I gave it all up to do this. You didn't." I looked at her life and thought, "Wow! Look what I missed." And, she was enviously looking at my life. How ironic.

Presently, I'm putting together a real estate team because my goal is to manage a team, and not have the hectic hustle that previously brought me to alcohol. I love the new teamwork method. It's working and truly producing. Also, I have custody of a nine-year-old nephew, and my fiancé has a fifteen-year-old, and we have three dogs—an instant family. I cannot imagine how my mom did it with three kids and a full-time job. My life has become quite different from what I had pictured previously. My hustle-and-bustle lifestyle wouldn't work without my new team effort on the job. I'm trying to reorganize everything to make all my pieces fit together. I am fortunate enough to be with the love of my life, my soul mate. We knew each other a long time ago, and now we are together. We are currently talking about the possibility of having a baby. We are going to get married next year. Then we'll decide what to do from there.

We plan on being retired at fifty-five. And following, we are going to live in New York for a year; then, we are going to travel and enjoy our retirement. As much as I like to work, I don't want to work forever. I want to travel and sleep in every day.

Soon, my company is moving me to an office in downtown Minneapolis. Then, I will start to build around it. It has been my plan for a long time.

And, I'm prepared for those inevitable obstacles and interruptions that keep on occurring. Because, for whatever reason, every time I get going on a plan, something happens. Impermanence is a fact of life we must always take into account. The first time I started to build a team, it was right after I got sober. I hired an assistant and took on more business. Then my mom got sick, so I cut back on my hours. I had to look at what was important to me. I let everybody go. The second time I tried, there was another downturn in the real estate market. So my timing got thrown off.

Today, I'm crazy busy, and it's what I like. When I'm busy, my house is the cleanest, my car is clean, and my laundry is always done. Over Christmas, when I didn't have anything to do for a month, nothing was done for a month. My house was a mess. I got so lazy I couldn't get moving.

I think I learned early on if you want something, you have to go out and get it. I got into real estate at the right time, because, back then, anybody could sell a house. You didn't have to be real smart, or real good. You certainly didn't have to do much because the times and the market were so crazy. I got licensed in 2001 and, by the time the market crashed in 2008, I had a database and enough business to keep myself going during the downturn of the real estate market, and I survived.

During this time, I was able to look at pulling systems together, and organizing myself so when the market did come back, I would be ready for it. Now with the market coming back, I feel real good about what is happening.

You have to believe you can do it, which is the big part. Believe in yourself. Sometimes my committee starts in my head. These are all the people in my head who tell me:

- "You're not good enough."
- "You're not smart enough."
- "You're not pretty enough."
- "You're not successful enough."

I have to learn to shut them off in order to get the things I want, knowing there is a battle going on all the time.

I think it's important for a person to set realistic goals. I write out my goals each month: 1) This is how many houses I am going to sell, 2) This is how many listings I'm going to get, 3) This is the amount of money I'm going to make, and 4) *All of the above is exactly how I am going to keep going.*

To reiterate, I think success means:
- Set realistic goals for your personal life and your business.
- Write down the goals and review often.
- Shut off the negative messages in your head.
- Surround yourself with positive people.
- If you want something, you have to go out and get it.
- If your mind's eye can see it, your body will achieve it.
- Have balance in your life.
- Be willing to change job/career if it is no longer fun.

Unlocking the Secrets of Successful Women

- If you are not happy, determine what you want in your life, and make sure others around you know what that is.
- Work where it does not feel like work, where you look forward to every day.

www.TaraOBrien.com

If you are not happy, determine what you want in your life, and make sure others around you know what that is.

CHAPTER 10

One Day at a Time

If you want something, you'll find a way.
You can be anything you want to be. It's up to you.

—Paul William Sellars, my father

Marilyn Sellars

Born at home on small farm in Southern Minnesota, I was the first daughter, and second of five children. My singing "career" started in church at about age three when I sang "Oh What a Beautiful Morning" at the top of my lungs during the sermon, to the delight of all around precocious little me.

I was a performer all my childhood, and with siblings and family members, we entered singing/performing contests in the area, almost always winning top or close-to-top honors. From age thirteen to eighteen, I studied voice with Gertrude Boe Overby of St. Olaf College, which was near our home.

While attending a one-room country school with three other girls as my classmates through eighth grade, I was fortunate to have a wonderful teacher whose husband was an executive for the Land O'Lakes company. Her daughter, who was a librarian in Washington, D.C., shipped us boxes of used books. With all these books, I was in heaven as I loved to read—and we didn't get a TV until I was thirteen. My life was what today is a "fairytale," a very Laura Ingalls Wilder lifestyle. Having heard about the singing going on at school and other places, our teacher's husband suggested having all the children who wanted to sing, do a jingle about chocolate milk for a radio commercial. What a thrill it was to hear us sing on the radio.

After graduating high school, I moved to Minneapolis. As my father drove me to a rooming house near the U of M, he said, "I know you want to go to college, but I can't afford to send you. But if you want to go, you'll find a way. You can be anything you want to be. *It's up to you.*"

I believed him, and still do. Such empowerment was the defining moment of my life.

Once settled in, I took a retail job at Dayton's downtown as a sales clerk in the camera department. I continued my voice lessons at MacPhail Center for Music, and at the same time, tried out for every possible beauty contest or pageant. I had been Miss Northfield at age seventeen, and a finalist in the Miss Minnesota Pageant. I would always win the talent portions, which helped to get jobs singing with bands at night. I had an interesting variety of jobs after Daytons, including an ad agency, elevator operator at Northwestern Bank Building, a stewardess for Northwest Airlines, and finally to a brokerage firm as a receptionist, where I met my first husband, who was an attorney and businessman.

In 1962, when our first daughter was only two months old, the Leamington Hotel came calling, having heard of me because of my various singing gigs around town—and then my piano bar career was born.

I took the job because we needed the money to buy our first house. For the next twelve years, I worked six nights a week, four or five hours each night, all in the best hotel lounges and nightclubs in Minneapolis.

During those evenings, I played piano and sang for *almost 19,000 hours* in that time period. Plus I was doing occasional corporate and private parties.

During those years, I had the opportunity to talk with traveling businessmen and women from all over the world, between singing songs they had requested. The audience chatting me up every night between songs also included the "cream" of the local business and sports world. It was an incredibly valuable learning experience, besides which I was challenged to learn a great variety of music.

I was playing at the Hub Cap Pub when my third daughter was born with spina bifida and hydrocephalus. She lived nine months, with many hospitalizations. Many nights I would go see her at 1:30 in the morning after working all night. The hospital was so kind to let me in since my days were full with the other two girls and maintaining a home. I was also dealing with many other things in my life because our marriage was not going to survive my husband's depression and addiction issues.

I remember vividly being upset one night, not finding my baby in her bed. I ran out to the front desk where the nurses apologized for frightening me. Because she was so adorable, they enjoyed having her in a baby seat on their desk so they could "talk" to her. I still remember how she would wake up and smile at me when I would come home from work and go check on her. Truly one of God's angels.

I did have a full-time live-in woman, without whose presence in our home I could not have worked and pursued my career. She did not drive, but was utterly trustworthy, and she loved my girls wholeheartedly. She also had some hospital training, which helped a lot during my third daughter's brief life. She remained with us until my two daughters graduated from high school. I was so fortunate to be able to afford to have her.

After my divorce, I knew I needed to work harder at my career. With the encouragement of my fans at the Mandalay Piano Lounge in the Ambassador Motor Hotel, where I ultimately played for seven years, I made my first album in 1972—a collection of pop and country songs.

Through various connections, I entered the world of local radio, first on WCCO (830 AM) where Denny Long was the brand-new music director. Boone and Erickson and all the other personalities played songs from my first album *every* day and night. Next local TV shows contacted me, and I appeared on all of them, sometimes even guest hosting. I received a lot of attention from Minneapolis and St. Paul newspaper columnists, and many smaller stations played my album.

The "break" came in early 1973. A country "Disc Jockey of the Year" from Iowa picked up my album and played the classic country song, "Welcome to My World," sung originally by Jim Reeves. Also, then many major country artists, such as Glen Campbell and John Denver, were contributing to the mainstream popularity of country music on TV.

My "fans" started telling me I needed to go to Nashville and "be a star." I told them I appreciated the thought, but I did not have the means to do it. Several wonderful people insisted on giving me the money to make a demo. Another still close and much-valued friend from Minneapolis volunteered to help. He had experience with recording and Nashville, and covered the fabled "16th and 17th Avenues" in Nashville, known as Music Row, literally walking in with my demo and first album and looking for a manager/producer for me.

Entering the Jim Reeves Enterprises, he met Clarence Selman, a (very) slow-talking Texan who had been managing the Reeves offices for some time. Clarence liked what he heard on my album, especially the Jim Reeves song. But what he liked most was the opportunity to introduce a new voice in Nashville, and what that could mean for both our futures. Nashville was in the process of becoming more "pop" sounding, with Glen Campbell and Kris Kristofferson on national TV along with many other new stars making country more mainstream, not just "Opry."

Clarence spent the better part of a year looking for material and a record label to release a new album for me made in Nashville. Meanwhile, I kept working in Minneapolis, raising my girls and hoping for a break.

This is when I learned what being "a star" could mean. I was able to guest on the Original Grand Old Opry, which is still in use today in downtown Nashville. I made many appearances anywhere Clarence could get someone to listen to me.

Being an avid golfer came in handy because I started to meet many of the country stars who are still my friends today. I was invited to play in tournaments, where after the stars played golf all day, we'd then entertain. I still receive invitations to such events, and especially enjoy being able to see my friends I've made through the years.

The break came when Mega Records signed me. On the last week of December 1973, I recorded my first Nashville album called, "Marilyn Sellars: One Day at a Time." We made the record using all the very best musicians and backup singers available. "One Day" was the most-played jukebox song in the Midwest in 1974. It sold over one million albums worldwide, changing my life forever.

I was thrilled when my single, "One Day at a Time," became No. 1, and the song hit all the national charts, crossing over from Country to Pop and Easy Listening—and finally, Gospel. It had an amazing forty-three weeks straight on Billboard charts, even overtaking an Elvis Presley album. This earned me numerous honors for being the first to record such a classic song. It was a great thrill to sing it on the new Grand Old Opry—which opened in late 1974 in Opryland, and national TV shows like "Name That Tune."

It was the beginning of thirty-plus years of entertaining worldwide.

It's still amazing to me to think about how far all this was from a farm in southern Minnesota, where as a child I listened to the Grand Old Opry on the radio.

How did I get that song? The best answer is being in the right place at the right time. Marijohn Wilkins, who wrote the song, had just finished writing it at a time her husband at the time, Clarence Selman, my producer and manager, was putting together material for my first album on Mega Records. I was spending as much time in Nashville as I possibly could while getting ready to record this most important project. One day Marijohn asked me if I'd like to take a ride on her boat on Old Hickory Lake outside Nashville. She wanted to play a new song for me. She brought one of the very first small electric keyboards on the boat, and there I heard "One Day at a Time" for the first time. I told her I thought it was a lovely song, and I'd love to record it.

When we got back to the office, Clarence was not happy. He felt "One Day" did not fit with all the other songs being chosen. All of them were quite country or pop-oriented. Most were never recorded before, and the best writers at the time wrote them. He felt "One Day" was too "gospel" for our project.

As it turned out, they were both right about the song. When the new owner of the record label sided with Marijohn and chose the song to be the title song for the album, it was quite an interesting situation. Many country radio stations did not want to play it because they felt it belonged on gospel stations because of the phrase "sweet Jesus." However, fans called in demanding to hear it anyway. This was a win/win for everybody—especially for Kris Kristofferson, who Marijohn gave half writer's credit to for helping her with a line of the song. She was also a very savvy businesswoman, and she knew his name on the label would make radio stations give it a listen, while not recognizing my name or remembering hers. He was certainly well known then, having written big hits like, "Help Me Make It Through the Night," "Me and Bobby McGee," and others. She was right, because after all these years, he is recognized as the writer of the song.

Both Clarence and Marijohn have now passed away, and I still miss them. Marijohn was truly one of the pioneer women in the music business with the natural gift for writing songs, as well as being a successful businesswoman. Clarence was a very talented people person coupled with a very bright and astute business mind.

"One Day" was released March 1974, and by October, it was a number one album, and I was swamped with work. It was so exciting, but also exhausting.

I continued at the piano bar in Minneapolis when not on the road, singing all my new album songs, plus patriotic songs—from the 1930s forward, particularly from WWII, plus Broadway, country, and gospel. I played piano and sang songs people loved to sing or hum along with—songs that took them down memory lane.

With the success of "One Day at a Time," I was invited to perform at corporate shows, county and state fairs, and TV and nightclubs coast to coast. I was kept extremely busy, along with returning to the Ambassador between those jobs.

I had been invited to be on the Grand Old Opry, but couldn't accept because I didn't live in Nashville. In those days, they wanted you to be available there every week. So I made plans to move to Nashville to pursue the options there. The decision was made easier because my live-in helper agreed to go with us. The girls were just about to start junior high school, making it the right time to move.

In 1974, I faced the biggest life-changing decision of my career and personal life.

Unlocking the Secrets of Successful Women

I met my second husband Peter, who was the "extra man" at a dinner party at my house. I love to cook and plan parties—and still do. I often joke I had to marry him because he was the only man I ever dated who my daughters liked. As much as I wanted to continue my career, it was also more important to me to share my life and my daughters with the man I cared about so much. As of this writing, we have been married thirty-seven years. We have eight grandchildren and two great grandchildren. I have absolutely *no* regrets about my decision to choose family first. For me, it was the right decision.

Along the way, I've met a lot of fun and famous entertainers, many of whom I got to know while doing some shows in Branson, Missouri in the nineties, and others from the many golf tournaments I've played in, too many to list. I will share one fun story:

One of my favorite people is Tommy Cash. When he and his band were on their way to a gig in Duluth, they stayed at our home. I'm quite sure I'm the only suburban Minneapolis housewife who answered her home phone to this: "This is John Cash. Is my little brother Tommy there?" Both Peter and I were privileged to be introduced to Johnny Cash by his little brother several years ago.

I sang at so many fundraisers I can't count them all, and in doing so, I met three Presidents when they came to town, including President Ronald Reagan a couple times when I sang at a local event he attended. He looked everyone in the eye, pleasantly greeting each person to whom he was introduced. He even put his arm around me for our photo, and I'll never forget how thrilled I was to meet him.

Another most memorable person was Vice President Hubert Humphrey, who occasionally came to dinner at the Ambassador when I played there. He would have a corner table right next to me reserved for him and his wife Muriel for after dinner, which allowed them to listen for a little while without being disturbed. I have some fun photos of us at a festival called Cornland USA in Olivia, Minnesota, where we appeared on stage together. A very special man.

I had a "wonderful life." When my career was at its strongest, I was performing coast to coast and also internationally:
- National TV, including on "Name That Tune"
- The Grand Ole Opry—and was one of the first to appear at the New Grand Old Opry in 1975
- Orchestra Hall and for the annual Symphony Ball
- Most every country club and supper club in the Twin Cities

- Every major corporation and business in the Twin Cities hired me, at least once; many multiple times
- County and state fairs all over the Midwest
- Ten years of singing the national anthem for the Vikings
- Celebrity golf tournaments and fund raisers
- Dinner theatres
- Political conventions
- Nightclubs from Bermuda to Hollywood
- An amazing month shared with my husband, performing on cruise ships on China's Yangtze River
- Performed in nearly 40 countries–from China to Jamaica
- Entertained on the Orient Express, the stages of Disney World, the theatres

Awards and Honors:
- "One Day at a Time" Album—43 straight weeks on Billboard, crossing over from national Country charts to Pop Charts to Gospel Charts.
- Minnesota Rock and Country Hall of Fame, inducted in 2004
- Minnesota Music Hall of Fame, inducted in 2009
- Cashbox Magazine Best New Female Artist of the Year (1975)
- Academy of Country Music Best New Female Artist Nomination (one of five)
- ASCAP award for "He's Everywhere" in 1975

Success to me is: Being able to make people happy. Performing in front of audiences is an amazing experience. I get to watch their faces and see how they react to what I say, sing, or do.

If you don't think about and choose what you want to do, you risk getting bogged down in a lifestyle or circumstances that keep you forever sidetracked from living your dream.

CHAPTER 11

A Love of Art Drew Me Into Living My Dream

*All life is an experiment.
The more experiments you make the better.*

—Emerson

Pat Lindquist

As a young girl, I learned to say yes to projects that allowed me to use my artistic talents and interests, from artsy-craftsy display cases in the school hallways to painting banners and signs for school events. Years later this would lead me to the title of art director in the business world. As the oldest child in my family, I had also been active at home and in school, from student council to volunteer committees. My dad was active too, and we learned to raise our hand, volunteer and again, say yes to help with any project. I also learned to take photos with my dad's old Brownie camera, which would later become my passion.

As an art major in college, I was thrilled to meet the famous printmaker Malcolm Myers who taught me not only how to make prints and etchings, but gave me a handle on creative thinking: to think outside the box, take risks—and say yes again, to creative challenges. I would continue to follow those rules for years, when promoting art, artists and celebrities, with my commercial art knowledge and photos, featuring them in my news stories, and later, to promote restaurateurs, chefs, food and drink and more. I even mounted a Myers Art Exhibit and Sale twenty years later with this art mentor of mine, and I am proud to have six of his prints on my walls.

Other wonderful art and photo memories of my next twenty-five years surround me on walls and shelves. This includes local artists like Jim Conaway, to nationally renowned Peter Max, to famous chefs I have worked with and their cookbooks—the likes of Wolfgang Puck, Emeril, and Marcus

Samuelsson. I found my first job at the *Minneapolis Star Tribune* when I was searching the want ads during the holidays for part-time work, and spotted a listing under the "Artist" category for a job as a keyliner at the newspaper. I didn't know what a keyliner was, but I said yes to the job, and found myself sitting at a drawing board, learning the basics of printing, layouts, advertising and retail as I prepared ads and pasted-up copy (called keylining) for local department stores like Dayton's and Donaldson's.

When a job for layout artist at Donaldson's opened up in 1970, I took the leap and got the job. This put me at a drawing board in the advertising/art department right in the heart of downtown Minneapolis, at the corner of 7th Street, on the newly constructed Nicollet Mall. During the early seventies, they were building the famous fifty-two-story IDS Tower, across the street, and I was there every day, amidst the growth and excitement of all the new skyways connecting downtown buildings.

This was a pivotal time for my step into the world of news. I was at the right place at the right time, and women were getting more visible and more vocal.

Jan Werner, Donaldson's Special Events Director, asked if I might like to be a freelance writer and report on the busy, changing social life downtown and in the skyways for the new *Skyway News*. This was dropped in my lap. In 1970, Sam Kaufman, the owner of a well-known PR firm, Kaufman & Spicer, decided to publish a free newspaper to be handed out weekly (eventually twice a week). Again I said yes, even though I never took typing. Before I knew it, I was writing a weekly column, as well as rubbing elbows with our local movers and shakers in the community. I was also meeting music and movie celebrities traveling through our city on junkets and promotions. In those days, we had no other free city weeklies. This was before the *Twin Cities Reader* or *City Pages*, and before monthly magazines like *Mpls. St. Paul Magazine* or *Minnesota Monthly*.

I wrote my first column in long hand on yellow legal paper, and Jan Werner typed it for me. Jan became editor at the *Skyway News*. She told me they couldn't pay much, but I would receive a lot of comps. I recall asking, "What's a comp?" Jan said it's a free dinner or theater tickets, press invites to free previews, and sneak previews or VIP events. Sounded great.

I named my column Pat's Potpourri, a French word I first saw as a category on the new Jeopardy TV show, meaning: "a collection of miscellaneous or diverse items." Magic! I could write about anything I wanted: food, wine, bars, theater, movies, and events—the works. As the years went on, I was invited to press night openings at the Guthrie and Chanhassen, as well as new VIP restaurant openings or movie previews. At the time, I didn't even know there were VIP restaurant openings, and I had certainly never been a VIP myself. Over the years, I also became a movie reviewer, attending screenings, and choosing the top ten movies each year, and meeting stars who came through town. I even interviewed the likes of Gregory Peck, who in fact, became a friend, but that's another story. I truly was living a dream … a life I could never have imagined.

In real life, I was also named the art director for Powers Department Store, earning my full-time salary to pay the rent and raise my daughter while I continued freelance writing. It was a wonderful whirlwind of fun and frivolity throughout the seventies and eighties, and I learned I was considered part of the "Fourth Estate"—the news media. Remember: There was no social media, no Internet, Facebook, blogs or twitter, where everyone considers himself a reporter or writer today. And, as a working girl and reporter, having fun drinks after work would also bring me fodder for the column, which I called research, and still do.

We were just a block from the historic Murray's Restaurant, and I was lucky to meet the grande dame herself, Marie Murray, and son, Pat, who ran the business. We would stop in on Friday nights after work for their famous free garlic toast and ladies night. A happy hour glass of champagne cost just thirty cents. I could wear my "girl reporter" hat, have fun with friends and share the news of other popular restaurants and nightspots in the seventies. I also met women who were leaders in the community, which gave me more knowledge about business and operations in the hospitality industry. Many made a name for themselves in the food business, like Mama Coronado with her authentic Mexican cuisine over at La Casa Coronado, and on the river, Reiko Weston lead the way with her daring move to the historic river's edge with Fuji Ya Japanese restaurant.

Weston's daughter Carol, who went to high school with my daughter Lisa, continued to operate Fuji Ya with her husband, Tom Hanson, after Reiko passed in 1988. They are now located at the busy Lyn-Lake intersection, which I also helped roll out. Fuji Ya taught us how it was done, and paved the way for more Asian cuisine, and Reiko who had been a dear friend, mentored me to understand the challenges women faced in the business world.

One of my biggest influences then was Louise Saunders, since I was a fan of the nationally acclaimed Charlie's Cafe Exceptionale. It was an award-winning steakhouse for decades, and the hangout for local celebs, politicals, plus judges and lawyers from the government center, across the street. Louise took over ownership after her famous husband Charlie Saunders passed away, and ran it until the mid 1980s when she chose to retire—and closed their doors. Louise also became a real mentor and a good friend. She was active in the community, the Minneapolis Downtown Council, and on the National Small Business Owners Advisory Council to President Carter in D.C. during the period when our own Walter Mondale was Vice President. When she had heard I was also doing some weekly radio gossip on events with DJ Glen Olson on his WCCO Radio show, Louise asked if I would consider writing radio commercials for Charlie's as a sponsor for my Radio News Events. I said yes, another lucky twist for me.

To meet the radio requirements, I had to join the American Federation of Television & Radio Artists (AFTRA) and my title of "artist" took a new spin. In the late seventies, Jim Toscano recruited me for the Society of Fine Arts, the membership organization for the Minneapolis Institute of Arts (MIA), as their Marketing/Membership Director. He read my column and heard me on radio, and felt I could be a good communicator and spokesperson for the MIA with groups and special events, and help them grow their membership. I said yes—and we did! Three years later, after the MIA had grown from 8,000 to 12,500 members, I said yes to a new offer by the owner of C.G. Rein Galleries, to be their Marketing Director, and rolled out new galleries in Texas and Colorado.

After four years with Rein, in 1984 I took another leap and opened my own agency with the support of Clayton Rein, who was my first client. I was forty years old, my daughter was nearly thru college, and I now owned my own business in a field I loved, wearing many hats, from both the layout and design for ads and PR to the media side of the communications industry. I was thrilled with the challenge, afraid of the risks, and yet excited by the potential of being my own boss with so many choices for the road ahead. I was an "entrepreneur"—another French word that came into my lexicon: "taking initiative, ready to accept the risk of failure, managing a new business." I was living the dream of owning a business, fifteen years after I had pasted up my first keyline at the *Star Tribune*.

In addition to support from Clayton Rein, I pitched two favorites, Bridgeman's Ice Cream Parlor and Lund's Grocery Stores, gaining their business and support. I also continued to work with many local retailers like Ribnick's Furs, and new retail and food businesses from the regional rollout of Applebee's to local entrepreneurs like Famous Dave's Dave Anderson and Leeann Chin. Both also became dear friends and mentors. And the world around me was changing. We had left the era of electric typewriters, copiers and the fax machine of the eighties and nineties, and by 1999, I took the risk of learning how to add computers to my business. The next decade was spent keeping up. I said yes to "techie" changes, including a new digital camera and cell phones, and I love it. Technology is now a crucial part of my everyday life for my clients and me—from iPhoto on my laptop where I use thousands of photos and Facebook. We all live on our iPhones and our Internet connections.

Now with nearly thirty years under my belt with my own business, these are my thoughts:
- I was lucky to be at the right place, at the right time.
- I was never afraid to say yes to change and risk.
- You have to be flexible and fearless (well maybe just don't show your fear, eh?), but be able to adjust your dreams and goals too, by keeping reasonable expectations.
- Do not be afraid to work hard.
- Be grateful for your good health.

Good friends and family have always made it easier to say, yes, and have made me happy to share the rewards and success of my business.

You have to be flexible and fearless, well, maybe just don't show your fear. Be able to adjust your dreams and goals too, by keeping reasonable expectations.

CHAPTER 12

How Five Became Eighty

Put it before them briefly, so they will read it, clearly so they will appreciate it, picturesquely so they will remember it, and above all, accurately so they will be guided by its light.

—Joseph Pulitzer

Connie Anderson

In 1997, five women met around a kitchen table, talking about writing over lunch. They were writing books about business, poetry, their lives, or their passions. These women became friends and strong support for each other. After a while, one asked if she could bring a writer friend to the group—and then so did others. Each visitor brought new life and a new story. Those who cherished the group felt a strong connection and started sharing. Soon you could see the kinship reverberate throughout this new sisterhood.

Quickly, this small but growing self-managed group decided to move to a restaurant.

Such was the modest beginning of our writers group that eventually became WOW–Women of Words. "Wow" is what we often shout when we hear a great story or a good idea. WOW women willingly share their victories—and just as readily share their mistakes, with the belief we help each other most with our honesty.

Over the years, at more than one lunch, a member has told us she has been diagnosed with a critical illness or is facing a major setback. We let her speak. Then after a communal deep breath, the next woman takes her turn, and we go back to talking about writing. We're supportive but not suffocating; we're caring, but understand that is not the focus of the gathering.

Rule #1: We do not talk about personal issues, period, unless they are pertinent to our work. Rule

Rule #2: We listen but never judge, offering our thoughts only when, and if, relevant.

As more guests became members, it was immediately apparent as every woman revealed her "own story," some stories would develop into memoirs, business books, self-help books, or passionate treatises about personal causes. Some stories bring tears; others produce varied responses from the rest of the women, emotions like disbelief, anger, sadness, and often, joy.

Each woman's forthright manner of talking and supporting others has made this lunch the most important day of the month for many WOW members, including me. One woman recently wrote me: "I can't even remember what my life was like before I became part of this amazing group of women." I strongly agree.

As deep friendships have developed, each month it gets more like "herding cats" to get them to break up their conversations, sit down and order lunch. Time management became essential as the group grew, each woman taking three minutes to tell us about her project, ask questions of the group, and seek help with contacts, ideas, etc. A timer impartially keeps things on track, its annoying beep reminding each member her time is up and to wrap up her thoughts and sit down.

Most of the women have already been, or will be, independently publishing their book. Some sell it at the back of the room after their speaking engagements, while others attend book clubs and do readings, knowing that writing a book raises the bar on how people view their expertise. At one time or another, we all have had the dream some agent will fall in love with our book, find us a publisher, and get us a huge advance payment—but then reality sets in. Mostly, we write, publish, sell and market our stories, and then we bask in the glory of telling them to others.

The scope of the group expands exponentially with each new member. Thanks to several WOW women willing to stretch themselves, we now have a professional retreat each fall where we share our expertise in greater detail than at our monthly meetings. Each year we invite outside guests so they too could learn from our expertise. The speakers include our members as well as other women who have special experience in related fields such as marketing, social media, platform development, publicity, and literary law.

In 2011, we established our own closed Facebook page where members can post articles, coming events, and good and bad news. With just one post, all 80-plus women can read and respond. Many of our women have been interviewed on radio or TV, and we support them by listening or calling in to the program. We read each other's books, writing and posting reviews. Just today one woman said she had stage fright and asked for ideas, contacts, and individual help if possible. Within an hour, eight people told their own stage-fright story and shared how they overcame their fears.

From the initial five women, our invitation list grew to over 40 names, and more were asking to join. But meeting time constraints forced us to limit the size of the group to ensure everyone had sufficient time to speak. A second group was started, and within 18 months, more than 40 women joined WOW2.

Inevitably, the *right* women attend; the *right* people feel comfortable sharing their issues—and the *right* women reach out to help their sisters. The women may be in different stages of writing their books, and many may have spent years working on them, but once they become active in WOW, they tend to produce a book more quickly. They like the idea of getting a book written in a timely manner. The encouragement they're given, their sense of "accountability" and, above all, their desire to make their fellow writers proud of them, lights a fire to warm us all.

It is my honor to facilitate these two groups, and I revel in the feeling "this was the best lunch group ever," which I say, without fail, twice a month, every month, after both the WOW1 and WOW2 meetings.

WOW truly is the "village" that helps turn writers into authors—all eighty of us.

www.WordandDeedsInc.com

At one time or another we all have had the dream some agent will fall in love with our book, find us a publisher, and get a huge advance payment. But reality sets in. Mostly we write, publish, sell and market our stories—and then bask in the glory of telling them to others.

Unlocking the Secrets of Successful Women

CHAPTER 13

Yes, Please

*You can't be that kid standing at the top of the waterslide,
over thinking it. You have to go down the chute.*
—Tina Fey

Molly Cox Ziton

"I'll do that for you." I said to Tom, the general manager of a Holiday Inn in Indianapolis, Indiana 28 years ago. What I offered to do was to teach the new customer service program the hotel chain was rolling out. For Tom, speaking in public was paramount to what Indiana Jones felt about snakes.

Growing up in a house with four over-achieving siblings, I looked for places to stand out and be heard. I wanted my own audience. Perfect! And, if I were training, I wouldn't have to make cold calls—what a clever girl I am.

So, that's how I stumbled into professional speaking, which led me to write a book on the principles of improvisation and produce a film on self-care for the caregiver. I know—so predictable.

Here's the thing. When you say yes to something, a new door opens. I said "yes" a lot, perhaps because I've always had a curious nature. This path has mostly worked, except for my first marriage; the one time I shouldn't have said yes.

Although, now when I think about it, had I not said yes, I wouldn't have my beautiful, smart, oh-so-funny daughter. The main thing I learned from that experience: something good can come out of something bad, unless it's a lousy haircut.

I moved back to my home state of Minnesota and took a job at a very fancy hotel. After two years at the sales helm, the hotel closed. (It's an incredible ego boost to be the sales and marketing director when the hotel closes. *Good job!*) The owner thought I was "so good with people," he chose me to be the one to knock on hotel doors and tell people they had to check out because, well, *the hotel was closing.*

Me: Knock. Knock. I'm so sorry but you will have to check out of the hotel today, Mr. Smith.
Guest: What? Why? When?
Me: In one hour. The hotel is closing. I'm so sorry.
Guest: What the %$*&! What kind of a ^&%#@ is this?
Me: Yes, well, still sir, you have to leave. May I make a reservation at another hotel for you?
Guest: Fine! Yes! What choice do I have? &6%4*# (repeat 67 times).
Me: Okay, very well. And, um, you should put some clothes on because as I mentioned, the hotel is clos—
Guest: SLAM.

I'm the kind of person who wants to be smack in the middle of the action. But even for me, that was a bit much. And yet, it taught me something: I was capable of doing horrid, embarrassing and degrading work in exchange for a paycheck. And I would have a funny story to tell at a dinner party.

Working at the hotel, for what turned out to be a psychopath millionaire, was good training. My lesson? I learned to work for—and with—jerks, but also some very cool people. Here's the thing … when you work with at least one professional and extremely funny person (which I did), you can get through anything. The worse the situation is, the funnier it can be. It's an attitude I embrace.

I was promoted to general manager of the club. *What were they thinking?* I learned to read a profit-and-loss report, manage twelve departments, and when you run the joint, you can demand kick-ass customer service. I also learned it's possible for two club members to have an affair in a tanning room. True story.

Our service was so good other companies would ask, "How did you do that?"—and, "Could I do it for their company?" So, I trained a lot of people and wrote a lot of training manuals. Then, I learned about the National Speakers Association (NSA). I joined, quit my job, and became a professional speaker. Who knew you could get *paid* to talk? Here's the thing, when people continually tell you you're good at something, listen. It can change your life.

Many people in my audiences commented on my use of humor and my ability to think on my feet. More than a couple people asked if I'd ever taken improvisation (such as Second City). My thought: Hmmm, maybe I should take improv. I did, and it changed my life. I also took other classes—*a lot* of classes, including attending Disney University. Nothing happens until you take action on your own behalf.

I met a couple of hysterical and talented guys in my improv classes. One was my teacher who quit the improv company to go into business with me. Lesson: Align yourself with talent. If you're always the best, what's to learn? Of course you'll want to have something to offer that complements the relationship.

We had a wild ride for six years. We wrote a book: *Improvise This! How to Think on Your Feet so You Don't Fall on Your Face,* went to New York and secured a publisher, ate and drank, wrote and performed sketch comedy for companies and associations nationally. Lesson: It is possible to have fun, love what you do, and make a living doing it.

Whoa! A twist and turn of life. A couple of twirls and I was a solo speaker again, and at the same time, being the caregiver for two aging, ill parents. Cancer and Alzheimer's disease came along, and my life dramatically changed. People said, "You should help others, and speak on this whole experience." Lots of "shoulds" were flying my way, but they did make sense. I produced an award-winning film about self-care for the caregiver called, "Note to Self."

It's worth pointing out this period of time was not the highlight of my career. But you probably already knew.

In case you ever find yourself in this situation, and about 60 trillion/bazillion of us will, (actual numbers reported by CNN), it's important to note caregiving is the most important work you will ever do. But, it's never going to show up in your plan. It just happens. Luckily I had a flexible business plan that fits nicely onto paper the size of a cocktail napkin. Okay fine, it's actually on a cocktail napkin. It reads: Get up and do something. I realize it's a bit heavy on detail, but it's worked like a charm.

In my line of work—funny business—it's a lot harder for women than men. You have to fight for the money you earn and know deep in your gut you're worth it. Confidence is everything. There are still men who think successful, confident women are narcissists. Women who have wild, fun ideas, and who are driven, are often labeled as "crazy." Women like Tina Fey, Amy Poehler and Bette Midler are as important as Rosa Parks. (Okay, a bit of a stretch, but you get the idea.) Take time to thank a woman who's made it easier for you. Thank good men, too. My point is, thank people.

I don't claim to have all the answers, but I know what's worked for me. Say "yes," listen to what others tell you, and stay true to yourself. When you're lost, ask yourself, "What would Betty White do?" She's going strong at 90—she's just got to be onto something.

It is possible to have fun, love what you do, and make a living doing it.

CHAPTER 14

H2O for Life–
Youth Changing the World

Never doubt that a small group of thoughtful, committed citizens can change the world. Indeed it's the only thing that ever has.
—Margaret Mead

Patty Hall

In 1995, I had the wonderful opportunity to travel to Kenya with my mother and 17-year-old daughter, Katy, to embark on a "dream-of-a-lifetime" safari. A strong connection was made, and we fell in love with the country and especially its people, and felt very fortunate to be able to go back later to help build a health center. While volunteering with Global Citizens Network, we lived in Keumbu, a small community where we noticed the effect of inadequate sanitation and hand washing within rural communities. We also saw what an arduous task it was to collect water, and once collected, the dirty water then had to be boiled. In the U.S., we rarely think about our easy access to clean water, but for people in the developing world it is an *every-day* concern.

Over the next twelve years, my family continued to visit Kenya and brought medical supplies for clinics and delivered books and supplies to schools in communities we visited. We looked forward to our volunteer activities in Kenya, and as a small group of individuals, we did what we were able to do to help the friends we met there. We helped complete several health centers, not through skilled labor but by carrying bricks, digging foundations, and hauling water for cement.

More than ten years after our first visit, in the summer of 2006, I received a desperate cry for help from Christopher Mutuku. Christopher, employed as a driver for a safari company, became our driver on all of our visits to Kenya. He had become a cherished friend. Chris told me his village, Kathungu, needed help to create a permanent water source. Their children and animals were dying due to lack of water. Who did I know who could help them?

My first instinct was to say, "There's nothing I could do," and move on. Then I remembered Mikhail Gorbachev's much-quoted remark "If not me, who? And if not now, when?" **I began to think about how could I, just one person, fund a water project in Kenya.** I decided to start with the teachers, students, and friends at my school, Highview Middle School in New Brighton, Minnesota. I found several teachers who said they would help me. At our first faculty meeting in 2006, I shared about how several teachers and classes were going to help me raise funds to bring water to a village in Africa.

The response of the entire faculty surprised and thrilled me. Mary Kuritz, a fellow teacher, asked why all of them couldn't participate. So we began our work. We had wonderful support from the entire faculty. Language Arts teacher Maureen Haqq, who motivated her classes, and a parent volunteer who brought her marketing skills to the table, were rock stars. Our students nearly doubled our $7,000 goal, and over the course of the year, raised $13,000. It was transformational for our school. We had worked together on a common goal, and in the process, changed our school environment to be more welcoming and inclusive. Every student had the opportunity to participate. Our corps of student leaders planned events centered on the value of nickels, dimes and quarters. After all, in Kenya, a dollar was a typical daily wage.

I visited Kathungu Village for dedication of the water project and returned with photos and the villagers' thanks. This was my ah-ha moment. Students said to me, "You mean, if I went to Kenya, I could see this project?" The project became real to them, and the students learned what a difference their actions had made to the community of Kathungu. So often, students are asked to donate to a cause, but they never see the outcome of their efforts. Through photos and letters from the community, our students realized the impact of their efforts.

As a teacher, I realized the power of youth engagement around a compelling global issue. We decided to partner with another school in Kenya the following year. During the course of the next school year, our students investigated the global water crisis. They created PowerPoints, organized concerts, created a website, and participated in water-related events.

Then I met David Douglas at a National Service Learning Convention in New Mexico. He was the founder of the Water Advocates (now known as WASH Advocates), an organization based in Washington D.C. David was to change my life. He was amazed when I told him about the success of our school project. He asked: "Can you get me ten schools next year because I have ten water projects?"

I hadn't planned to do *one* more project, let alone ten. His confidence inspired me to co-found *H2O for Life*, a nonprofit organization named by my students, with a mission to engage and inspire young people to learn, take action, and become global citizens. Founding an organization is not a one-man show. Fellow teacher Maureen Haqq and a parent volunteer were co-founders and hardworking board members.

During our first year as a non-profit organization, school year 2007-08, H2O for Life enlisted sixteen school partners. How did we engage these sixteen schools? We asked them! Sometimes a simple ask yields great results.

My own parents were a defining force in my life. I was fortunate they were philanthropic, and always welcomed everyone who came into their lives. My mother would talk to anyone and everyone. I remember having a political discussion in a shoe store in South Korea. Language barriers and all, we learned much of what one Korean man felt about Oliver North.

- I learned at a young age kindness and caring are important attributes.
- I was encouraged to pursue my dreams.
- My dad instilled in me the idea that I could accomplish whatever I set out to do.
- My parents also provided me with opportunities to travel and meet interesting people. As a result, I developed a love for the global world at a young age.

As a young child I wanted to be a teacher, and I have never wavered. I thought then, and believe today, teachers have one of the most important jobs in the world; we hold the future generations in our hands.

With the founding of H2O for Life, I was lucky to have Maureen Haqq, and others continue to be passionate and supportive of our adventure. Maureen continues to be a board member who is always ready to help. Many thanks also for the support of two family foundations continuing today to make it possible for us to provide materials, outreach and start-up costs necessary to organize a non-profit organization.

We were successful because of the hundreds of dedicated, amazing teachers across the United States. They understand the youth of today must be engaged in relevant, meaningful actions, and must have opportunities to actively participate in service that can change the world.

Starting a non-profit organization was challenging. None of us had experience in non-profit business, and we learned from our mistakes along the way. From the beginning, H2O for Life was blessed to have the financial support that assisted to further our outreach. For the first three years, we worked out of our homes to connect schools and facilitate projects around the world, squeezing the work of H2O for Life in after already long workdays. All of us were working full time at various careers, and it was exhausting and exhilarating.

Eventually, I retired from teaching and became a full-time volunteer. My son, Steve, became our Director of Schools, responsible for communicating with teachers and connecting with the non-governmental organizations implementing the projects.

Ramping up our funding for operations was a business learning experience. The economy took a nosedive, and schools were decreasing their fund-raising goals. As a result, grants for operations were becoming more competitive. To combat the challenges, we knew we needed to engage more schools and meet more people. We began to attend educational conferences to meet large numbers of teachers through exhibits and presentations. As a result of my travels, I have met remarkable teachers and leaders in the water sector who have become friends for life. Many have continued to introduce H2O for Life to their students for multiple years. We've had our struggles and times where we weren't sure what the future would bring, but the organization is solid, and now we are on the verge of explosive growth.

I was extremely proud of our school when we surpassed our fund-raising goal. I would have been content to know our actions changed a community. Today, I am amazed at the growth and scope of H2O for Life. We are a nationally recognized non-profit with a voice in the water sector. It is gratifying to be asked to speak at World Water Day events and to be asked to represent youth engagement around the country.

Visiting the project at Kathungu Village was life changing. The community was grateful for the funds, and could hardly believe kids raised the money. Never did I dream that H2O for Life schools would help bring water to over five hundred schools. I am proud of the work, and gratified to know our educational materials and the service learning experiences are not only changing lives for students in developing countries, but are changing the lives of students in the U.S. Students understand their actions matter—and their actions can change the world. This makes me ecstatic. But supporting an organization, developing materials, and providing the program is serious hard work. On days when it is overwhelming, I remind myself of the important work being done because of all the wonderful teachers, students, supporters and the office staff at H2O for Life. Then I take a deep breath and press on.

Many attributes lead to success. For me, determination, passion and action are key. My mentor and friend David Douglas, who challenged me with a simple statement: "Can you get me ten schools, because I have ten projects?" was a pivotal moment. Once I make a commitment, I am *determined* to see it to fruition. My biggest disappointments today are when teachers, students or schools choose projects, and then don't meet their goals—often not following through at all! Schools and NGO partners are counting on the funding, and sometimes we are letting them down. I cannot understand it. Making a commitment and sticking to it is important, and a lesson that should be shared by all.

I adopted the mantra of former President Bill Clinton and his Clinton Global Initiative: "Do something, and do it now," for kids around the world cannot wait for water. They are dying. I knew we would deliver ten schools and ten school projects if at all humanly possible—and we did.

Passion: When visiting Kenya prior to our first project, I met four young girls collecting water at a muddy water hole. Cows were standing in the water nearby. It was mid-day, and these girls, ranging from seven to twelve, were not in school. This vision stuck with me and opened my eyes to the global water problem. I began to do research and found over 1 billion people didn't have access to clean water, and two billion people lacked adequate sanitation. I also discovered women and girls share the burden of collecting water. Girls often spend hours every day walking for water, missing many hours of school, if they attend at all. Upon reaching puberty, if there is not access to an adequate latrine, girls tend to stop attending school. Studies have shown that educating girls is essential, and will lead to community change. Water, sanitation and hygiene education for schools became my passion.

I realized if our U.S. schools could change the circumstances for one school at a time, we would be changing the lives and creating opportunities for students in developing countries. In the process, our service learning project is also life-changing for our U.S. donor schools. Philanthropy must be taught through providing opportunities to give. H2O for Life provides that opportunity at a young age for youth in the United States. My goal is to work as hard as I possibly can to engage more U.S schools to investigate the global water crisis, while also taking action that truly will change the world.

Action: The mission of H2O for Life is twofold. We educate youth in the U.S. about water, and we provide the opportunity to participate in global action to provide water, sanitation and hygiene education to schools. Our educational materials provided to U.S. schools focus on local and global actions focused on the water crisis. As I began to study water, I was surprised at what I didn't know. I think my generation didn't focus on water while in school. Today, the issue is paramount. We cannot ignore the water crisis, and today is the day to take action. Students learn about local groundwater and wetland protection, how to conserve water, and how water is interconnected globally. The United States, in general, uses more water than most people in the world. As population expands, our water sources are being critically challenged. We must educate our youth to take actions to ensure future generations have access to a safe drink of water.

We encourage students to raise local awareness in their communities about local water, through service learning and action. Our world water crisis is serious. By 2025, it is predicted two-thirds of the world will be facing water shortages. Without local action—taking actions to change water usage and conservation, and without global action such as donating funds—things will not change for world water security and for schools in developing countries.

Advice: I think women more than men are driven by passion. What do *you* really care about? Define it, and figure out a way to embed it in your life. If you love what you do, it no longer becomes a "job," it becomes a calling. My work with H2O for Life is the most fulfilling work I have ever done. It combines my love of education with an outcome that feeds my passion. H2O for Life consumes my time, sometimes more than it should, but my goal is to move it to the stage where our *mission continues* far into the future.

Now, almost twenty years since my first visit to Kenya, the mission is solid, the business plan is solid, and there is more work to be done. We have a project with your name on it. *Join us today!*

www.h2oforlifeschools.org

I think women more than men are driven by passion. What do you really care about? Define it, and figure out a way to embed it in your life. If you love what you do, it's no longer a "job." It becomes a calling.

CHAPTER 15

Making Hay:
The Journey to Entrepreneurship

Nothing will work unless you do.

—Maya Angelou

Linda Hachfeld

My life journey began on a farm in west central Minnesota. I'd like to say it was a dairy farm, but back in the sixties and seventies, small farms had a host of animals—a few pigs, chickens, sheep, beef and dairy cattle. Life centered on the cycle of perpetual planting and harvesting. We toiled.

The earth took our attention. We turned the hard soil to plant a garden, cultivated the larger fields to plant corn, oats, sorghum, rye, and soybeans. And, while those crops were growing throughout the summer, it became haying season, time to cut the alfalfa, windrow the cutting, and bale the hay.

I recall the John Deere tractor pulling the square baler, which, in turn, pulled the wooden hayrack. We'd creak over every inch of those hayfields from one end to the other until we had piled every bale as high as the back of the rack (well over eight feet). And, then we'd drive slowly and carefully back to the farmyard, and pull up next to the barn where the hay elevator rested against the open doorway leading into the haymow (the upstairs of the barn).

Three sets of hands handled every bale. First, my dad pitched them off the hayrack onto the ground next to the elevator; then, he climb down and place them, one after another, onto the elevator. Next, my siblings and I removed the bales from the elevator as the bales fell and landed every which way in the haymow. The job for us children, who ranged from ages thirteen to six, was to organize the chaos caused by the ever-flowing bales, falling helter skelter at a pace seemingly impossible to keep up with—but we did.

We carried those bales across the haymow floor, stacking them into neat rows, end-to-end on one level; side by side on the next, creating a strong basket-weave foundation so the rows wouldn't topple as we climbed higher and higher until we could touch the underside of the barn's roof. There was a system to it all, which we created as we went along. We were always being mindful that a stairway of bales leading from the highest row to the lowest had to be arranged. This was so we could exit through the door cut in the haymow floor leading to the lower level where the cows were stanchioned for milking.

Looking back, I realize how "making hay" was a good "entrepreneur-in-training" proving ground. Who could have guessed making hay could give one the very life skills needed to start, grow, and tend a business? I count five character-building skills:

1. Believe in yourself,
2. Be present,
3. Work as a member of the team,
4. Stay on task, and
5. Don't give up.

When we're young, we know we can do anything. As a youthful farmhand, I just "did the job," without actually thinking about it.

Later in my mid-thirties I started a company called Appletree Press, an independent publishing firm with the mission to develop, publish, and market books and tools to encourage and promote a healthful lifestyle. Twenty-five years later, Appletree still publishes nutrition education books and tools for people who want to eat and live well. Along the way, my writing and publishing efforts were recognized for excellence nationally, winning two Benjamin Franklin Awards; one as Best New Voice, and another for Best Marketing Initiative.

Youth has a purpose. We believe in ourselves—we know "we can" do it. Even if we question our abilities, the thought is fleeting because our physical energy knows we're up to it; the "if there's a will, there's a way" thinking is unshakeable.

Ever work so long in a day, when you look up its dark outside, and you didn't even see the day's end coming? I call that "being present." When I develop the habit of being present, the work at hand "flows"—without concept of time. Hours tick by—at my desk, on the phone, at the keyboard—writing, rewriting, editing, and revising. Does seem like work. Upon reflection, I'm grateful to be handling words and not hay bales. Eight hours stretch to ten, sometimes twelve. Sweat equity counts. Yes, it a different type of "sweat," but if you want to have a business, you have to show up and stay to finish the job.

I may be at my desk, seemingly alone, but do we ever do anything "alone"? Truth is, on the farm, without every member of the family pitching in and working as a member of the team, we could not have "baled hay." This is not much different from starting and running a company, even if you're a "solo" act or a workforce of one.

A peek behind every entrepreneurial curtain exposes the "team." My team includes an attorney who helped structure the company, reviews contracts, and gives me the legal backbone to move forward with confidence. I have an accountant who helps me master the incoming and outgoing numbers, keeping the numbers organized in translatable rows, in order to build a firm foundation. There are authors and freelancers who share and discuss with me their ideas about building, shaping, and designing new products that did not exist before. The readers, who make this all possible, allow me to show up every day with purpose, driving me to be better.

Success is never the work of one. It takes a team.

I firmly believe in the power of community, and I am an avid volunteer with nonprofit organizations to address women's economic well-being, support leadership development, and empower women.

Focus. Okay, I admit, this is my "prickles and stings," my Achilles' heel. After doing what I've been doing for this long, it becomes easy to drift, get distracted, and leave the track. But, wait. Stop. I ask myself, "Why … why am I doing this? What am I here to do?"

Reframe what is difficult. Either I have to admit life has become too easy, and I've grown complacent, or life has become so hard I've lost confidence to do what is difficult.

I recall the relentlessness of the bales pushing me to find my energy to stay on task and avoid being buried. I recall wishing I had a "shut-off" valve. Do I have one now? What are the never-ending bales in my life? What keeps me flowing, to stay ahead of it, or on top of it, and not be overwhelmed? Rediscover what in life pushes you, or what is so enticing it pulls you.

When is the job done? When do I exit a company where I've been engaged for forty percent of my life? I write this before I know the ending. Or is it a "new beginning"? The future is unknown, but I have a yearning to return to simple pleasures. I've reawakened to the concept of all things have a season, a natural cycle to life and to a business. Perhaps the question I need to ponder most is, "Am I in harmony with the season of my business"?

Some points of success to me are:
- Believe in yourself. Hard work and commitment inspires and keeps your energy flowing.
- Be mindful of what it will take to accomplish the goal. Plan ahead. Identify the things you need to do to stay on target.
- Build relationships. Make room for others to participate.
- Reframe what is difficult. A responsible attitude directs our thoughts and behavior.
- Rediscover your passion—what pushes or pulls you. Take risks that add meaning and passion to your life.
- Persevere. Don't ever give up. Multiple efforts often are needed to get you to where (or who) you want to be.

lindah@hickorytech.net
www.AppletreePress.com

Who could have guessed making hay could give one the very life skills needed to start, grow, and tend a business. I count five character-building skills: boundless energy, accept long hours, work as a member of a team, focus, and don't quit until the job is done.

CHAPTER 16

Success–A Daily Journey

*And in the end, it's not the years in your life that count.
It's the life in your years.*

—Abraham Lincoln

Roxanne Zoet

I got started early on in life by joining the military. I have to attribute my success to the teachings and discipline I learned while making a career out of defending my country. It was not easy at first. I worked with so many people, mostly men. You had to develop your own style of leadership and management.

I learned quickly that leadership was the art of getting people to do what you wanted them to do, not because they had to, but because they wanted to. It also did not mean being friends with your subordinates, but gaining their trust and earning their respect. You had to get to know the people who worked for you, and you needed to know what they set as their goals and aspirations. I also learned you needed to serve those who worked for you. If you met their need, they would meet yours. This could be as basic as getting them connected to the right school to help them further their education, or even ensure they had the right job match, and they are fully trained to complete their jobs with the right skill sets.

In my military career, I found myself in many different leadership positions. I was in charge of an office environment where I managed the people, resources, and government funds—and the day-to-day operations of a particular function. Other times I was in a deployed environment in a war-torn country and had to manage more than just resources, but also the daily emotional and physical well-being of the people who were under me. While I was deployed in Saudi Arabia in support of Desert Storm and Desert Shield, I found myself in charge of people who did not have the skill sets required to operate sufficiently. This meant I had to train the personnel and give them the confidence they needed to work long hours in a high-pressure environment. It was exciting and rewarding to earn their respect. Giving them the confidence they needed helped to develop a solid working environment. This allowed us to not miss a beat in support of the aircraft that were a valuable part of the mission.

During my first time in Baghdad, Iraq, I found myself in a completely different situation. I was in the middle of a war where rockets, mortar attacks, and daily bombings were all part of the normal working conditions. This added to the high-pressure environment where those under me needed constant moral and emotional support. You learn rather quickly to trust those around you, and follow directions to the letter. Your life clearly depended on it. In this environment, I found myself bonding quickly with those around me.

In my first deployment, I dealt only with others from the Air Force. In this deployment, I worked alongside members of the Army, Marines, and Navy, as well as service members from other countries, and the State Department. Each service was operating under its own unique set of rules, and working alongside one another, all for the common purpose of rebuilding Iraq. This also brought on new challenges—and all were met under intense pressure. The lesson here is no matter whom you work with or for, be honest, fair, consistent, punctual, respectful, and above all, be confident.

In every situation, I had the opportunity to get to know those individuals who worked for me, and ensure they were being taken care of right. I found in order to be successful, you had to be honest with yourself and those who worked for you. If you did not, you found yourself in a position requiring a lot of hard work to build back up relationships you had once had.

Several people who laid the foundation for me include my parents who set a great example to follow. Many bosses also took the time to make sure I knew where I was and where I wanted to be in life. There was even an occasional bad boss who endeavored to make sure I did not act or treat people the way he or she did. I think everyone has had someone in her life who is a bad seed, and we can also learn from these people. As long as we continue to grow and improve ourselves, I think a person can attain a level of success.

The military is not an easy career. Being a woman in a male-dominated career has its disadvantages. If there ever was such a thing as a good-ole boys club, this is where you would find it. You have to push yourself and work a little harder to prove yourself. If you had an idea or a new strategy, you had to struggle to be heard. If you went against the status quo, more often than not, you were ostracized and not taken seriously. The key was in knowing how to work the system. Get to know those who you were selling your ideas to, and make sure you win them over. Sometimes that meant having a meeting before a meeting to make sure you played your cards right.

I had always wanted to join the military and be a part of something bigger than myself, and serve my country. I served for twenty-six years and enjoyed every moment. It had it ups and downs like any career, but in the end I wouldn't trade any of it. It made me who I am today.

In order to be a successful, I believe a person has to have the drive and determination to want to succeed at whatever it is they do best. As I climbed the ranks in the military, it was clear taking care of the enlisted troops underneath me was what I did best. I found myself in positions where decisions were made that would affect the lives and careers of those who were serving in the military. I tried to make sure that commonsense prevailed, and the welfare of others was always top priority. I looked at every situation as it pertained to others and not me. I made sure everyone else was taken care of before me.

I have helped many people through the years, but the stories sticking out the most are those individuals who were going through rough periods in their life. Everyone always says don't bring your personal life into the workplace, but how can we separate ourselves from who we are. It is a fact that people come to work with their problems—and it can affect their productivity. I learned early on to read the signs of human behavior. As I mentioned, if you do not know your people or those who work around you, you will not be able to pick up on the subtle differences they will display, without even knowing it. Everything affects others differently. What might bother me may not necessarily bother someone else. What I hold dear may not even be a footnote in someone else's life. What a person perceives to be true may not be a concern for another. Keeping all this in mind helps me empathize and understand the needs of others.

I had one individual who had a bubbly and out-going personality. Slowly but surely she changed. It wasn't overnight, but I saw some slight variations to her behavior. Because I made a point to talk to the people who worked for me, it was easy to see a difference. Of course, it is never as easy as walking up to someone and asking, "Is something wrong?" and they blurt out their problem. It takes time. If they trust you, respect you, and know you are genuine, then it seems to quicken the process, but it is never easy to open up to someone about a serious personal problem. It turned out another higher-ranking individual was sexually harassing this individual. It took time, patience, and trust but ultimately the situation was resolved, and the individual who was sexually harassing her was punished. I learned she had gone to others for help, but they had put no stock in what she told them. They knew the accused, who was in charge of all our sections, and didn't believe he was capable of the accusations. She was very grateful I had taken the time to listen and believe in her. She had lost faith in the system and found it hard to trust anyone anymore.

As with that experience, I have found myself in other similar situations where issues arose concerning friends and respected colleagues. There will always be hard decisions to make when it comes to leading people. One situation while I was in Iraq had multiple people involved. I was the superintendent at the time and didn't have anyone working directly for me, but I was still responsible for around twenty-five enlisted personnel in the office itself. Several were lower-ranking officers who worked alongside the enlisted and reported to the officer-in-charge. After I arrived, I got to know everyone as best I could. I always walked around to the different sections to observe and take part in the daily interactions of individuals who worked in each section. It was easy to see some sections clicked while others did not. You ask questions and try to get a reading, but knowing the individuals and seeing how they behave helps to notice when something was not quite right. Again, here is where trust comes in and knowing your people. One individual came forward and took me into her confidence. Afraid of backlash, she wanted to remain anonymous. However, this was a start. I knew something was not quite right, and now I had something to go on. I had to do so in a manner to protect the individual until the whole story evolved. Little by little others came forward, and the issue was brought to light. One of the lower-ranking officers was abusing his authority towards the enlisted and was mistreating individuals. The biggest problem to be addressed here was all the individuals involved were lower-ranking enlisted personnel away from home and loved ones. They were thrown into an office environment where they are now working with individuals who they do not know. Also, bombs and rockets were going off around them. It was a very stressful situation, and you want to be able to trust those with whom you work.

My difficulty was in dealing with the officer in question because I also had come to know and respect him. Not being on the receiving end of the abuse, I was surprised and shocked when the situation came to light. After the officer was removed from the office, the working environment changed drastically. You could actually feel the burden lift and see productivity soar. It is never easy when dealing with and trying to resolve issues, especially when there is controversy. I have seen other people in this position just sit back and hope the problem would go away. To begin with, most of the people who do wrong are not going to think or believe what they did *was wrong*. There are those who will support the person that others perceive to be in the wrong. It is not easy. At times when I was dealing with a situation, I would feel overwhelmed by the injustice of what others were saying and doing. Then I asked myself two questions. First, "Can I look at myself in the mirror and be proud of my actions?" and second "Can I lay my head on my pillow at night with a clear conscience?" If I could answer yes to both questions, I knew I was on the right path, and no matter how hard the problem was, or how tough the situation got, I knew I could make it through and be successful.

Over the years, I have taken a lot of leadership courses and read many inspirational books by successful people. One of my all-time favorites is *Lincoln on Leadership* by Donald T. Phillips, which I read many years ago, and read it again every few years. The timeless writing speaks volumes today as it did for President Lincoln. The other book I refer to is *The Servant: A Simple Story About the True Essence of Leadership* by James C. Hunter. This book taught me about being a leader and being successful by treating those under me as if they were above me. I needed them as much as they needed me. There is a saying: if you have to tell someone you are in charge or constantly remind them, then you probably aren't.

The best advice I could give other women on achieving success is
- Never give up your dream.
- Keep pursuing what it is you want.
- Find a person who you would consider a mentor and follow his or her lead.
- Make sure you are honest and open with people.
- Any decision you make will not be firm until you do something about it. Action strengthens your confidence.

Any decision you make will not be firm until you do something about it. Action strengthens your confidence.

CHAPTER 17

From Survival to Joy

Be yourself—everyone else is already taken.
– Oscar Wilde

Gloria VanDemmeltraadt

Calamity changed my life and its direction; I started to lose my hearing at age fifty-five. This opened up a whole new world to me. For much of my life I was a singer, and a pretty good one. I sang in nightclubs when I was young, did musical theater, and sang in church choirs and as a soloist for fifty years. The hearing loss, which was hereditary, does not respond well to hearing aids. Singing became increasingly difficult, and I had to stop. With time on my hands I turned to writing instead.

Writing has always interested me, and I wanted to see if I could do it, so I took a couple of writing classes. I especially loved an on-line class. I began to be more observant. I started writing down my thoughts. I even wrote singing telegrams for a couple of years when my children were growing up.

My children had long wanted me to capture my life on paper. Three of them had lived through some turbulent and hard times as young children. My first husband left us when my little boys were three and four years old, and I was pregnant with my daughter. Four years later I remarried a widower with two teenagers. All of a sudden my children had a new dad, a new house, a new brother and sister, and a mom who stayed home instead of working two jobs. What an adjustment for all of us, to say nothing of a new baby on the way.

So in 2007, when I started writing about myself, it was like a catharsis. At first I just wrote down everything. When I realized some of it had become my way of getting anger and frustration out of my system, I decided those pages were just for me. However, the book was for my family to read, so I began some heavy editing, searching for a way to pull the stories together. I came up with the idea of associating the stories with food as a "binder," even though food had never been important in my early life. It worked. I added recipes and made it both a memoir and a cookbook.

I was sixty-eight years old when this memoir, *Musing and Munching*, was published. Others have told me my little book is a story not just of survival in difficult circumstances, but a joyful one of perseverance and determination. Others say that it is inspirational and very rewarding.

Starting to write late in life was not an easy transition. I am so grateful for my husband's incredible support and encouragement, as well as the positive backing from the rest of my amazing family. Another important source of inspiration and encouragement for me was the writers' group Women of Words (WOW), which I joined after my memoir was published. Through WOW, I found new avenues for my writing, and new outlets for my creativity.

When people began telling me I should keep writing because I was good at it, I was astounded. I knew then the determination and dedication it took, the endless hours and hard work to complete the memoir, was all worth it. I began to see writing as "living my dream."

Today, I write life stories for hospice patients. Both the hospice stories and my own memoir have led to my second book, launched in April of 2013. It is a history of the town of Lake Elmo, Minnesota as told in personal stories. My best sources have been some amazing people in their nineties with perfect memories, and I have learned so much in the course of my interviews.

I will continue to do the hospice life stories, and now that *Memories of Lake Elmo* is published, I'm going to switch my focus and try my hand at writing fiction. That will be my next challenge and adventure.

As to success, it can be defined in many ways. I may never attain financial success, and it is far from my mind, since much of what I do is as a volunteer. I have always been what you might call an "overachiever," working harder than I needed to and focusing on "getting the job done."

For me, success is:
- Seeing the gratitude and joy on the faces of the families of hospice patients for whom I write life stories.
- Knowing these stories will be there to help grandchildren get to know more about their grandparents and to provide insights for future generations.
- Having passion for what you love to do, confidence you can do it, and staying power to get the job done.
- Found within us; it is not in the eyes of others.

- Taking risks, because we have to follow our own individual dreams, something not always easy to do.
- Asking for help, if only to confirm you're on the right track.
- Taking action, and continue trying, in order to make it.
- Best accomplished by persistence.

www.gloriavan.com

Having passion for what you love to do, confidence you can do it, and the staying power to get the job done.

CHAPTER 18

Attitude Is Everything

Never, never, never quit.
—Winston Churchill

JULIE KAY

When I was about ten years old, my parents and I were redecorating my bedroom. I remember sitting at my desk and drawing up plans as to where I wanted the furniture. I actually created a style board, with wallpaper, flooring, lamps and furniture. When most kids were shopping for clothes, at twelve, I was going to furniture stores. So this inspiration had become ingrained in me, but thinking back, I didn't know it then.

Later on, in high school, I took a course in interior design and loved it. But there came a time when we had to do a lot of math for measuring carpeting and wallpaper. Math was not my strong suit, ever. Not being overly strong in those math areas, suddenly I was scared away from continuing. At seventeen, I didn't want to determine square footage.

I also wanted to become a teacher. I knew teaching and decorating were my two loves. To be a decorator, you didn't need a license, but to teach, you do.

At college, I chose teaching with the hope I could do decorating on the side. After receiving my degree, I got married, and we bought our first house. I had so much fun redoing it. Friends would come over and say, "Gosh, you certainly have a knack for this." "You're extremely good at this." At the time I thought, "Anyone can do this," and I believed they didn't need me, but all the time, others told me that wasn't true.

After teaching a couple years, I became friends with one of the teachers on my team. Her parents lived in an older rambler and needed help with their house. She asked me if I would help them, but only if they could pay me. I felt weird about it, saying, "I don't know if I can do that." They had me over to look at the house, and basically, over the next ten years, I redid every room.

With this first job, it was difficult to see things and say it like it is. You can take it or leave it. There is no in between, no going halfway. In their sixties, her parents had lived in the same house for years. When I would say, "This is the way we'll proceed," then the wife would say, "You'll have to talk to my husband about your plan." At first he would say, "What wrong with the woodwork, it's dark, it's oak. Why would we ever paint the woodwork?" "What's wrong with the carpeting? I think it is fine."

I have a way of talking to people—and they listen. I build up a trust very quickly. In the end, the husband listened to me.

When someone asks me to make over a room, I can immediately see what needs to change and what needs to be removed. It pops into my head, and I'm usually saying to myself, "Okay, this chair needs to go!" I usually sugarcoat my words for my clients, and many times what needs to go is something to which they were personally attached. Sometimes before I speak I ask my clients, "Does this bench or chest mean a lot to you?" If it does, then we try to repurpose it somewhere else in the house.

My husband and my friends have helped me to be successful in what I do. My friends were the instigators, telling me I should share my gift, saying, "We can't do this, we need you to help us." They were adamant about wanting me to have a business. These were the people who believed in me. The clients I have today are connected to that first tier of clients.

I think *I* was my biggest challenge in decorating. It was trusting I could do it. Fifteen years ago, I didn't have the experience behind me. Now I can walk into a room and say it like it is: "This is what I see. I can draw it out for you, or just do it." In the past, I would say, "This is what I think you should do." Through the years, what I have learned has made me feel validated.

The second condo I was blessed to redecorate in Sanibel, Florida, is an example of a space where I knew immediately what needed to be changed. The previous owner had been a woman in her eighties, who had lived there with her sister for years. This meant they likely hadn't redecorated at all recently. Even in its time, it probably needed a lot of help.

My clients had inherited this apartment from this woman who they knew only from renting another condo in the same building for a few months each year. They were neighbors. Both my clients and the woman were from Minnesota, although they didn't know each other prior to Florida.

My clients would occasionally bring her jam from Minnesota when they came down to rent. They would also bring her homemade cookies. My clients were simply being sweet, doing a few random acts of kindness over the years. Before they left one spring to drive back to Minnesota, they delivered one last batch of warm chocolate chip cookies. When she greeted them at the door, she asked them to step in for a bit, and sit down. Then she proceeded to tell them she had made the best decision of her entire life; she had decided to will the condo to my clients. They immediately began crying with tears of shock, happiness, and gratefulness. Their hearts were full.

Now, back to the Sanibel condo. When I walked in, I felt so claustrophobic seeing the huge cabinets in the front entry. Continuing, I saw a room overstuffed with furniture, pictures in random spots, old carpets, heavy draperies closing off the beautiful Sanibel view, and a desk and freezer in the kitchen area where a table should be. It goes on and on, and it was all wrong.

My client wanted a true "beach feel" in the condo, so immediately upon viewing the condo, for the first time, I could see through the madness. My mind took me to the calm, serene feeling of a relaxing beach condo. I saw khaki-colored walls, crisp white woodwork, sea-grass headboard, granite kitchen counters on top of new white cabinets, whitewashed kitchen chandelier with sea grass shades, sisal runner, sailboat pictures, and seashells. In the living room, I saw large soft-blue floral rugs, simple accessories, long wooden boat on the buffet filled with sand, seashells, and a small wooden scoop. In the bedroom, I saw crisp white bedding, with sea-blue wave-like pillows, etc. All of these ideas bounced around in my head as I walked through their condo

I am able to share with my clients what I am visualizing, and they trust me as they have a hard time visualizing. I know most people's brains don't process rooms and decorating the way my brain does. Sometimes I feel like, "Well duh, this is simple, the room will feel much better if we move the furniture around like so." But I have to remember what hits me as the obvious usually doesn't occur in other people's minds. However, I'm there to do something about it. My clients don't know what that "something" is. That "something" usually wakes me up at night with constant inspiration, and it's key to keep a pen and paper on my nightstand so I can write down my middle-of-the-night decorating thoughts. It's hard to shut off my brain because I love what I do—and it energizes me. If only I didn't need sleep, and the stores stayed open all night for my convenience.

A great design allows your eye to sweep fluidly around the room without getting stopped or drained by something. Also, in a well-designed home, you could take an item from one room, move it to another room and it completely works and blends well in there to create a nice flow throughout the house. By keeping the same integrity throughout the house, you create a pleasant continuity.

In my world, I have a few personal rules. Less is more, simplify and de-clutter, for example, too many things on counters will drain energy out of a space, and doesn't allow the eye to rest. If a person is interested in decorating, aim for the "look for less," which is what I do for my clients: high-end look, low-end prices.

The advice I would give any woman is
- Don't take "no" for an answer.
- There is always a way ... but you need to persevere.
- Have a get-it-done attitude.
- Think outside the box and act upon it.
- Have extremely high standards.
- Be nice, but be persistent.
- Settle for nothing but the best.

Don't take no for an answer. There is always a way. You just have to persevere.

CHAPTER 19

If You Feel Scared, Do It Afraid

Worry is like a rocking chair—it's always in motion but it never gets you anywhere.

—Attributed to Corrie TenBoom,
but frequently said by Joyce Meyer, author, Bible teacher, and speaker

Victoria Kriz

After going to college in Wisconsin for two years, I decided I wanted to move back to the Twin Cities and try something different. I came home to Fridley, Minnesota, and told my parents I wanted to do hair. My dad was not pleased. He said if I finished school I could live at home for free, drive their car and eat their food. However, if I went to cosmetology school, I was on my own.

Frustrated, I realized it was a no brainer for me to finish school. I attended the U of M and earned a degree in Retail Merchandising and Marketing. I worked for about a year at a large corporation. I wouldn't say I was unhappy because it takes a lot to make me unhappy; I was simply not satisfied. I knew another career path waited for me out there. I wanted to go back to school and be a cosmetologist, a teacher or a counselor. I figured a cosmetologist was a perfect career for a young person. I could be a teacher or a counselor later in life; little did I know you become *both* of those things as a hair stylist.

When I told my boss I was quitting, and the reason, he couldn't believe it. Shocked, he spoke down to me, "You are leaving this company with all the benefits, and our retirement program for *hair*?" And I confidently said, "Yes I am." It was almost like a confirmation. I knew I didn't want to be at such a company. When I walked out of there, it felt great.

It was time to decide where to go to cosmetology school. Visiting Aveda, I knew this was it, and attended there for ten months. I asked one of my teachers who the best hair stylist was in the city. When he said, "Jon English," I decided I would go there. I walked into the Jon English salon, and I knew immediately this was where I needed to be. Jon took me under his wing. I went through an apprenticeship and advanced training with him, watching him work, shampooing, and even sweeping hair. He taught me many valuable techniques. However I had to adjust to a new technique since Jon had a different approach to cutting than most people learn. I had left school thinking I was very good, so this was humbling. It became clear to me that doing hair in school for ten months does not give one enough experience; it's crucial to keep practicing and to learn new techniques. Although the change means less income for the additional time, it's worth it. Jon taught me everything I know.

I am most grateful to Jon English, and I worked at his salon for seven years. When I had my first baby, Sophia, I worked only three days a week. With reduced commissions, I realized I needed to work smarter. Between the lower income and missing Sophia, I knew it was time for a change. It broke my heart to leave my baby, and each day co-worker Hector would ask if I was ever going to come to work without eyes puffy and red from crying.

While still working at Jon English, I started doing a few people's hair in my kitchen, to get the feel of it. Most of them were my friends. When Jon stopped doing hair himself, he passed his clients on to me. I respected him too much to take them over to my home business. I only took on people there who came to me directly; mostly friends and family. I continued to work all day at Jon English, and I worked at home on my days off. Time to take the plunge.

When I made the decision to give up Jon's clients, I was scared. My clients became my family, yet they were also my income. So I was letting my income walk out the door. My dear friend and manager at the time, Natalie, would whisper in my ear as I said good-bye to clients, "God blesses integrity." All I thought was: I hope so.

My husband Aaron and I talked a lot about starting my own business—and the fears involved. Working at such a high-end salon, with Jon helping me a great deal, brought a lot of security with my client base. Thankfully Aaron has a secure job with incredible benefits, which made it easier. I also left on excellent terms with Jon; it was reassuring when he made it quite clear I could come back at any time.

I believe if you leave somewhere well, you will be blessed the next place you go, which my situation is a testimony. Within a few months, I was back up to 150 clients, all on referrals. Clients who referred someone received $5 off, as did the new client. I often wrote cards thanking my clients for their business. I was grateful and still am for every single client. I let them know it, and as a result of all of the wonderful referrals I have an amazing client base. Usually when people refer someone, they are similar because they are friends. If you are starting with some good people, before you know it you are blessed with a wonderful group of people. I am daily humbled, and thank God for my amazing clients.

The cost of daycare was considered because we were paying a lot while I worked at Jon English salon. I think it's cheaper to have your kids in daycare fulltime, but since we were paying hourly, it was spendy. I was most thankful because the woman who watched Sophia lived across the street from the salon, and I could run over and feed Sophia on my break ... worth every penny.

The pros of our discussion about having the salon in our home were obviously having Sophia at home, not having to chase before and after work to daycare, having more flexibility with my schedule, and reducing our cost of daycare. The cons we discussed were putting money into building it and buying all of the equipment and then it not working, getting enough clients, and having people/hair/chemicals in our home. We installed an expensive vent in the salon which took care of the chemical concern, but I also don't do permanents because of the horrible smell and time it takes. Even if you talk about everything, when you know God is leading you to do something, you just step out in faith and go for it despite the cons.

The pros very quickly outweighed the cons. I love the saying: *sometimes you have to step out to find out.* I also think if you walk through the worst-case scenarios in your head, you realize the worst is often not so bad, and you just need to try.

Then, despite the fear, I did it. We hired someone to build the salon. He was a friend of a friend who agreed to let my dad help too, allowing us to save some money. After a significant amount of paperwork involved with the licensing, we opened the salon on May 1, 2005. What a special day—one I will never forget. It was great; I was home, and my baby was upstairs with my friend Natalie.

When we opened up the salon in our home, I had two good friends nanny for us. Even though we were still paying a lot, the cost went down significantly.

When our second daughter, Violet, was born, I wanted a larger house with bedrooms on the same level. We started looking. We'd find a house we liked, but there would be no space for a salon. We'd find a house with a perfect place for the salon, but we didn't like the house itself. It was challenging. Unexpectedly, my parents told us they were planning to move, and asked us if we wanted to buy their house. My immediate answer was: absolutely not. As far as I was concerned, no way were we going to buy a house in which I grew up. Aaron, on the other hand, thought it was a good idea. I agreed to think about it. Quite honestly, I was only being nice, and respectful. Aaron said, "Great, let's go look at it." We looked at it as if it was an actual "showing," even opening closet doors. Going downstairs, I opened the door to Dad's workshop. Immediately I saw my salon. The house was perfect. It had three bedrooms on the upper level, and a space for a salon in the lower level. Exactly what I wanted, and I am grateful Aaron pushed me to do it.

The salon was built while my parents were still living there, so I didn't miss a day of work, nor did I lose any clients by changing locations. We moved in on a Saturday, and I opened for business in the new house on the following Monday. It wouldn't have worked out as perfect if we had bought any other house. Although it all worked out very well, before I knew it, I was working way more than I wanted to be, and giving far too big of discounts to friends and family. I was completely out of balance.

I realized six to eight appointments a day were a perfect balance. One day, after I had had ten clients, all with long, thick hair, I ached all over. I literally crawled up the stairs because I was truly hurting. I complained to Aaron this was the worst day I ever had. I was surprised he didn't say, "Let me rub your shoulders," or "Let me pour you a glass of wine." Instead, he asked: "Who made your schedule?" Not what I wanted to hear—but what I needed to hear.

It was all about balance, and I was the one in control. I told myself, "Stop letting life happen to you." I thought about the quote, "Other people's lack of planning is not your emergency," and knew I had to get those words ingrained in my head. I used to say "yes" to an appointment on my days off, but I complained about it all week. It may have seemed like a good idea two weeks away, but as the time came closer, it certainly wasn't. I would say to myself, "I can't believe I said yes." My yes was not a yes. In the Bible it says, "Let your yes be yes and your no be no." Today I say, "Let me call you back," because I want time to take the emotions out of it and make a wise decision.

Today I no longer work on my days off, and I try never to take more than eight appointments in a day. I still have some work to do in saying yes too much, and allowing my schedule get overbooked.

After we moved to Fridley and re-opened the salon in our new home, we were close to my sister who had just moved here from Winona. So my kids have been blessed to have their auntie watch them while I work. At first she came to my home and watched them; after a couple years, my head was ready to explode between work and kids in my home. The timing was perfect to make a change since my sister had just had her third baby, and I started bringing my girls to her house. Work became a very peaceful fun place to be again. It added a little more chasing around getting them there and back home and off to activities, but I needed a break from all the activity in my house. When she came to my house, my sister helped me with washing the salon towels and making calls to confirm appointments. Taking the kids to her house added a little more work for me, but it was worth it for my sanity.

My laid-back, wonderful husband didn't have different expectations because I was at home. Actually it was me who had way too high expectations—something I still have to work on. I often try to run upstairs the second I get done with work and straighten up the kitchen and get dinner going, or run up in between clients to start dinner. I used to apologize to Aaron when he walked in because the house was a mess. We have been married ten years, and just recently I learned the one thing he cares about is the TV room (of course, the girls are always playing in there). He has a hard time relaxing at night if it is all messy. All of these years I had been apologizing for a messy house, cleaning up the kitchen, and making dinner, but the one thing he cared about was the TV room, which I never even noticed. One day I was relaxing for a few minutes before picking things up. However, when he came home, he started picking up the TV room. I took it personally since "I was home," and became quite hard on myself, and we ended up getting in a fight. He told me that he didn't expect me to have it clean, but if he came home and cleaned it, not to take it personally. He was *not* saying, "You're not doing a good job," he just likes it clean. We are most opposite because I like to relax and then clean up—and he can't relax until he cleans up. His one and only expectation is (and it's not an expectation, more of a desire) is if I have a few minutes, to pick up the TV room, he certainly appreciates it. And if I don't have time, not to get offended if he comes home and picks it up. I have recently started to give myself some slack and realize I am working almost full-time, and I don't have to kill myself to make it seem as if my only job is cooking and cleaning.

It's hard because technically I'm "at home," but I definitely have realized I can't have the same expectations on myself as if I was at home—and not working. Sometimes I come upstairs from work and want to cry because toys are everywhere and dishes fill the sink. One time, I had my own pity party about how other people come home from working all day, and their house looks the same as when they left in the morning. Most people don't have to walk in from work to a disaster. One Saturday after an extremely long day at work, I saw a TV commercial about kids with cancer while I was cleaning and grumbling. Ahhh, the ad put my life in perspective. The house was messy because I have two healthy children who can play all day. I was humbled and changed my grumbling to thanking God for my children.

Another thing I've learned is: communication is key. Aaron is very much

Unlocking the Secrets of Successful Women

into electronics, and he has a special speaker all hooked up in my salon to make the music sound great. When it broke one day, he replaced it. Because we put it in when we built the salon, we couldn't get the old one out of the closet location without taking down the door. The speaker sat in the corner of my broom closet for a couple of weeks. Because it wasn't in my way, it didn't bug me one bit. One night Aaron said, "I can't believe you haven't noticed I got the speaker out of the closet." And of course it was on one of my tired, exhausted nights. I replied "It wasn't bugging me; if you want me to notice something, do the dishes on Thursday nights." Okay, I admit what I said was not the most kind way to respond to his comment, but clearly coming up to a messy kitchen every weeknight had been bugging me, and bam, it just came out. Thursdays I am not done until eight or nine in the evening. So I usually walk up the stairs exhausted and hungry. And every Thursday as I walk up the stairs I talk to myself about being appreciative that Aaron fed the kids, helped them with homework, and got them into bed … and how *not* to focus on the kitchen. Ever since my outburst, the dishes are done every Thursday. Just like I didn't even know that it bothered Aaron when the TV room was a mess, he didn't know that it bothered me when I came up to a messy kitchen. I think it's important to find out what is important to your spouse. Instead of cooking and cleaning a room he doesn't even care about, spend a few minutes doing something he will appreciate.

Now I am at the stage of the kids being in school, but home in the summer, so it's changed again. The great thing about my job is as the girls grow up, I can make changes right along with them to fit our schedule. I don't need day care during the school year now, except for Saturdays, because Aaron works as a letter carrier on Saturdays as well. Then I rotate between a few young girl babysitters, and also grandparents and auntie. I am usually just finishing work or have about an hour left on Mondays and Tuesdays, and the girls just come down and say hi and then head upstairs. I try to run up in between clients and have a snack waiting for them. On my late-night Thursdays, I try to schedule my break when they get off the bus so I can visit and see papers and stuff. If Aaron is working late, I quickly get dinner ready for them before heading back down. I think why Thursdays used to be so exhausting is because I was being two people all day long, and by the end of the night, I had nothing left in me. It's much easier now as they are getting older because everything gets easier, and they are fine hanging out while I'm working.

I still struggle with balance because even on my "days off," I'm getting/ordering products, washing towels, making confirmation calls and returning client calls. Technology is a great thing because I can do a lot via text and email, which doesn't take away as much time as phone calls. Although nine-year-old Sophia tells me I text too much, I need to be aware when it is time to take a break. I used to text clients back while hanging out with Aaron watching TV at night. Then I realized most salons are closed by nine p.m., and I should put away my phone, close my book and return the call the next day. I need to be smart about setting some boundaries so it doesn't affect my family. I tell all of my clients I will always get back to them within twenty-four hours. Of course they all understand because they've been in my chair when my phone is beeping and another client is waiting.

Along the way, I have had different role models for different things. I call my friend Kristine for any spiritual questions; for in this area, she is the wisest woman I know. My friend Dayna is extremely wise financially, so anytime I have a financial question, I call her. My friend Bridgette is so creative and gifted she helps me with all of my graphic design or creative things. My sister is so good with children, so anytime I am struggling with my children I call my sister. I never call the same people for all my questions, and I seek out those I know will have good insights because they have been successful.

Another thing is to have direction. If you want something, don't ask the person who is on the same level as you—who is struggling. Ask somebody who is where you want to be in life, and ask her how she got there. Be smart and ask people who know what they are doing.

In the book, *The Principle Path*, it says, "Good intentions don't get you somewhere; direction does." Nobody gets into a car and says, "I'm going to get lost today." Your intention is to get to where you want to go, but if you don't have good directions, you are going to get lost. If you want to be successful and you don't have direction, your good intention is not going to get you there. So make a plan, get good wisdom and direction, and go for it.

Jon English would tell me, "If you follow money, you will be miserable, but if you follow your passion, money will follow. If it's your passion, you will try harder. You will be good at it, and you will be excited about it. You will want to try new things. If you follow money, you will never be happy, but if you follow your passion, you will succeed, and the money will follow."

If I had stayed at the corporation, I would have been following the money and would have been miserable. When I worked at Jon English, I showed up and did hair, which was the fun part. Once I came home, I was done. Owning my own business is hard work. Now I'm also dealing with client calls, ordering products, washing and folding towels, paying taxes and invoices. It's more of everything, but the benefits outweigh the extra work. My children are welcome in the salon, and while I make sure they have boundaries, they always know if they need me or just want to say hi, they can come down. At age thirty-six, I am blessed with such an amazing job for this stage of my life with young kids at home.

People often want what other people have, but they aren't willing to do what it takes to get there. In Beth Moore's book, *So Long Insecurity*, she says whatever we are insecure about, we look at someone else's life with that quality—and decide their life is perfect. So if we are self-conscious of our weight, we decide the thin woman we saw somewhere has a perfect life, not knowing maybe she has a horrible marriage or some other problem. A person who struggles with finances looks at someone who has money and decides he has no stress. They never stop to think of all of the hard work, wise choices and discipline it took for her to get there, or about anything going on in her life then.

Comparing ourselves to others, or being jealous, is such a snare. During the message at church one Sunday, they encouraged us to "Stop comparing your life with other people's highlight reel. You're not watching how they got there." There are always obstacles when starting a new journey. Mine were my emotions, prompted mostly by the initial lack of support from my dad. Yet it was my dad who ended up helping to build my salon, and is one of my biggest supporters today.

I continue on my journey to find balance, keep boundaries, and not have such high expectations of myself. Every year I learn something new and make changes for the better. The key is to keep growing, learning and changing for the better! I was completely out of balance when I started my business, but I'm figuring out what works as I go. I guess it's true that with experience you gain wisdom; now I just have to make sure I apply what I learn! As Joyce Meyer says, "I'm not where I need to be, but thank God I'm not where I used to be; I'm okay and I'm on my way!"

My advice to anyone opening her own business is to start with firm boundaries and pricing. You can always give discounts or make exceptions, but it's much harder to make adjustments the other direction. And if you are feeling overwhelmed, don't forget to ask yourself: who makes your schedule?

Learn to say "Yes" when you want to say yes and "no" when you need to, so you have the energy to work toward your own goal.

CHAPTER 20

Roaming with Ellajane

Nothing great was ever achieved without enthusiasm.
—Emerson

Ellajane Knott

For 88 years, it seems I've lived in two Americas, or seemingly more accurately, on two planets. I've juggled the carefree but tough environment where people were the magic formula to creating a strong country, as well as equally strong families. I accomplished all of this with compassion for others, a healthy imagination, and steadfast work ethics. College degrees were rare for our immigrant families as they were deigned to rise to their potential on their own merits, and resolve to build a better nation—which they did without fanfare or complaint. They did it together with fellow Americans who took much pride in themselves and their new country. It all culminated in the creation of a dynamic and humane society we all share. I began there so many years ago, and it's been a magnificent journey.

Today, technology has taken over with its cold, mechanical approach to world problems, leaving behind much of the beauty of our culture, as well as its human touch. Of course, this comes at a great price to those students struggling with school loans and finding jobs, though the benefits to the world have been spectacular. Gone are the days of personal inter-relationships with the human race. Now we talk to each other less and use technology more, depersonalizing our lives. Today a college degree is imperative in getting a foothold in today's industrial world.

My assets were meager by any measure: an over-abundance of energy, healthy imagination, love of people and life, tenacity, and a sense of the ludicrous side of me. The greatest asset of all was an incredible father who gave me such self-confidence that nothing would prevent me from following my dreams, never even considering the possibility of failure. This was achieved by his being an exceptional role model, not only for me, but people he met throughout his life. His formula was simple: integrity, heart, strength, and an Irish sense of humor. How he achieved these characteristics as an orphan, living with relatives who treated him as the "hired help," is a mystery, but he walked with confidence, comfortable in his own skin, treating everyone alike. He was tall in stature at at six foot, two inches, and tall in spirit and honesty. For me, his youngest daughter, he was a giant in every sense of the word.

A hands-on dad, he not only encouraged me to choose my own dreams but backed them with physical help, and when needed, cash. Without the toys children enjoy today, we had to entertain ourselves by using our imagination. After attending dance classes for several years, I decided at age ten I would stage a show for the neighborhood. I began my first job teaching children dancing, particularly Hawaiian dances, and named, the soon-to-be production, "Hawaiian Fantasy." I took the idea to Dad who agreed to produce it by hiring the hall. He was with us from planning to curtain time with his encouragement and applause. We had accomplished something to be proud of just as he had done in climbing the ladder from orphan to being superintendent of Truax Traer Coal Mines in North Dakota, located a short distance from Velva, which was a tiny town with little to help build dreams.

The future for young graduates of that era was uncertain and frightening, with many of the male students opting for military service in World War II upon graduation. Many never returned, including brothers James and Robert. Even so, there existed an overwhelming feeling in our whole nation: we were united as one family, with everyone helping one other and the war effort itself. Everyone was willing to help anywhere it was needed.

For me, the "what now" of graduation seemed an easy choice. My sister Betty was studying nursing and stayed with married sister Dorothy at her home in Minneapolis. She later joined the army, serving in a Mobile Army Surgical Hospital (MASH) unit in the South Pacific. Without local contacts, I decided modeling was a natural way to meet people, and enrolled in the McConnell School of Modeling, a choice that would have longtime effects on my life. It was the start of my amazing and colorful career, which scanned several fields of endeavor. I worked with world-famous people, but it all started in a little coal-mining town in North Dakota as the coal miner's daughter's career took "wing."

I recall to this day the thrill of facing my future as the train exited the border of North Dakota into Minnesota thinking, *"Look out world. Here I come."* I was ready.

Following graduation in 1943, I began a career in a field in its infancy, working the runways and doing photo shoots. Sounds glamorous, but in fact one would need another more stable income to survive. At five foot, four inches, I lacked the height to be in contention for many jobs, though I did fairly well. However, it was irritatingly slow to harness engagements, and I decided to do something about it. Contacting and meeting models in both Minneapolis and St. Paul, I suggested we start our own "union," so to speak, though I dubbed it the Twin Cities Models Guild. When we elected our officers, they voted me president.

In introducing the concept of treating models with more respect—and modeling as a profession—both to the public, and particularly prospective employers, I started a media campaign that proved to be popular, complete with models' photos. Employers then believed models should be satisfied at being *chosen* to walk the runways—and shouldn't expect anything but paltry pay. We intended to show them modeling should be treated as a profession, deserving of decent salaries—and we did it.

Nurse Sister Kenny, of polio treatment renown, was in the middle of a major fund-raising campaign. When I suggested we hold a Models Guild Ball, with all proceeds aimed at raising monies for those suffering from polio, she was delighted. The ball was a sensation as the beautiful young models appeared in eveningwear, and joined local, state and national politicians in making the evening a rousing success. When we repeated the performance later for the coffers of the United Nations, then-Senator Hubert Humphrey joined us as our celebrity guest for the evening.

When I was twenty, I was working at McConnell's School of Modeling as an instructor, desperately trying to appear older and more sophisticated. I always had my eyes on New York. I thought I'd find a niche in the modeling community, even though I was short the physical credentials to do so. Traveling to New York City, I did work the runway daily at a plush women's-wear shop, The Tailored Woman, and spent my evenings ushering at a neighborhood theater. I don't know what I had been thinking—if I was too short for the Twin Cities market, did I think I would shoot up vertically enough to compete with the statuesque models? Also, New York proved I was living "above my pay grade," and I decided to head home.

My return garnered some pleasant publicity, and a local department store offered me the position as fashion coordinator in staging style shows. In the interim, I learned there would be an opening for a new publicity director at the Hotel Nicollet, and I set my sites on getting it. Initially the manager was lukewarm on hiring a model, thinking my work ethic would be lax, but I made it my mission to prove him wrong, haunting him weekly with fresh ideas in implementing a successful public relations program for the hotel's plush supper club, the Minnesota Terrace. Ultimately I wore him down and he agreed, saying, "You have the energy of four people, and should be able handle the pace."

In post war years, America took on a glamour and excitement in the pursuit of after-hours' entertainment. Night clubs sprung up around the country, and high-test performers began the circuit to perform in packed rooms with guests donning their best finery to enjoy a night out with pianist Liberace, comedian Victor Borge, actor Pat O'Brien, cabaret singer Hildegarde, and many others. My job was as exciting as the time itself, hosting evening press parties, driving celebs to media interviews, writing press releases for local, state and national outlets, supervising lighting, and myriad of duties connected with the show itself. It was my dream job, exhilarating, exhausting, and fun. Adrenalin did its job, and I ended up in the hospital twice for exhaustion, not realizing I was so worn out.

Later in the year, public relations would have a personal meaning. During a press party at Hildegarde's opening night, I was introduced to the most amazingly handsome man I had ever met. A Marine Colonel, veteran of two wars, he had been ordered to take over the duties of commandant at Fort Snelling. I was certain he would play a significant part in my future. Life was brimming to overflowing for me during my tenure at the Hotel Nicollet.

The job itself was a fun-filled challenge, and I knew it would provide me with the credentials to take my career in new directions. One day, two advertising men came to my office to discuss a photo-features spread they were planning for a national magazine. After a week of being interviewed about my duties and unique experiences, Hildegarde and I posed and talked our way into an incredible cover photo and four-page spread in the renowned *Hotel Management* magazine. They later told me the idea came to them to make it a cover story because of my modeling background, and the energy I expended.

A year and a half later, the Marine pilot, Gordon Knott, had become an after-hours' fixture at the hotel, and wanted to get married as he was to be relocated to the Quantico Marine Air Base at Arlington, Virginia. On very short notice, suddenly a career seemed less important, and I said, "I do" at a small family service. A week later I flew out to meet him and be introduced to the well-known "esprit de corps" of the United States Marines—men and their families who would play a momentous part in my life for years to come.

Several years later when our sons were all in school, I decided it was time to get back to work, holding a series of interesting positions, one leading to another. One was as a PR assistant at the American Heart Association, where I authored a TV special on the history of the Association. I was public relations director for *Minnesota Calls* magazine, where to herald our first issue, I invited statewide media on a boat trip down the Mississippi, complete with a band. I also handled publicity and sales for the newly built Ambassador Hotel. Moving to Mound, Minnesota, luck was with me in finding a career change. One day I walked into the local newspaper to ask the editor for a job. His offer came as a shock as my only claim to writing had been in public relations and publicity pieces.

At any rate I was hired, and began a twenty-three-year sojourn as a columnist/reporter for the *Minnetonka Pilot* newspaper, later to become a part of the Sun Newspaper chain where I covered everything notable in the community, features, my "Roaming with Ellajane" column, including every facet of the area and its citizens. In addition, I served as secretary for the Mound Chamber of Commerce, heading the committee in staging a 100-unit parade for our annual festival. Vice President Hubert Humphrey provided great excitement as he rode in the lead car waving to his fellow Minnesotans. In order to keep abreast of local news, I offered my services for many local organizations. It was a "battery-charging" job, and gave me a way to stay in touch with my sons as I covered school activities, without guilt.

In retrospect, I doubt I would change any part in my career. I had selected creative, rather than technical choices in mapping out my career, not needing a college degree to rise to the pinnacle, just with energy, imagination, and love of my fellow man. To say I designed my career would be an overstatement. Somehow today it feels as though I just floated over it on an exciting roller coaster, giving me much happiness in the journey.

There is much to be said on behalf of the personal touch, dealing with people rather than the stereotype of becoming savvy with the newest technical devices in making a name for ourselves in the professional arena. It is certainly less expensive and surely more fun.

Enthusiasm is the necessary ingredient for success. Little is accomplished without it.

Unlocking the Secrets of Successful Women

CHAPTER 21

Fit 2b Well

I've learned that people forget what you said, people will forget what you did, but people will never forget the way you made them feel.

—Maya Angelou

Julie Lother

For five years, I worked at a hospital fitness center—after having worked at a fully equipped, state-of-the-art fitness center. At the hospital, we had just one room and a few pieces of equipment. I accepted the job there because the person who interviewed me made me feel so welcome, as did everyone I met. It felt like the place for me.

In 2008, the hospital was struggling financially and had to lay off some 350 people, including my three staff members and me. I had a newborn, and having lost my mother in a car accident when I was nine years old, I was not very confident about becoming a mother myself. Now the lay-off caused me to feel somewhat lost.

Then ... I met Joan Kennedy. She had been a speaker at our Women's Professional Group in Hudson, Wisconsin. Something about her intrigued me. Later, after my daughter was born, I read Joan's book, *What's Age Got to do With It?* The motivational content was exactly what I needed in my life. More later.

When hospital personnel asked if I'd like to start my own business and run it out of the hospital, I said yes. The hospital was family to me, and I wanted to maintain the relationships I had formed there. Losing the hospital job led me to start my own business, something that always had been my dream. I had researched, jotted down notes, and met with people who had their own businesses. It had been my passion, but I never got it started because I had become comfortable with my hospital position and, after all, I had received great benefits. But now the job was gone, and I was finally driven to establish my own business.

This was my chance, and all of the above had become a blessing in disguise.

The part of my job I had loved best was talking with people, creating personal relationships, and working with them one-on-one, exactly what I was about to do in my own new business.

At first it was rough to have no co-workers. When I first started, the fear of the unknown was daunting. There I was with a new baby daughter, Dianna, and a new business, all at the same time. But, I still felt it was the place for me. Loving what I was doing was my motivation. I liked helping people with their goals, encouraging, motivating and inspiring them. I would tell my clients, "Internal inspiration equals external results. It has to come from the inside, and the outside will change."

Joan's book was my inspiration, helping me both personally and professionally to become who I am, and not try to be someone I am not. I am grateful for Joan Kennedy in my life, for I believe it is she who has helped me become successful.

I talk to my clients about being the people they were meant to be—beautiful, unique, and themselves. I emphasize if you stick with your passion and values, success will follow. *It* will chase you; you won't have to chase *it*. One simply has to take action if one wants things to happen.

My mother was also my motivator. She, too, helped me to be who I am today. At the time of her car accident, she was working at the Central State Prison. After she died, the inmates sent my dad and family a card and poem about my mother. They said, "Dianne always treated us like we mattered; not as just *matter,* she treated us like people." My mother didn't care what crime they had committed or who they were. She was kind and loving, overlooking their flaws. I practice this idea in my life and my cherished relationship to all people, not just friends and associates.

I was pursuing my passion, and I had come to understand and accept what was *my number one value*. A lot of people say their family is their number one value. I tell people my number one value is *my health*. If I have my health, I can certainly take care of my family and my relationships. I do value my family and friends, but if I didn't have my health and my well-being, how could I give my energy and my happiness to others?

My grandmother was a nurse, so I started college in Pre-Nursing before switching my major to Exercise Science. I especially enjoyed learning about the muscles and applying such knowledge to exercise.

I developed a passion for getting people healthy. In nursing, I realized I would be helping people who were sick; what I actually wanted to do was to keep them healthy after recovery. I saw from being in the hospital, while nurses care for others, they don't care for themselves—and this is the culture I'm trying to change. If nurses care for themselves, they will be better able to care for others.

I encourage people to:
- Use your time, not as a schedule, but as time itself.
- Take a step back a moment, even if it means you stop for a while on the way home because you need to take a few breaths.
- Otherwise, look for something that excites or relaxes you. Stay there for five minutes.
- If you take time for yourself, it will bring back more quality time, you'll have time for others, and you'll get more done.
- Be focused.
- Be mindful and stay in the moment.
- Don't worry about stuff you can't control.
- Surround yourself with loving, kind people who fill you up with joy and compassion.
- Don't surround yourself with empty, self-centered souls who drain you.
- Have a positive attitude.
- Connect with your spiritual self, your mental self, your emotional self and your physical self—for it's a lifelong journey.

I know I was put on this earth to help people, so that's what I do. I do it my way. I am who I am. I know if I fail, I will pick myself up and move on for this is how one grows.

Surround yourself with loving, kind people who fill you up with joy and compassion. Don't surround yourself with empty, self-centered people who will drain your energies.

CHAPTER 22

Find Meaning in a Midlife Career Move

The best parts of a good person's life are the small, nameless, unremembered acts of kindness and love.

—Walt Whitman

Mary Treacy O'Keefe

There is not one single thing I always wanted to "be." I attended a women's college where the only options for majors were education, nursing, occupational therapy, and home economics. Because I had always loved history, I became a social studies teacher. However after it was apparent I did not enjoy, nor was I effective at teaching seventh and eighth graders, I quickly realized I was not meant to be a teacher.

I soon realized what I truly loved was selling, as long as I believed in the product. Since I loved travel, my first "products" were the vacations I sold as a travel agent. Every job I've had since then has involved selling in some way.

After I left teaching, I answered an ad for "travel counselors" placed by a tour operator called Your Man Tours. Unlike most travel agent positions, this one was primarily commission-based, so my motivation was in part financial. But more importantly, I loved helping people plan vacations often as celebrations of special events, like anniversaries, in their lives. So I often did extra research to offer helpful advice about the destination, and this resulted in repeat business and referrals.

One of the many people who helped me the most was my first boss, John "Doc" Dolan, the owner of a Mr. Steak restaurant in St. Paul. I loved working there as a waitress, plus doing so enabled me to pay for my private high school and college tuitions. Doc taught me the importance of offering excellent customer service by caring for and enjoying each person I served. I always left the restaurant feeling good about the interactions I had with the customers, plus for a part-time job, the pay was terrific.

My dream changed in midlife. I had been working in a job I'd loved for years as the sales and marketing manager for one the top creativity consulting firms in the country. Despite selling an outstanding product to various Fortune 500 companies, after five years, I no longer possessed the passion and enthusiasm for the work itself. Rather than being energized, I was drained at the end of each day. I now realize this shift in energy was telling me it was time to leave. So I did. And then I developed a new dream, one motivated by finding meaning and making a difference, rather than making money. So what might have been perceived as a challenge or obstacle became an opportunity for profound spiritual and personal growth.

While working in the corporate world, I sensed that at some point I would work with people who were at the end of their life. So I began attending seminars on death and dying. Eventually, in 1998, I became a hospice volunteer. My first patient encouraged me to become a spiritual director, as did my own spiritual director. This coincidental encouragement, from people who knew me fairly well, seemed like a "sign" I was supposed to become a spiritual director. I decided to attend graduate school despite not being sure where a Master's Degree in Theology would lead me. But I felt I was beginning a journey I was meant to take, and it felt right and good. During the first semester, I was diagnosed with breast cancer. After experiencing holistic therapies to help heal myself, I ended up volunteering as a healing-touch practitioner and spiritual director at a nonprofit wellness center until it closed in 2002.

Two years later, I co-founded Well Within, a nonprofit holistic wellness center where we provide low-cost and free integrative therapies, classes, and workshops for people living with various health challenges, including some with terminal illnesses. Because of my commitment to people living with life-threatening illness and other challenging situations, I am passionate about helping individuals become "well within," and live as fully as possible—especially when they or their loved ones are facing health crises and other transitions.

I also love giving presentations and hosting an Internet radio show called Hope, Healing and WellBeing. These activities have provided the opportunity to help people reduce stress and anxiety and to foster hope, healing and spiritual growth for a variety of audiences. Working at Well Within, and later, writing books, provided more opportunities for "selling" various tools, techniques and ideas that enable people to heal in mind, body and spirit. I've loved everything I've done since 1999, and have found it all to be very fulfilling and rewarding.

For the past nine years, I have worked as a volunteer at Well Within, and I don't make much as an author or speaker. So success for me is not determined by salary, job title, or prestige. Thus, regardless of what someone earns, a person can be considered successful based on other things.

Success to me is:
- Discovering where your passion lies and using your gifts and talents.
- Creating a career that manifests what you believe you are called to do or be.
- Finding a good mentor and being an excellent mentor to others, especially other women.
- Keeping your professional and personal life in balance by practicing good self-care while helping others also do so.
- Finding the opportunities within challenging situations
- Having fun
- Creating a warm and welcoming environment for coworkers and clients
- Providing excellent service to your clients
- Contributing to the greater good of society while doing meaningful work you love.

www.marytreacyokeefe.com

Discover where your passion lies and create a career that manifests what you believe you are called to do or be.

CHAPTER 23

God Always Had a Plan; I Just Forgot to Listen

Dance like nobody's watching; love like you've never been hurt. Sing like nobody's listening; live like it's heaven on earth.
—Mark Twain

Devie Hagen

When I was young, it was the standard for women to become teachers. I think every kid goes through a couple of different professions. Then you dream about your big wedding. I had my daughter's name picked out when I was ten years old. I said when I have a little girl I'm going to name her after my mother, Anna. I was very traditional in terms of what I thought I was going to be when I grew up.

Once I was in high school, I wanted to go to college, but women often didn't go to college in the sixties. My parents didn't have very much money, and they couldn't afford it. So I thought, I'll be a flight attendant because it will be so glamorous. So after high school, I went to Northwest Airlines and applied for a job. They said, "No, you have to be at least five foot, two inches and must be able to reach the overhead bins. I missed by a quarter of an inch (I was 5ft., 1¾"). In the past, a flight attendant was hired based on how you looked, your weight and height.

Today, airlines have normal people like us. I like that. They are there for our safety. Although I miss the glamour of the white-glove service, cocktails in a glass, and meals served with a warm washcloth to wash your hands, I do get upset when I see people in pajamas and sweats in the airport because I think it's so tacky. I always dress. You never know who you're going to meet.

I started college classes at night, and I went to work at Unisys, where my boss was a very powerful man. I wound up dating and then marrying him. I was to stay home and make the meals, clean the house, and be in a dress, waiting with a cocktail when he came home. I found it so stifling to be his vision of the perfect wife. My husband wouldn't let me go anywhere or do anything. I think then I was the most depressed I've ever been in my life. After a year, I couldn't handle it and (almost) went crazy. I knew I had to work and have a fulfilling career. We had a child, but separated in a year and later got divorced.

I think what was tearing at us back then was the women's movement, which was going on at the same time as the hippy movement. The big question was: do you want this free lifestyle, or do you want to be a nurturing person with, at the time, a traditional lifestyle. Does wanting a career path make you a bad mom? I think looking back I always knew I wanted to be independent—to take care of myself. I didn't want to depend on anybody because there were always the "handcuffs" involved—which I didn't like.

Today, I work with a lot of students and different mentoring groups, specifically focusing on the lessons I learned throughout my career and life. One of the things I tell them is about all the nights I stayed late at work because I felt my clients needed me and my employer expected it, thus missing my children's events. Those clients don't remember I stayed late to accommodate them, but my children remember every single event I missed. That is one of my regrets, and hopefully people will learn from my life. You have to have balance in your life.

At the time, I didn't realize the importance of balance because we lived on a farm—and my father raised me. When I look back, my mother had been working three jobs. My father, bless his soul, wasn't a very good farmer. So in order to bring in the money needed to sustain the family, my mother had to live in another city. She would come home on Friday night to spend the weekend with us. While she was home, she would do all the cleaning and the laundry. On Sunday night, she would drive back to the city and work two jobs. She worked during the day in a factory and as a waitress at night. Now when I look back, I say, "Oh my God, I'm just like my mother." I've always worked two or three jobs. I feel she was a frontrunner even though she did it to sustain the family.

Growing up with a lot of confidence, I was not afraid to seek out people I admired, thinking I want to be like her or him. I would ask, "What was it that made you successful?" Many times I heard, "Luck," or "keeping an open mind," or "listening to what was going on," and "not being afraid."

When I was in my thirties and forties, and my sister was still alive, she would call me every day, saying, "Let's start our own business." I'd think, "Are you nuts? I need a steady paycheck. With two kids to raise, I need health insurance, stability, etc."

For twenty years, I was in hospitality sales and management and did a lot of traveling. And all of a sudden it hit me: This isn't fun anymore. I wasn't sleeping well, I was lonesome, I missed my family and my friends—and I quit. How dumb is it to quit at age fifty-eight with no retirement benefits, and no health insurance—or was I finally listening to God's voice. Work should be fun and fulfilling. We give the best of ourselves to the office, and if you're not having fun, I'd tell people, "Get the heck out." I saw an interview with Dick Clark back in the seventies when he was asked, "What has made you so successful?" And he said, "I'm having fun, every day I get up and it's fun, and when it stops being fun, I'm gone."

After I left that job I had no idea what I was going to do, but I knew I didn't want to be in the hospitality business. One day a woman whom I had hired out of college called, saying, "I hope you won't be offended, but I thought of you. We are looking for someone to do telemarketing for us. It's for the next six months. We have all these old lists of clients that have never been called. Would you consider doing it?" I thought this income might be enough to pay the bills and start a business. I wanted to ensure I went into this new venture with no bills. So I told her I needed this certain dollar amount, I will work these many days a week, and she'd provide a computer. She said, "Fabulous!" What a gift! God was watching out for me the whole time.

After twenty years in the hospitality industry as a meeting planner and sales director for major hotel, resorts, and conference centers, four years ago, when I was in my late fifties, I started my own business, Élan Speakers Agency. It was probably the worst time to go out on my own because there was a recession. But I was never afraid, and was always joyful and thankful for all my clients. I thought if for some reason this didn't work, I always had other options. I could tend bar, I could pick up a phone and do telemarketing, or I could work at Walmart, as a greeter. There were always options to put food on the table. "No risk, no reward." My sister was right all along—I just wasn't listening.

When I started my own business, I went to people who I respected and asked them what would be helpful to make their jobs easier and make them a star in the process of securing speakers. Whatever profession I'm in, I ask the same thing:

- "What can I do to make you successful?"
- "What is your process and criteria?"
- "How can I help to make it easier?"

People remembered me because the biggest compliment is to ask somebody how she or he got somewhere, and genuinely appreciate her or his adventure and advice. Yeah!

Starting My Business
I determined how many speakers I would need to be successful, and it just all fell into place. I started putting together a focus group of meeting planners from associations, corporations, government, and non-profits. I asked them, "What are your biggest challenges when you're booking a speaker?" and, "How can somebody support you in that process?" So they helped design my business. The speakers also told me what they needed. I listened and put their needs into action in my business plan. All I did was figure out the dollars and cents, and what I needed to pay the bills, and again it was "pure luck"—or was it because I finally listened to that voice.

Now I had the money to start my business, as well as the business plan, and support from meeting planners and speakers. The day I opened, the clients that were part of my focus groups called, "Are you booking yet because I need a speaker? Wahoo! It hasn't always been easy. There are time periods where I won't get anything going for a month or so, and I'd start thinking, "What am I doing that I don't have the bookings coming in, or people returning my calls or emails?" and, "I'm a failure." But I have trusted friends, who are my clients. I can call and say, "What am I doing wrong? Is it my marketing, is it my website? My phone isn't ringing—and I need your help." And without fail, every time I do that, the phone starts ringing. You'd think I would learn to be patient and confident. I have a difficult time with patience. I just have to go back and remember that as long as I am doing the work of planting the seeds, the plants will grow. Just keep planting. This is always the tough part for me.

When I think back, I didn't know what my dream was. I think now my dream is to be a great mom, a good friend, and a trusted business associate. I want to feel very good about what I have accomplished at the end of the day of following my business plan, making a difference, and having fun. It's important when one becomes successful to give back. I'm a big believer in being a mentor. Anyone can do this. Also, I am always so joyful that I receive as much back from mentoring as I give. I think life is a continual learning process … a fun learning process. I don't mean to be a "I'm going to take a class in psychology because I need to be learning." You can take dance lessons, learn to do the zumba or get to know different companies and the responsibilities of your clients. You can expand your mind in many different ways. Just go out and do it, and not be afraid. Just remember, God is always talking. We just forget sometimes to listen!

Success to me is:
- Having balance between work and family demands.
- Not being afraid to ask others what made them successful—and learn from it.
- Stopping doing something when it is not fun anymore.
- Sometimes accepting jobs/opportunities for where they will lead, not just the present.
- Knowing there are always options for putting food on the table.
- Doing what it takes to make other people's jobs easier—and you'll be rewarded.
- Appreciating your own accomplishments.
- Realizing that life is a continual learning process.
- Remembering God is watching over you all the time, so keep listening.

www.ElanSpeakersAgency.com

Don't be afraid to ask others what made them successful—and learn from it.

CHAPTER 24

The Russian Express

*A dream you dream alone is only a dream.
A dream you dream together is reality.*

—Yoko Ono

Zhenya Melnick

When I was a child in Russia, I wanted to have my own dance company, choreograph dancing, and to dance. I did ballroom dancing, waltz, tango and the cha-cha. I absolutely loved performing. I think I started when I was seven or eight, and I stopped when I was about thirteen or fourteen. Even though it was always in the back of my mind, I knew it was not going to happen. It was just a dream—but it would be nice. I simply never developed the proper training. It was just ... fun.

My next dream was to be a psychologist because I am fascinated with how people think and what motivates them to do certain things. I am most fascinated with digging into people's minds to try to understand them. Even now, I read a lot of books about psychology. It's interesting to try to understand just how and why people behave the way they do in social situations. Why do they make their particular choices; how do they decide? I continue with this special interest, reading and investigating and watching people, applying the psychological perspectives. But, once again, it has become just another interest and hobby.

In 1998, at age sixteen, I moved to the United States to pursue my undergraduate degree in business, greatly influenced by my mom. Mom was convinced life abroad could offer more opportunities than a newly changed and developing Russia. Sharing her dream for a better life, I did not hesitate to make the leap. A decade and a half later, I have no doubt it was the right choice for me.

Mom was already a successful businesswoman. At the time I came to the U.S. to study, she was the director of a regional office in the Russian Far

East for an American company, headquartered in Seattle. This international fishing company owned and operated a number of fishing vessels in Russia as well as other areas of the world. Mom was managing the regional office and responsible for sales in the area. Thriving in largely a man's world, she became a perfect example of what success was for me—overcoming seemingly impossible circumstances to make it to the top *in spite of gender* odds.

Business seemed like a good and diverse field to go into if I wanted to be able to find a decent job after I graduated, and there was no better place to study business than the U.S. While in school, I particularly enjoyed the subjects involving economics because it has a lot to do with cause and effect.

After I graduated, I worked at a number of start-up companies. Being intrigued by both ambiguity and indeterminacy, I enjoyed these positions because:

- I was a part of building something from the ground up with lots of unknown factors by which one can be challenged according to structure and formation.
- This ambiguity about shaping a new company afforded opportunities to try your hand at a lot of different projects. In such a manner, one can observe your own impact upon the development process.
- I also enjoyed being among highly entrepreneurial people who had an immense drive to succeed, along with the passion for and in-depth knowledge of what they did.

My last job before going to graduate school was no different. Initially, as a second job, I became a hostess at a brand-new restaurant located in a popular tourist location in Seattle. It was the family venture of a chef and a general manager who saw more potential in me than merely as a hostess. A few months later I became their full-time marketing manager. I was responsible for booking the banquet room for private events, and building awareness about the restaurant in the local community through networking events and trade shows. While enjoying my job, I realized I wanted to learn more about marketing in a structured way, so going back to school seemed like a natural way to do so. I went to the University of Minnesota–Carlson School of Business.

Since I am in business now, I see a superficial, yet quite appealing notion of being a businesswoman—having the power to make decisions, run a business, or be a manager. From today's vantage point, a difference exists in the marketplace:

- Twenty years ago, fewer women were approaching leadership roles within most business communities.
- Many of us have risen to top management levels and are quite successful in our achievements.
- Gender equality in both leadership roles and salary adjustments across the board is still virtually non-existent.

For a woman to be in business and become successful, it takes education. Being able to think and speak the same way a man does is a huge factor in being perceived as an equally talented individual. So I can honestly say getting my MBA was a big step for me—in making the leap from where I was before I went back to school, to where I am now.

I've learned these most-important business facts:
- Gaining trust: Having the ability to gain the trust of people around you in the workplace, and having the opportunity to take on challenges, first you have to find a few people who truly believe in you. These would be folks who want to see you succeed through your skillset and hard work: managers or co-workers who would place you into situations where you might find excellent ways to show what you are capable of doing.
- Support with resources: Yet, at the same time, you would need their support with resources. If you are exploring an unknown territory (and you are not exactly certain what you are doing), it would be incredibly helpful and valuable to know your co-workers and managers are standing behind you whenever you need them.

I have a boss who is absolutely fantastic, and I am lucky to have him for these reasons:
- If I'm not sure about something, I can bounce my ideas off of him. He may approve of some of them; sometimes, he may not but he will always be open and honest in his feedback, always striving to find opportunities for my development.
- He may provide recommendations I haven't thought about, and it goes both ways.
- Sometimes I just need a little reassurance what I'm trying to do makes sense.
- Sometimes I need guidance about what it is I need to do.

For a woman to have a better chance of being successful, she has to have good support at home from someone who wants her to succeed. This someone would have no expectations that whenever he arrived at home, he would immediately find dinner already prepared for him while she magnanimously greeted him with a glamorous face and beckoning smile. These are different times. It takes two cooperative, hard-working breadwinners to run a household today. Things just don't work out the old way, at least not for me.

I was lucky to find "my special someone" who appreciated my drive, and who admired my intelligence and determination to succeed. Part of our initial attraction, this grew into our mutual desire to work together to build our life into something which would make us proud. This understanding meant a lack of expectations I'd be a wife in a traditional sense—but an agreement to work together instead, in our home and outside of it, to create the life we wanted. Now, eight happy years later with a baby on the way, my husband and I reflect on everything we have achieved together and take an immense sense of pride in the partnership and support system we were able to create.

My mother did not stay home. My grandmother was the one I most remember from my childhood. It was wonderful to have her with us. Now I want my mom to do the same thing for my child. I want her to be here, to take care of the baby because I think family values are incredibly important in the development of a child. I do not choose to have strangers taking care of my child. One should desire such a bond to exist between Grandma and baby. I would like to have the ability (and the option) on a professional level to go back to work.

I have very good prospects to potentially keep moving up the ladder at my current position. Taking on more responsibility, I am managing additional people on my own team. There seems to be a lot of trust in me; I feel others recognize I am a talented employee whom they would like to keep and continue developing.

It's fantastic and wonderful.

I also now know different paths exist to get where you want to be, and this one works for me. But everyone is different. Some women need to be able to do it by themselves. They don't want any help. For them it's a process of getting there and being independent—which they value. What I have gone through may not be applicable to them at all. I value the support system, and I need it to succeed. But some women are motivated by being independent and to be able to do it alone. I also think it depends on the company. It has to be a match between what they value and what you value because, if the culture is not a good match, you are going to be miserable—*no matter what you do.*

Overall, as I have attempted here to illustrate adequately, in order to achieve success in any field, one must be motivated, one must acquire an adequate education and have the necessary support, but most of all, one absolutely must be *driven by passion*. "You've got to really want it!"

For women in business to become successful it takes education. Being able to think and speak the same way a man does is a huge factor in being perceived as an equally talented individual.

CHAPTER 25

The Artist in Me Finds Her Wings

All you have is this moment, right now. Make it count.
—Sharon Wagner

Sharon Wagner

I am an artist, mother of three sons, wife and twin sister, who was raised to be kind and fair. When we were young, my sister and I would sit with our mother and draw. Even in grade school, art was my favorite subject. Oftentimes, we abandon dreams we don't even remember we had.

I am blessed to have been married to the same man for thirty-seven years. We have moved fourteen times and lived in eight different cities, all of which helped make me the person I am today.

For seventeen years, I was a school cook in the Anoka Hennepin School District, first at an elementary school, next the middle school, and my last ten years at Blaine High School. At the same time, all three of our boys went to school there, which was a great time for me.

I had to survive in this normal, sometimes dismal, work-a-day world almost all of my work time. When the last of the three boys graduated from college, I looked at my husband and said, "I am fifty years old. I can either stay as a school cook, and die inside—or be an artist and ... *thrive.*

My dream has been to be an artist and start my own mural business. I have never had a formal education in art, but I have taken classes. My talent is natural.

My husband supported me completely, and with family and friends telling me to "Go for it," I did.

My biggest challenge in starting my own business was losing the security of a steady paycheck and group insurance. My husband's check helped, and his insurance took up the gap. Then it was overcoming the fear that maybe I can't do this. At the beginning of each new job, I was filled with fear of failure, but I did it anyway. In the end, it was some of my best work. Now I can approach any job without the fear, and without so much stress, all my energy goes into creating the project. Next I had to find the right way to get my name out there to generate business. Finally, I had to learn to spend money, when I had it, to grow my business, and not to spend money when I didn't have it. Being debt free has allowed me the freedom to get through the slow times.

I have formed an excellent relationship with many Sherman Williams paint stores, and I send my clients to them whenever I can. For the thirty years before I started my business, I had been painting murals for friends and family, and also doing canvas artwork, and portraits of people and animals. So I had artwork to put in the various display sample books Sherman Williams' stores have available for customers to review.

No specific form of advertising has worked well for me, and word of mouth from happy clients is the best way of promoting my business.

I also belong to an invaluable national group of artisans called National Territorial Artisans (NTA). As a solo businessperson, I turn to two of my sons for help. When I have a large job, I am able to take it on with the help of people in NTA, and pay them as contractors.

I started small and within a few years, I was making more money than I did working as a school cook. I have had to expand the skills and type of painting services my company offers in order to keep it going. But the added variety of painting walls, removing wallpaper and faux finishes means no two days are alike.

Getting to a point where I had complete confidence in my ability to do a good job has made the work more enjoyable. It is wonderful to face each job now without fear. It is hard work, and the days are long when you are your own boss. Because of the added confidence, the flexibility and rewards are worth the added effort.

As far as advice for anyone going into business for herself I would say: The more support systems you have when you start out will help you a lot. Be willing to roll with the punches, because, when you are the boss, customers come to you only if there is a problem. I have always been able to work through anything with reasonable people, however; some people are not, and you have to just let go. If that is your passion, nothing will keep you from reaching it all. Life is too short not to be living your dream.

To be successful, I have found that your most valued trait is to go with the flow. I call on my Higher Power every morning, and I'm willing to go where it takes me.

My ability to hold joy in each day, and leave love behind in each home, has evolved. Having learned to visualize and project my dreams into a kind of "Now Reality" is what certainly changed my life. I simply wake up and "keep going" with love and light in my heart.

I still have a lot of ideas of how I would like to move forward into my own artwork for sale. It is still in the baby stages, but it will also be born one day.

Success to me is:

- Overcoming the fear that I cannot do something.
- Finding the right way to get your name out there to generate business.
- Spending only the money you have, not going into debt.
- Realizing word of mouth is best business advertising.
- Having a strong and reliable support system established.
- Learning to roll with the punches—and go with the flow.
- Having quality and trusted resources to share.
- Showing pride in what you've accomplished.
- Never burning bridges with suppliers or vendors.

www.muralsbysharon.com

The only way to get rid of the fear of doing something ... is to go out and do it. Take the risk of being who you really are.

CHAPTER 26

From Adversity to Success

Sometimes I think my life would make a great TV movie. It even has the part where they say "STAND BY". We are experiencing temporary difficulties.
—Robert Brault

Nancy Chakrin

As I approached the skyline of my hometown, Minneapolis, from Interstate 94, the seventies' hit, "I Can See Clearly Now," pulsated from the radio. I turned it up and sang along at the top of my lungs.

After thirty-four years, I had finally garnered the courage to take back my life from an ill-fated marriage. My future was about to unfold in ways I could never have dreamed possible.

Success is finally taking charge of one's life and not giving away your power.

My failing marriage was not my first encounter with adversity. When I was fifteen, a serious back injury and surgery forced me to bed for an entire year. As a result, my childhood aspiration to be a nurse crashed. My devoted mother, Dorothy, cared for me daily, lovingly encouraging me and supporting my healing process. During college I still tried to work as a nurse's aide, but transferring patients caused severe back pain.

Although fate may have stomped on my nursing career, I recognized the blessings of ever-present family talents in the visual arts and leadership. After some fifteen years of working for corporate advertising and marketing firms, my passion for healthcare, graphic design, photography, painting, and public relations resurfaced into one eclectic package. In 1980, I birthed my own business, NRC Graphics LLC.

Success is finding another path when obstacles get in your way. Believe in yourself and set goals for new outcomes.

Back in Minneapolis and newly divorced, I was catapulted into the caregiving role, and my childhood passion for nursing was fulfilled in a manner I had not anticipated. For the next twelve years, my mother suffering with Parkinson's disease, and my father dealing with cardiovascular illness, required my daily nurturing and relentless advocacy.

As my parents moved from our family home, to senior apartment living, to nursing homes, to hospices, until finally death, I was by their sides every step of the way, providing for them the best quality of life possible. Assuming the role of passionate healthcare advocate, not only for my parents and two aunts, but also for two of my condominium neighbors, I reinstituted the family council at the nursing home to give voice to needed changes.

Often I took Mom out of the nursing home and engaged her in the extraordinary Struthers Parkinson's programs, other community events, and day trips. Even six weeks before she died, I wheeled Mom, strapped into her wheelchair, onto the Minnesota State Fair grounds—a tradition she never wanted to miss.

Witnessing my mother's deterioration was heart wrenching. For inspiration, I attended the Parkinson's Progress and Possibilities Conference to hear Pauline Boss, author of *Ambiguous Loss: Learning to Live with Unresolved Grief*. Her talk provided important information regarding the Parkinson's patient: *"psychological absence can be as devastating as physiological absence—a loved one is often present, but as the disease progresses her mind is not."* She encouraged families to *"celebrate the part of their loved one that is still present and mourn the part that is lost."* I felt successful when both Mom's nurse practitioner and her doctor said to me, "Nancy, I only wish all my patients had a caring daughter such as you. You enriched her life and made a significant difference."

During the spring of 2000, I took on yet another challenge, breast cancer. This time I was my own healthcare advocate. I questioned everything. My past work history at the University of Minnesota Medical Art and Photography Department propelled me to do thorough research. I even visited the hospital pathology department and viewed my cells microscopically before scheduling surgery at Mayo Clinic. Radiation treatment followed. I chose the traditional allopathic approach but began to learn more about alternative and complementary healing practices.

Turn your wounds into wisdom.
—Oprah Winfrey

While recuperating, my dearest friends encouraged me to find serenity by returning to my love of painting. After a twenty-three year hiatus, I questioned my ability to still be able to create anything on canvas with a paintbrush. The confidence I required came by entering an unusual competition, chair painting. For three weeks, my chair and I bonded as I lovingly painted it with landscapes and quotations.

Spontaneously, I sent a photograph of this painted chair to my former husband. Extremely taken by the depiction of the country road we had lived on, he commissioned a large painting on linen canvas and included money for the best quality oil paints. He sent a check for this painting and subsequent commissions followed.

Surprise! Surprise! My former husband transformed into one of my most ardent supporters. He is the most influential person in my life. While our marriage was often challenging, I recognized his many brilliant gifts with respect to business and education, legal and financial matters, medicine and medical research. I learned from him about operating one's business life with integrity, honesty, ethics, and humor. We have let bygones be bygones, and for the past seventeen years now we have enjoyed a most cordial relationship via email, U.S. mail and telephone.

Happiness is not something ready-made. It comes from your own actions.
—Dalai Lama XIV

Prolific, calming landscapes with billowing clouds or tranquil views of rivers and lakes seemed to roll off my paintbrush. Soon I exhibited in galleries and juried shows. "Healing Blue Waters," my traveling landscape exhibits, continue to be viewed in medical and wellness centers. Also, I received a commission from USA Track & Field Adirondack for the 25th Anniversary of Freihofer's Women's 5K Run in Albany, New York. They invited me to attend the event where I autographed some 3,500 posters of the original painting of the 2002 race. My art is now a part of international private and corporate collections.

Learn to get in touch with the silence within yourself, and know that everything in life has purpose. There are no mistakes, no coincidences, all events are blessings given to us to learn from.
—Elisabeth Kubler-Ross

My desire to nurture others led me to coach three significant women with remarkable projects over a seventeen-year period. Mentoring these women has enriched my life in ways I could never have imagined while also contributing to community and global changes.

Barbara Lee Friedman, of Music Memories Inc., has a passion and a special gift that allows her to awaken in the elderly their love of music from times gone by. As co-chair for Music Memories fundraising events, within two years my efforts had burgeoned her concert attendance by 400 percent. I helped her produce a CD and a laminated songbook, "Forever Young at Heart," for use in nursing homes. We even created several videos of families gathered around loved ones in hospice settings during the last days of their lives. Not only did these videos become family heirlooms, but Alzheimer's Speaks http://www.alzheimersspeaks.com, and Alzheimer's Speaks Radio, have featured our videos on international YouTubes. http://www.youtube.com/watch?v=WAZ6_67zH5Y This video has received over 33,000 hits.

Denise Meyer, of SignBridge Language System, was there for me during my trials with cancer. Later, with my photography, graphic design and project management skills, I reciprocated and helped her formulate a multilingual system based upon the American Sign Language which included ten languages: Spanish, French, German, Chinese, Russian, Hmong, Korean, Somali, Japanese, and Arabic. Besides many presentations, Denise and I exhibited at national conferences. I helped to promote her training programs for early child-caregivers, elementary teachers, parents of internationally adopted children, and ESL and foreign language immersion teachers. http://www.signbridge.com.

Laurie Ellis-Young, founder of Breathe The Change LLC & BreathLogic™ Inc. has become my special friend and business partner. For my sixty-fifth birthday, I accepted Laurie's invitation to attend an annual wellness/yoga/breath retreat in Guatemala. This was stretching far beyond my comfort zone for a topic I knew nothing about, and it was taking place in a third-world country. Nonetheless, I needed a vacation so I took the leap to this photographer's paradise. http://www.breathethechange.com

Attending this retreat turned out to be one of the five best decisions that I have ever made in my life. This experience changed both our lives. I was most impressed by Laurie's phenomenal, peaceful teaching style, her calming voice and compassion for others. I encouraged her to share her gifts with the world, but she disliked the idea of marketing, so I stepped up to the plate.

Upon returning to the States, I designed her first business card, and then began coordinating her many workshops, retreats, corporate lunch-and-learns, conferences and presentations in medical, educational and business centers.

The fun thing about getting older is finding younger people to mentor.
—Mike May

In Guatemala, I had photographed Laurie and her friend, Jen Gori, doing morning yoga. Little did we know one of those photographs would be the cover on our 2010 book, *FRIENDSHIP: The Art of the Practice* published by TRISTAN Publishing. For this book we did yoga photo-shoots in several locations: Hawaii, Arizona, Colorado, the National Parks, and other locales of beauty. This included solo and partner poses with women ages 10 to 100. Inspirational friendship quotes accompanied each pose. We jumped for joy when Midwest Independent Publishers Association (MIPA) awarded our book a gold medal in the Arts category.

In conjunction with our book, we produced experiential traveling photography exhibits called "Yoga ON and OFF the Wall," which several medical and wellness centers in the Midwest display. When Laurie is in the country, she makes the images come to life.

Creativity comes from looking for the unexpected and stepping outside your own experience.
—Massaru Ibuka

Feeling the desire to expand our work on a more global level, I applied for and was awarded The University of Minnesota's 2012-2013 Buckman Fellowship for Leadership in Philanthropy based upon our multilingual and multicultural *Breath Awareness* integrative medicine project.

This fellowship provided me with the courage, skills, and knowledge needed to launch the non-profit organization, BreathLogic™, with Laurie. I have taken great delight in helping my co-author (and yogini model) focus her dreams of bringing the *Power of Breath* to the masses. Once our 501c3 non-profit status is approved, we look forward to receiving funding for the programs and developing tools to expand this vision.

Initially, our plans include a multilingual pilot study at the Park Nicollet Health System in Minneapolis, Minnesota, and an educational/peace/wellness model curricula to be developed at both the King Abdullah University of

Science and Technology (KAUST) in Saudi Arabia and at the American School London (ASL) in London, England.

To me, success is knowing that I use my talents, determination, abilities, and skills in many ways to serve and benefit others. It provides me a sense of joy. I am living my dream life with passion and purpose.

And lastly, other success stories involve my photography business and community service activities. Photography has been a passion since childhood, and I have volunteered my services for many non-profit organizations. Each situation has provided exciting opportunities with new connections through my camera: polar explorer Ann Bancroft; David Gergen of CNN; Drs. Andrew Weil and Deepak Chopra; E-Bay CEO John Donahoe; Rabbi Harold Kuschner; and His Holiness the 14th Dalai Lama.

In Guatemala City, I helped create a YouTube video for the organization Asociacion de Superacion Educativa. http://www.youtube.com/watch?v=gH4gFjawZt0. Founded by Lucrecia Godoy, this fabulous organization helps educate impoverished girls past sixth grade, providing them with safe drinking water, life-changing skills, and inspired family values.

I feel very fortunate to live in the Twin Cities' community ranking first in the country for volunteerism. I belong to several healthcare, arts, publishing, and women's organizations, and have served on the boards of the United Nations Association of Minnesota, the Park Nicollet Struthers Parkinson's Center, and now BreathLogic™.

For four years, I have served as the email community connector for the Wise Women group begun some fifteen years ago with just a handful of friends. By default I ended up increasing this inclusive list to almost four hundred women. It has become a well-respected list of Women Helping Women, not only in the Twin Cities, but often receiving worldwide requests and services. The success stories are heartwarming.

The more you invest in others, the greater your harvest will be!
Your life will always benefit from multiplying someone else's life.

—Verna Price, PhD.

We all have dealt with crises, adversity, misfortune, and challenges in our lives. What matters is this: How *do* we make lemonade from lemons. How *do* we create success from our mistakes? "Research shows hardiness is the key to the resiliency for not only surviving, but also thriving, under stress. Hardiness enhances performance, leadership, conduct, stamina, mood and both physical and mental health." (From "Turning Lemons into Lemonade: Hardiness Helps People Turn Stressful Circumstances into Opportunities," American Psychological Association, December 22, 2003.)

I hope this story of creating my "lemonade" will inspire others. In my seventh decade of life, I am thriving with such joy and happiness, hardiness and resilience.

To achieve success:
- Take charge of your own life. Do not give away your power.
- Believe in yourself. Then be a mentor for others.
- Learn all you can about business, law, and medicine.
- Set goals for new outcomes when obstacles hinder your path for success.
- Be more than reliable. Go the extra mile; surprise your clients with more than they expect, and they will never forget your dedication.
- Surround yourself with fabulous friends, *especially* a friend who is different from you.
- Open your heart to synchronistic events for they *may* change your life.
- Adversity builds character.
- Discover your purpose! Ask yourself, "Am I making a difference?"
- Take risks. Leap beyond your comfort zone.
- Never burn bridges.
- Have fun. Laugh a lot. Breathe consciously.

NancyChakrin.com
nancy@NancyChakrin.com
Midwest and Northeast Oil Paintings by Nancy Chakrin

Success is knowing that I use my talents, determination, abilities, and skills in many ways to serve and benefit others.

CHAPTER 27

The Career Path of a Creative Woman

Creativity requires the courage to let go of certainties.
—Erich Fromm

Melissa McGath

From very early on I knew I wanted to have my own business, and I achieved this goal on January 2, 2012. I also knew I needed to position myself academically and financially to do so—to gain the education, experience, and financial wherewithal that were the stepping-stones in my master plan.

I have always been blessed with a knack for seeing things differently than most. Talented artistically and with many interests and passions, I found my artistic lens made me a great problem-solver as well as a perfectionist.

An education in art and design was my logical path. After graduating from college, I landed what I thought was my dream job as an illustrator for a greeting card company in North Mankato, Minnesota. After a four-year stint, I moved on to work as a graphic designer in the marketing department of a Twin Cities hospital, while simultaneously earning my BA in marketing.

The relationships I developed were crucial. I received many referrals for illustration and design work, and one of my biggest accomplishments, both for my career and in helping relieve me of debt in my mid-20s, was illustrating a children's book series called, *Who Grows Up Here?* In 2003, while still working full-time for the hospital, I was able to turn my freelance work into a part-time business, M.J. Carpenter & Co., for which I designed a logo, business card, letterhead, website and even a branded invoice.

This was major progress towards my goal. In time, my freelance business grew, and my hours at the hospital were cut. When they said, "We have to cut your hours due to the economic downturn," it turned out to be a blessing. In December of 2010, I decided to resign from the hospital and focus on my freelance business. In doing so, I was able to continue my work with the hospital, because it became my client instead of my employer.

Prior to starting M.J. Carpenter & Co., I often second-guessed my career choice as a graphic designer, thinking I would be well suited to be a craftsperson, designing and making furniture and cabinets. While working at the hospital, I was surprised to find my true passion was branding—helping companies tell their story by connecting them to their target audiences both visually and emotionally. I leveraged the visual side of branding with my design skills, and the emotional side of branding with my marketing skills.

So I felt quite confident and knew I was on the right track. It truly seemed like the perfect fit, and I was very excited to move forward. That's when a friend introduced me to Tom Dupont, owner of Kazoo Branding in Minneapolis.

We met for the first time in October of 2009 at a coffee shop in Northeast Minneapolis. Tom, a 60-something with thinning hair, and me a 30-something with big sunglasses, swiftly discovered our personalities were an immediate match. I was anxious to show him my portfolio in the hope we could work together in some capacity. As it turned out, our common interest in do-it-yourself home improvement projects quickly took over. We shared numerous stories and became friends. Tom supported me in my decision to pursue self-employment.

Once I became a full-time freelancer, we started working together informally, helping each other out as needed. We kept in close contact and talked openly about the business decisions we were each making. We officially became partners in January 2012 in a 50/50 partnership under the name Kazoo Branding, Inc. I was proud to be able to make that investment without incurring any debt.

Surrounding myself with people who encouraged me was instrumental as I reached for my goal. These were people who gave it to me straight without fluff or a disingenuous pat on the back. It was from these close friends and family members I got wise, honest counsel, and I trusted they were not just being cheerleaders. I knew they truly had my best interest at heart.

My husband, Adam, has been my biggest supporter. He's been my best friend for more than fourteen years and has listened to me share my dream and watch it become a reality. He taught me a lot about dealing with people—whether they be friends, acquaintances or customers.

- In both your personal and business life, follow the golden rule: to do unto others as you would have them do unto you.
- Put the needs of others in front of your own, but this does not mean people take advantage of you.

- When customers see you want what's best for them, this is when true relationships are established, and lasting business relationships are formed.
- The importance of expectations: Never expect a good deed or favor to be reciprocated, but to do it with a whole-hearted giving mentality, and there will be no disappointment.

In addition to having the support and shared wisdom of others, it was very important to me to be fiscally self-supporting. I had read that one should save a year's salary before taking the self-employment plunge. I then began my research and crunched the numbers to see what it would take for me to live conservatively, yet comfortably on a monthly basis.

- I did an analysis of previous spending and future added expenses, such as health care insurance, given I would no longer be under an employer's health plan.
- I looked at bank statements and credit card statements over the past couple years, and came up with a monthly number that seemed reasonable without sacrificing a social life or skipping any meals.
- Once I established a financial goal, I was able to determine how many clients I needed and how many billable hours a month it would take to maintain a modest living and lifestyle.
- By breaking down my goal into sub-goals, my plan became feasible and realistic.

In my marketing classes we learned about SMART goals: Specific, Measurable, Actionable, Realistic and Timely. In order for a marketing piece to be effective, it has to be SMART. For example, I have designed and written numerous direct mail pieces. Each piece featured a nice image, headline, maybe a subhead, content about the product or service, company logo, contact information, call to action and a time limit. However, without a plan for measurements, its success would be unknown, and the piece would be worthless. The same goes for the success of individuals. They have to be SMART in setting their goals.

The "when" for starting my business was not a specific date or year, but rather an attained dollar amount. I knew how much I wanted to save before becoming self-employed, and worked aggressively at meeting my goal. The dollar amount became my timeframe because I knew how much I could afford to save, and picking up freelance jobs along the way only helped expedite the process. As I drew closer to the number, the actual date became clearer. I began to put the specifics of my plan together, including the number of clients and billable hours I needed. My goals were specific, measurable, actionable, reliable and timely. Without goals in mind, I would still be working for "the man," instead of attaining my goals.

To summarize success in my experience:
- I made it a habit to never execute anything until I felt at complete peace about it.
- As a woman of faith, I prayed regularly about direction and decisions in my life, and can thankfully look back knowing I made each decision without regret.
- Education, experience, passion, motivation, planning, goals and finances, are all ingredients to "success soup," but without a sense of peace to seal the deal, decisions can be guided by fear.
- It is important that each of my business decisions was made with information based on well-researched facts and understanding, so it can be made with clarity and confidence.

http://www.linkedin.com/in/mjmcgath

When customers see you want what's best for them, this is where true relationships are established and lasting business relations are formed.

CHAPTER 28

A Life Focused on Health and Wellness

Find a job you love and you'll never work a day in your life.
—Confucius

JANICE NOVAK

I can't recall "always" wanting to be or do anything specific, and my idea kept changing throughout my childhood and early adulthood. I went to Catholic grade school, during which I wanted to be a nun. By the time I was a junior in high school, I definitely knew I wanted to be a teacher who focused on health and wellness, and I have been in the field ever since.

I did not have the resources to go to college immediately upon graduating high school. Instead, I went to work for Maggie Lettvin who had one of the first exercise programs on public television called "Maggie and the Beautiful Machine." Maggie taught me how to look at health and wellness with common sense, and from the angle of prevention. It made so much sense to me. I learned how to create relevant health education programs with information people can put to immediate use. I also learned how to translate medical research into plain English. I will be forever grateful to her for all I learned.

While working with Maggie, I decided I wanted and needed to go to college, and I wanted to keep going until I earned a Master's degree. However, I had absolutely no financial resources. I applied to several colleges as office help. If you were a college employee, you received a certain amount of free tuition every semester. Along the way, I was granted a few helpful grants and scholarships. I worked during the day and went to school at night. In May of 1990, I earned my Master's degree in Health Education.

Shortly after graduating college, my first book, *Enhancing Lamaze Techniques: Exercises for Pregnancy, Birth & Recovery*, was published by Putnam

Publishers. I began doing seminars and workshops on different health topics as well as TV spots—both local and some national.

I began my career in the posture field in my late twenties. At the age of fifteen, I had grown several inches over the summer, making me taller than almost all of the girls, and a lot of the boys. In my mid twenties, a high school friend showed me pictures of us at a party. I was horrified at how slumped and round-shouldered I looked. I know I wasn't born that way—I did it to myself in an effort to fit in. I then decided to see if I could undo all the damage I had done to my posture. Not only did I find that you can fix posture problems, I discovered it is not even so difficult. Anyone can do it.

I authored a book and companion DVD titled, *Posture, Get It Straight! Look Ten Years Younger, Ten Pounds Thinner and Feel Better Than Ever.* I teach posture improvement workshops for groups, as well as custom design posture improvement programs for individual needs.

Along with posture improvement workshops, I teach a variety of other health and wellness topics like: The Art of Aging Well; Women, Weight & Hormones; Stress Busting Strategies for Busy People; Overcome Your Carbohydrate Cravings; Vitamins & Herbs: Facts & Fallacies; and Building Better Bones, to name a few.

In these sessions, I present up-to-date info on pertinent health/wellness topics that can improve employee health, decrease sick days, as well as improve productivity, alertness, energy and motivation. I try to empower people to take action toward attaining better health. My easy-to-use techniques are informational and motivational and can easily be integrated into daily life. Many of my students tell me implementing the simple steps I teach have led to huge changes in how they look and feel.

My favorite message to impart is: You need to realize how much control you actually have over your own health. Every day, the body repairs and replaces billions of cells in your heart, eye, skin, kidney, etc. Even as you read these words, your body is pumping out millions of new cells. And the quality of cell you can make right now is very dependent on the raw materials you have floating around your bloodstream. For instance, any day you don't get enough zinc from your diet, is a day your immune system won't work 100 percent. It can't. It needs zinc to make its antibodies. And so on and so on.

This is exciting because it means every moment is another opportunity to make every system in your body as healthy as you possibly can. No matter what might be coming down your genetic road, you will be better off right now by making yourself as healthy as possible. We also must keep our muscles strong by focusing on strengthening exercises. I am a Baby Boomer. Scientists speculate lots of people in my age group will live well into our eighties, nineties, and many of us may even hit a hundred. Most days, I would not mind living to be a hundred; I just want to be functional when I get there. I want to be able to get in and out of my chair, and walk trails with my great grandchildren. This is not an impossible goal.

Since I do a lot of speaking, I always advise people just starting out in the speaking field to focus on the information they want to impart on their audience—instead of worrying about not making a fool of yourself. I also think to achieve success today you need to be especially savvy in social media. If you do not have those skills, it is important to find someone you can work with who does.

I am thrilled to be doing work I absolutely love. That's the key to success. Also,

- Love what you do, and you'll never work a day in your life.
- Your work will renew and replenish you while feeding your soul.
- Success also takes hard work and perseverance.
- Have a really good support system.
- Be prepared. It makes doing your job look easier.
- Tell everyone what you do; you never know who needs your help.
- Research new ways to share your knowledge and expertise.
- Learn to be comfortable doing public speaking and radio/TV interviews.
- Start writing articles and books about your expertise.
- Live in the future and forget about "should haves."
- Forgive yourself for past mistakes, and vow never to repeat them.

Janice@ImproveYourPosture.com

To be successful you must love what you do. It can't feel like a job, but rather something you look forward to doing.

CHAPTER 29

Healing on the Mountain

We must embrace the pain and burn it as fuel for the journey.
—Kenji Miyazawa

Meg Blaine Corrigan

People who think they have no control over their lives are correct. But we do have control over our attitude *towards* our life. We cannot change the past, and we may be powerless to prevent certain things from happening to us. But we can choose how we react towards the things that happen, which is an important difference. For me, it made the difference between lasting happiness—and an almost certain downward spiral into depression.

When my father died in 2002, I was sorting through old photos and found a picture of my mother passed out on the floor in a drunken stupor. Suddenly, I was flooded with memories of my horrific childhood, lived out in the shadow of my mother's raging alcoholism. My older sister and I spent our days trying not to set off our mother's violent temper, a rage she shared with our long-deceased grandfather. Short periods of sobriety always led to much longer phases of drinking, anger, and estrangement, as well as verbal and emotional abuse toward the rest of the family.

My father was a high-ranking United States Air Force officer who spent time in foreign diplomatic service, but we quickly learned the military was no place to turn for help. "Don't ask, don't tell" was the policy in those days for families who had any type of mental health problems. Because of our frequent moves, we had no extended family around us, and our family was not part of any kind of faith community. My father became secretive and protective of our family's "dirty little secret," and his co-dependency eventually became almost as overpowering as my mother's alcohol addiction.

In 1972, after completing a graduate degree in counseling, I was living and working in Colorado Springs, Colorado. My parents had moved to one state; my grown sister to another, and other than a few casual friends, I had no support system to deal with all of the challenges of being an "adult child of an alcoholic," as they are identified now. The phrase hadn't even been invented yet, and I was dismally deficient in knowledge about the systemic effects of family substance abuse. I was also more naïve than I would have admitted about surviving on my own. My salary paid the bills, but I had no specific values, goals or aspirations other than to exist from day to day. My social life was sparse as well; I lacked even minimal skills to maintain meaningful relationships with men or women.

On a quiet Sunday afternoon in a mountain park outside of town, I sat sketching scenery, not noticing the light was fading, and other people were leaving the park. A man wearing a bandana over his face suddenly jumped from behind a rock. I thought this was some kind of joke, and expected his buddies to come out, beer cans in hand, laughing their heads off. That's when I saw the gun.

The man forced me up higher on the mountain where he sexually assaulted me. He then pulled a heavy chain from a bag and told me to move to a large pine tree.

I knew I had to do something fast. Not believing in divine intervention, but desperate to try anything, I cried out, "In the name of God, don't do this!" The man's face contorted into a look somewhere between fear and cowardice. When he slammed the chain into the side of my head. I fell backwards into the brush.

"Don't talk about God!" the man screamed. And then he fled.

Driving myself to the sheriff's department in town, I found the investigating officer less than compassionate. Among other perplexing questions, I was asked what I had done to provoke the incident. The same treatment prevailed at the small local hospital; the attending physician refused to come to the hospital to see me, and had me sent home without a physical exam. Even in 1972, I expected better treatment.

The assault and the unconscionable treatment afterwards brought years of fear and uncertainty. Those brief moments of terror at the hands of one person changed my life so drastically, made my heart beat differently, and rendered me incapable of trusting anyone, least of all myself, for a long, long time. I knew two things beyond a shadow of a doubt: I could never endure another attack like this without going insane, and I could have killed the man who attacked me with my bare hands if given a chance.

Because of the unprofessional way my case was handled, the man was never found. I fled Colorado Springs with a road musician whom I later married—only to find out he was an abusive alcoholic. I remained married until our two children were out of high school. My emotional suffering during that marriage could be described as mysterious, overwhelming and solitary.

Then one night I attended a Christian revival service at the local high school, where I accepted Jesus Christ as my personal Savior. I discovered where the answers had been all along. After many years, I determined the pain and trauma I had been through would no longer define who I was. I am a child of God, holy, beloved and forgiven. This is when I truly began to heal. I left my marriage and began living out my life as a follower of Christ.

I have come to understand God was with me on that mountain the day I was assaulted. When a nonbeliever like me can call out to the Father on high and have Him answer in such a profound way and deliver me from the very clutches of a madman—indeed, from the brink of being chained to a tree and left to die—how can I do less than give Him my life, my heart, and my will? Why such drastic measures had to be employed to get me to change my life has haunted me. But I believe like Paul on the road to Damascus, I had to have my life come to a screeching halt before I would listen. It took a while, but I now understand God had plans for me, and recruiting me wasn't easy.

Writing my memoir *was* easy; the words just tumbled out of my soul. With my wonderful husband, Patrick, to support me, and a one-year sabbatical from the college where I worked, I was able to put the manuscript together in a few months. Through more of God's loving grace, I met my editor, Connie Anderson, and the amazingly accomplished members of Women of Words (WOW), who have supported me in spirit and skills.

Health problems plagued me during the publishing phase, and there were times I was sure I would not complete the book project. But my husband and the many good friends I have met over the last several years kept me going until the book was in print and electronic form.

I knew I was making a difference when I went on my first multi-state book tour and spoke to a group of male and female juvenile offenders. I told them, "Rape isn't about sex. It isn't about being macho or cool. It isn't about impressing your friends. It doesn't make you more of a man. It's a cowardly act, and it's only about power and control. And it ruins lives." By the way they were looking at me, I knew no one had ever talked to them that way about sexual assault. I knew I had reached them.

Healing came full circle when in 2012, on the 40th anniversary of the assault, I met with five members of the sheriff's office in Colorado Springs. None of them was there in 1972, but each of them treated me with respect and compassion. After listening to my story, three of them took me to retrace my steps, where the attack took place four decades before. We had a kind of ceremony at the place that once spoke terror to me. Revisiting the site, I had no fear in my heart; only sadness for what had turned a beautiful mountain scene into a nightmare. And I felt myself letting go of my rage toward my attacker. I saw him as both a crazed maniac and a defenseless child that day, and my only response as a professional counselor and a follower of Jesus Christ was to grant him my forgiveness.

When I walked off the mountain and rejoined these three new friends, I knew I was supposed to survive. I knew I had a message of hope following trauma, of hope outside of myself.

True success requires humility first, and then a great sense that we are built up by first becoming humble. We are all broken, but we all have a responsibility to be the best we can be.

Forgiveness does not mean the hurt never happened. It means we no longer want to hurt the person who hurt us, which is what frees us. The rest is up to God.

www.MegCorrigan.com

Forgiveness does not mean the hurt never happened. It means that we no longer want to hurt the person who hurt us, and that is what frees us.

CHAPTER 30

An Unwilling Expert

Happiness depends upon ourselves.

—Aristotle

BECKY HENRY

Happy. Happy is all I've ever wanted to be. I'm naturally good at it, still am for the most part—despite everything. As a child, I was happy, doing what I did best, which was playing, mostly outside. When adults weren't making me do other, boring things, I loved to climb, bike, jump, swing, read books, explore, do puzzles, dance, swim, watch clouds float by, and dream. I believed anything was possible, even for a little girl in the '60s, and when I was an adult, no one would be telling me what to do, and I'd get to play all the time, or at least do what I want.

By fourth grade, I found out life isn't fair. Back then it was something pretty innocuous. I started wanting to make things fair the day a boy shot a rubber band at my leg, but I was the one who got in trouble from our teacher, for making noise. Ever since then I've fought for fairness and tried to right wrongs by speaking up, even if I get reprimanded. It's taken a lot for me to find my voice again.

My husband and I had two daughters, born four years apart. At about age fourteen, our older daughter started disappearing before our eyes. Our typically delightful child suddenly seemed as if she was possessed. We'd find her sulking, laying on the couch for days without showering, and alternately having fits about the food being served. We noticed school friends were becoming a thing of the past, and seeing her school grades drop, became big red flags. Watching her only eat brown rice and peanut butter for a few weeks, and then consuming an entire cake, really scared us.

Two years later, we finally were able to confirm our fears: she had an eating disorder, and it was life threatening. This illness hijacked our daughter and turned her into a sad, angry, belligerent, difficult person. We found little-to-no resources for us as her caregivers, and back then, healthcare professionals told us we'd done enough damage and should back off. I knew something had to change.

During the two years it took to get a diagnosis, we visited the pediatrician and two separate psychologists to no avail. Later our daughter told me she'd lied to all of them. This was my first indication that this eating disorder (ED) monster was in fact holding her hostage. As the eating disorder told her lies, she told us (and her health care team) lies—and the health care providers treated us like the enemy. The eating disorder is the enemy, not us. In bed at night, we cried and worried, and while walking through our day, we worried: would she hurt herself? Our social life began to disappear as we were consumed with worry, just trying to deal with the daily dramas on our own. We had no one to talk with and no one to help us know what to say or not say and what to do or not do.

As the years of living in this black hole of hopelessness dragged on, not only did the healthcare providers judge us, but so did my family and friends. Often we heard hurtful comments such as: "She's just looking for attention, can't you just tell her to stop that?" or "Can't you just make her eat?" and "We want you to come for Thanksgiving but please don't bring (her) because her behavior is too disruptive and annoying."

We knew better than anyone how disruptive and disrespectful her behavior was. Our daughter was bulimic, which meant she'd eat a lot of food, and within a short time, vomit it all up. Then she was hungry again—and needed money to buy more food. Thus, money regularly disappeared from my purse, makeup was taken out of my bathroom, and stealing became a regular habit. It was insidious; we were in a living hell, watching our daughter be eaten alive by this monster. My husband and I would lie in bed holding hands and crying ... two very resourceful people, now at a loss—and the only advice professionals gave us was to not talk about food.

After putting the kids on the bus, picking up the phone every weekday morning for a year to call the insurance company was but one of the draining, time-consuming activities brought on by the eating disorder.

Watching our youngest daughter become very self-sufficient and independent as she sat quietly in her room two hours past her school night bedtime brought mixed feelings of guilt and pride. She now has anxiety, and we wonder if it developed from living with the mayhem and daily drama.

Special trips to the animal shelter, the ice cream shop and the park were part of what we did to try and normalize her life, but it was like pretending there wasn't a monster racing throughout the house terrorizing everyone.

Existing and getting through each day by breathing slowly and trying to have some humor and hope was all we could manage for a few years. Then we settled into a pattern of coping with chronic illness.

I had been trained as a professional certified life coach during my daughter's illness, and now decided to coach the parents of loved ones with eating disorders, in order to right the many wrongs. I've learned how to cope, how to support someone in recovery, how to fight insurance companies, and how to have joy and hope even when things are dire and dismal. Now I teach others how to do this.

Through these struggles and challenges Mom and Dad were always most supportive and believed in me. I also have my mastermind groups, other coaches, friends, and my husband. The families send me thank you notes from time to time about how much it means to them that I'm doing this work, telling me what a difference having my help has made in their struggles.

In pursuing my dream of coaching the caregivers of those with eating disorders and taking them on fun adventures to boost their efficacy in coping, I have dealt with the challenge of financing this in a grassroots manner. In approaching eating disorders treatment centers, I've found resistance to embracing my programs. It seems that a factor may be the lingering paradigm of healthcare professionals blaming parents, as well as treatment centers' resistance to bringing in outside help for parents. Just before the great recession beginning in 2008, my husband had quit his job and started a new business. We ended up selling our home and downsizing to support both of our businesses. Not good timing.

At the same time, the eating disorder convinced our daughter to quit talking to us. She was about twenty-five, and had been living away from us for about four years. I have been close to giving up many times while trying to get this business financially viable.

While writing my book, *Just Tell Her to Stop: Family Stories of Eating Disorders*, I wanted to quit so often—about every two weeks, and then once a week toward the end of writing and editing. I had interviewed over forty other families coping with a loved one's eating disorder, hearing story after story about their sick children, told by very frustrated parents. When boxes of my books arrived, my younger daughter was with me as I held the first one in my arms. I said to her, "Now you are finally a big sister." It felt like another baby had been placed in my arms. At the same time my first child—the one with the eating disorder—was still being held hostage by the eating disorder.

You need tenacity, faith, trust, collaboration, and clarity on what you want to do and be, as well as having a passion and purpose, in order to be successful. I've had to learn success isn't always measured by financial gains. My book and my services have helped so many families all over the world. Regularly I'm told what I'm doing is so important and needed. And when a parent in a tiny remote town tells me my book helped him or her feel less alone, or my programs made all the difference for his/her child's recovery, I know I have contributed to changing the world. To me that is success. I'm very fortunate in many ways, one being my husband is completely supportive of what I do, and has helped me to see that even though I'm still having to dip into our personal savings to keep this business afloat—what I'm doing matters.

When you are dealing with issues related to a child, it is important to do what you can do—and then give yourself a break. As much as parents want to, we cannot fix everything for our children. Sometimes we just have to "forgive ourselves," and go on.

Keep doing what gives you joy and know you have it in you to achieve your dreams and success. Read all you can on creating a successful business, and connect with other business owners who have been successful. Surround yourself with supportive people, and of course, have a business plan. Right now I'm reading, *Think and Grow Rich* by Napoleon Hill, and I wish I'd read it eleven years ago. It is filled with wonderful advice for anyone in any career.

I've never worked so hard in my life, as I have at this job. For a few years, I worked sixteen-hour days six to seven days a week … and wasn't showing any financial results. The saying is true: we must do what we love, and work must be our play.

www.eatingdisorderfamilysupport.com

Keep doing what gives you joy and know you have it in you to achieve your dreams and success.

CHAPTER 31

From Barely Surviving— to Really Thriving

Only those who risk going too far will realize how far they can go.
—Thomas Elliot

Susan St. James

In my teens, success was having enough money to buy cute clothes—and having a cute boyfriend. When I was in my thirties, it was being able to take care of my children, not just financially, but in all ways.

I've always wanted to live a large life, have a lot of experiences, and travel to many countries. I see myself as a serial entrepreneur, having several businesses of various types, even non-profits. They would ideally be located in different states so my hunger for travel is satisfied at the same time.

When I was thirty, making money was a high priority since I was a single mother without a high school diploma—the sole provider. I worried about paying for necessities like food and keeping the lights on, etc. I knew I was in trouble when McDonalds turned me down. Fear is a great motivator. My children had to eat.

Literally living dime-to-dime, I took the only job I could get, making $5.25 an hour. I couldn't give my children a Christmas that year. There were no presents, and our Christmas dinner was beans and wieners. We lived in a mobile home, and I could barely make the payments on it. I woke up one day and realized: I have to make a change.

Somehow I talked my way into a full-commission job. If I did well, I could make a lot of money, and if I didn't, I wouldn't get paid anything. I had to take the risk. I went from an income of $6,000 one year to a six-figure income the next. In 1987, I decided to learn as much as I could about the business of recruiting. I made a conscious choice that I was not going to fail. I was going to work as many hours as it would take to give my daughters the life they deserved. I read books on business, took the advice of good recruiters, and became very good at the job. Tenacity goes a long way. Eventually, I started my own firm. I surrounded myself with people who were willing to give me advice on running a business, and a lot of my learning came from making mistakes.

Although I never thought of giving up, I certainly didn't realize just how hard it was going to be. Many consider starting a business, but I believe the lack of tenacity keeps some from actually doing it. My advice is to surround yourself with mentors who can guide you, and then be smart enough to consider their advice. Want "it" bad enough to go through hell to get it.

While my daughters were young I worked a lot from home, which is one of the benefits of recruiting. Having a good work ethic keeps you focused. I never compromised my daughters' life for mine.

Coming up with the right niche meant spending considerable time learning and understanding business trends in order to find an industry that could support what I would create. I did this by having many, many conversations with others, and doing valuable research. It had to weather the economy's ups and downs since I wasn't interested in just cashing in on a trendy idea—and then moving on to the next big trend. I also knew I wanted something which addressed the aging population. The medical industry seemed a good fit.

Today I am President/CEO of Labrador LifeScience, a service with over eighty employees all over the country. We are a life-science consulting firm providing medical personnel—scientists, medical engineers and other specialists needed by the life sciences. Most of our clients are in the medical device industry, biochemical healthcare management, and pharmaceutical industries. Not bad for a gal who didn't graduate from high school. But honestly, I don't feel like I have even scratched the surface yet, I'm just getting warmed up.

A life of hard knocks has helped me the most. It made me tough and gave me the tenacity to work through the tough times. Last year I was part of a group of twelve entrepreneurs who met twice a month on a one-year program. We worked together to gain each other's vision and insight. It gave us the ability to take our focus off the day-to-day operations and look at the bigger picture—things that can have a major impact on our businesses. We were devoted to helping each other. We were also assigned a mentor. Mine was incredibly valuable and worked with me one-on-one for two hours a month on my biggest issue. I still meet with this amazing man every quarter.

Many entrepreneurs have similar challenges/issues such as: funding, employees, marketing, etc. Our mentors and fellow entrepreneurs would share how they had worked through these issues, in the hopes we might gain insight to a new way of gaining solutions.

Universities and mentoring programs in every city offer programs like this. Each has its set of rules and criteria businesses have to meet. Each has value, but is geared to particular types of businesses. For instance; a start-up would need different advice than one going for years. A business generating $1 million in sales has different needs than one generating $50 million in sales.

I have always had staff, with the goal to surround myself with those who know more than I do. I hire people based 50 percent on skill and 50 percent on personality. Skills you can teach, but personality you can't.

Like many start-ups, I had tons of obstacles—and these are just the big ones:

- Funding is always one of the biggest issues for small business owners.
- The dot com issues. NASDAQ stock index crashed from 5,000 to 2,000. Hundreds of dot-com-related stocks such as Pet.com, which once had multi-billion-dollar market capitalizations, were off the map as quickly as they appeared. Panic selling ensued as the stock market's value plunged by trillions of dollars. The NASDAQ further plunged to 800 by 2002. At this time, numerous accounting scandals came to light in which tech companies had artificially inflated their earnings. In 2001, the U.S. economy experienced a post dot-com bubble recession, which forced the Federal Reserve to repeatedly cut interest rates to stop the bleeding. Hundreds of thousands of technology professionals lost their jobs and, if they had invested in tech stocks, lost a significant portion of their life savings. Our clients froze with this news. They were not hiring, which meant they did not need us to provide them with people.
- 911 when all businesses were paralyzed. The nation stopped doing business as soon as terrorists hit the twin towers. Companies had only one issue to deal with, which was to defend themselves against cyber war and cyber terrorism. Once again, we were on hold.
- The current economic state.
- "Obamacare" healthcare mandatory program, and increased the taxes it will put on small business is coming up. This program has been put on hold.

Thankful for the life I have, I feel extremely good about what I have been able to accomplish. I am grateful all our employees make a good living. I don't think of this as my dream, but it is a wonderful life and a means to my dream.

It takes tenacity, drive, adaptability, risk tolerance, persistence, and a rock-solid business plan to be successful. The Internet has an infinite amount of advice on business plans, which I used as a guide. I also think passion drives the most successful businesses.

To me, success is achieving the goal you're passionate about, whatever that might be. Arm yourself very, very well with knowledge from people who have been there, prepare your plan, then … JUMP!

www.LabradorTalent.com

It takes tenacity, drive, adaptability, persistence, passion and a rock solid business plan to be successful.

CHAPTER 32

A Voice for My Mother

Trust your instincts.
—Ernestine "Teen" Johnson (Mom)

JACLYNN HERRON

I have always loved to write, but becoming a published author was not on my radar until I lived a story I felt compelled to share with a wider audience. Then, there was nothing else left to do but *write, write, write.*

Living the story: For eight years dementia gnawed at my mother's memories and abilities until it took her life in 2006. During those years, our family advocated for Mom's quality of life as she traveled along a continuum of care offered by a reputable healthcare system. During the first four years, assisted-living and memory-care facilities provided exceptional, resident-centered care, but once Mom moved to the nursing home, everything changed. Wheelchair-bound and silenced by her disease, she became extremely vulnerable in a care center configured more like a mini-hospital. Gone was the feeling of "home" she had experienced back at her memory-care facility. Each day I arrived to feed my mother her noontime meal, a task she could no longer do herself.

Each night I sat in front of my computer and journaled my mother's nursing-home experience—along with my fears, frustrations and grief, as she slowly slipped away. As the weeks turned into months and then years, journal entries reflected the highs and lows of nursing-home life. Good days involved compassionate care giving delivered by nursing assistants who treated Mom with tenderness and respect. However, systemic problems, such as high staff turnover, understaffing, and burnout, negatively impacted my mother's quality of life. Too often, inconsistency in care from one shift of caregivers to another, care-related injuries, breaches in the implementation of Mom's care plan, and concerns about her safety and the security of her belongings all took center stage.

Writing the story: After my mother's passing I quickly discovered my journal's account of business-as-usual in one of Minnesota's reputable nursing homes could not be buried as peacefully as her ashes. Mom's experience, I believed, was a story worth sharing. Using my journal entries, I began to weave our family's eldercare journey into a memoir.

Sharing the story: Once the story was written, edited and re-edited, the next daunting step was finding a publisher willing to help me tell an eldercare story that is heartbreakingly commonplace. Finally, in September 2011, *Singing Solo: In Search of a Voice for Mom,* was released. The memoir gives voice to the universal frustrations, fear, sadness, and helplessness experienced by families with aging or ill loved ones who are destined for nursing homes. It begs people to pay close attention, and to advocate for those who can no longer speak.

Reflections: My mother's experience with dementia was a sad one, yet a great teacher. I learned to value each day with Mom as she slowly disappeared behind a wall of dementia. I began to pay full attention to the world around her, as well as the internal reactions her circumstances set off inside me. Once dementia stole Mom's ability to speak on her own behalf, I became her daily advocate. Equally important, dementia taught me the definition of real heroes: the compassionate caregivers who understood Mom communicated in an unspoken language. They were the ones who looked at the position of my mother's disabled body and into her eyes, and they understood something as simple as a change of position or a drink of water could improve her quality of life. Then they delivered that much-needed care.

The goal of turning the journal entries into a bound memoir was another learning process requiring five years of grit and determination. An important first step was to verbalize this goal to supportive family and friends. Articulating my dream established it as a reality, not only to them but to me. Once I had declared my purpose, there was no turning back, even when I became tired and discouraged.

Years of dedicated research and writing fleshed out my journal entries into a full-blown memoir. Motivation to stay at the computer arrived often via the newspaper. I clipped every article about dementia, nursing-home abuse and neglect, and other eldercare concerns and taped them to the wall next to my desk. Daily, they reminded me Mom's story would reinforce the need to advocate for improvements in eldercare. I structured my days in order to make writing my top priority, and with supportive family members, especially my husband, Tom, I celebrated each step along the way, such as the completion of a chapter, a rough draft, a revision, even the arrival of my first rejection letter.

Valued mentors assisted me with every step along the process. Memoir classes at the Loft Literary Center in Minneapolis became my springboard. I applied each class assignment to my project and received effective feedback from teachers and writers. Others helped me understand the confusing world of publishing, and offered encouragement as rejection letters arrived from literary agents who did not want to invest time in an unknown writer. Professionals read the manuscript and offered blurbs for the back cover; a receptive publisher honed the final product and distributed it. A friend created my author website and taught me the technical aspects of maintaining it.

I was not prepared for my overwhelming emotional reaction the day the book, with Mom's picture on the cover, arrived from the publisher. A mixture of jubilation and relief overtook me. I opened the cover and turned to the acknowledgement page listing the names of those who had supported our family through both the living and the telling of this eldercare story. It truly takes a village, and I am filled with gratitude.

Now I am dedicated to the next step: giving the book a greater audience. Discussions of *Singing Solo* at bookstores, churches, libraries and dementia forums prompt other families to share their nursing-home experiences. Together our stories stress the importance of advocating for loved ones who are unable to advocate for themselves. These narratives encourage the discussion of a very crucial question: How can we make improvements in eldercare that will promote quality of life until the very end of life?

www.JacLynnHerron.com

Start each day with conviction, and trust your instincts.

Unlocking the Secrets of Successful Women

CHAPTER 33

Choosing Wisely

Well-behaved women rarely make history.
—Laurel Thatcher Ulrich, Harvard University Professor,
born July 11, 1938

IRENE M. KELLY

What is success? It is an assessment that implies different things to different people. To re-phrase Elizabeth Barrett Browning's sonnet, I'd suggest, "How do I succeed? Let me count the ways."

For almost as long as I can recall, success in my world has been grounded in doing what I love, what fires me up, what excites me.

From an early age, I refused to engage in things I didn't have passion for, and that did not provide meaning. Okay, to be honest, as I look back, waiting tables in my early years did not involve a ton of passion nor provide much meaning. However, growing up at the Jersey shore in a family hotel, bar and restaurant business, besides teaching many valuable lessons, laid the groundwork for a way to earn money for education.

As a young woman, I pursued my own path, rather than the one someone had already paved. I often found myself treading in new waters with folks I had never met because my friends were interested in only following "the path most travelled." New territory excited me, and learning a new way spelled success in my world. I often say, "I'm very happy in a room of strangers; I just make new friends."

Success meant being happy, feeling fulfilled, and serving others. Service has long been a key to my success—and sometimes it interfered with my happiness. Only when I learned that service must be grounded in staying true to oneself, rather than serving because it is expected, did I realize the true meaning of success.

Values play an important role in success. The role models I admire, people I count as successful, have been true to their values; those who veer from core values eventually face demise. I count parenting my two boys as the most successful accomplishment in my life. Choosing to put a full-time career on hold to parent was extremely challenging for many years. My husband and I had made the decision jointly. However, I still dealt with resentment for quite some time and struggled to decide who it was that I resented. I finally realized I *resented me*. While opting to be a full-time parent was my choice, back then, I wished I'd made it differently.

While I loved being a mom, baby talk day in and day out was just not enough. Yet, my strong belief around the importance of family led me to balance the baby talk with part-time work. And while my husband was willing to be the stay-at-home parent, our financial state would have had to be significantly altered had we chosen that path. I realized that time passes quickly and recognized the importance of my choice to be a full-time parent/part-time worker—and finally embraced the choice I made.

My choice for part-time work/part-time parenting allowed me to dabble in a variety of community volunteer endeavors, which supported me in developing my leadership skills. I cut my teeth as a community activist and leader by serving on a number of election campaigns, homeowners' association boards and even senior partner of an investment club. One year, I led a $27 million dollar school-board referendum. I was actually hired for a job because I had led the transfer of ownership of a homeowners' association from developer to neighbors. Turns out, my boss had led a similar effort and knew that those skills transferred to the job at hand.

The one thing I regret in this choice was not having enough of a plan—while part-time work in the marketing field provided me with "adult interaction," when I was ready to return to a full-time career, I found myself floundering. What might that be? I regret that I did not define what would be next, and then work toward a goal.

A very good friend shared that parenting is one of the most important roles we play. I somewhat dismissed that advice, and it took me time to realize she was correct. Looking at the big picture in hindsight, I recognize the years of "interrupted career" as time well spent. And, I count myself among the fortunate to have been able to devote time to parenting and spend quality time with my boys.

Initially, my major challenge was deciding to leave the workforce to be mostly a full-time parent for a number of years. When I was ready to re-enter, there seemed to be obstacles. I had developed as a leader through part-time work and volunteering. My skills and abilities had developed beyond entry level, however, having been out of the workforce for seven years, entry level was what I was offered. I overcame this obstacle by starting a business. Once I had that "credential," my credibility increased for other opportunities.

Before finding what I consider to be my true life's work, I made several stops. Each one was a stepping-stone leading to starting my coaching and consulting firm. Business ownership of a small women's fashion accessory business, C & I Unlimited, allowed me to make the mistakes of a novice business owner. As a manager at Globe Express Services, I learned the transportation business and honed my financial and technology skills. I built my sales skills at Redwood Signs where sales increased 250 percent, because of my efforts.

And then, while serving on a volunteer advisory board, I led an effort to bridge the gap between business leaders and educators, serving as the nonprofit, Executive Director of Habitat for Technology. Six years of service, personnel, and organizational changes, and personal transformational learning, all led me to resign from that position without a plan. I declared a three-month sabbatical for rest and reflection.

My sabbatical allowed me time to gain clarity about my life's purpose. As I looked back on life, personally and professionally, these things were clear:

- I am a connector—in each of the four states I lived, I made connections and connected others.
- I am a collaborator—WOO (Winning Others Over, in Strengths Finder language) is one of my strengths, inviting (or influencing) others to join me comes naturally.
- I create new things—professionally, from my first position out of college and each one that followed, I wrote my job description (and certainly that was true of parenting for there is no manual).
- I have a heart for serving others—I'm rewarded when I see I can support others to thrive.

The result of the clarity: the launch of Prisma, LLC., and this time, with a plan. Prisma is a coaching and consulting firm that specializes in working with leaders in education and business to create an environment where people work collaboratively and think creatively. Our mission is to help organizations realize the possibilities that will allow them to reach their peak. My coaching mastery supports clients to choose how they lead so they can positively impact their organizations. Most importantly, our clients have more trust, courage, resources and possibilities—and we meet them where they are and support them to *soar*.

When anyone asks which of my achievements I'm most proud, I answer: definitely, my two sons because I parented boys to become men who encourage and support women.

In the career realm, I am most proud of having coached and mentored many young people to become leaders who are self-aware and self-confident. In my coaching work, I have had the opportunity to witness the growth and development of many women (and men). Their growth led to self-awareness that fostered success. I am honored to be part of the journey of so many successful individuals.

Upon return to the career path, I have had many years of success. And in retrospect, I realize that success has come on many fronts.

For me, the "achieving" occurred as a wife; then as a widow. As a wife, I had a *very* involved spouse. We shared parenting responsibilities. When babies awoke in the night, he got up changed the diapers and brought the little one to me to breastfeed. My maternal instinct was tested by pure exhaustion. I did not always hear them wake, but he did.

We shared other responsibilities. He was a great "cleaner upper," doing most of the dishes and cleanup after meals. I believe we learn much more by example than words. Now I have two married men in my life (my sons, Brian and Matthew) who help with cleanup because they saw that modeled. And, we had a rule, whoever got up last made the bed; my husband made it most days.

And one day, unexpectedly he passed away. The boys were seventeen and twenty; one in high school, the other college. Quickly I had to learn how a single parent functions. After his passing, I realized just how much he had contributed when *all* the responsibilities for the household, children, and finances fell to me. It was quite an awakening to all of a sudden be the lone source of support, to have no one to share the decision-making process, and to be in a place in my life where major decisions were afoot.

From experience, I've learned two things everyone should do:
1. Always have a clear, solid plan
2. Never allow resentment to fester.

I learned the value of having a solid plan. While my part-time work satisfied my need for adult interaction and feeling productive, I was not intentional about that work. While I studied and learned, neither was it intentional. I learned the value of a plan and setting intention. In retrospect, had I been intentional, my work and study would likely have supported the next step.

I believe that lack of intention contributed to brewing resentment. Although I did not realize it then, the lack of a plan allowed the resentment about "what I was missing" (which in reality was nothing) to grow. It hampered me at times from celebrating "what I had."

Both women and men have been significant to my success. Along the way, in my career, two male bosses were extremely significant. Each was an advocate for my ability, and both were especially important in my development as a leader. The most significant lessons included: 1) being willing to make and acknowledge mistakes, 2) getting to know myself, and 3) allowing my heart and gut to lead.

Women have also had a significant impact, my mom being the first. She was a workingwoman in a generation when that was the exception. Several women "advocates" have also played a critical role in my success by inspiring me to reach for more than I thought I was capable, and encouraging me to allow my uniqueness to shine.

As a coach and mentor, I encourage young (and more seasoned) people to work toward their own success by knowing themselves, becoming aware of their life purpose and following *their* dream—not those created by parents or society.

I have had extensive training in coaching and leading, and I achieved several certifications:

- Completed Coaching for Professional & Personal Mastery at Villanova University; is a Newfield Certified Ontological Coach (NCOC).
- Trained as a Core Values Index™ Certified Coach/Trainer and member of the Taylor Protocols "Value-Added Relationship" (VAR) team.
- Participated in somatic and co-active coaching programs
- Participated in Courage to Lead training
- Participated in Beyond Diversity training

While I do not necessarily count success by receiving awards, I have received my share over the years. I am especially proud of two of them. The ATHENA Leadership Award®, received in October 2004 from the Eden Prairie Chamber of Commerce, is presented to a woman—or man—who is honored for professional excellence, community service and for actively assisting women in their attainment of professional excellence and leadership skills.

I was honored to receive the International Coach Federation (ICF), Minnesota Chapter, Elaine C. Gaston Award for Distinguished Service in September 2013. ICF Minnesota annually recognizes a member coach who has exhibited distinguished service to the coaching profession and to the chapter. The recipient demonstrates clear and strong leadership for the advancement of the coaching profession and integrity through professionalism and selfless service.

The Gaston Award was created in 2005 in honor of Elaine C. Gaston, a coach who initiated the first professional association for coaches in Minnesota and worked relentlessly to establish the profession. Elaine C. Gaston is a Master Certified Coach and a coaching instructor for the Coaches Training Institute. Still active in the chapter, Elaine's commitment to professionalism in coaching and service to the growth and development of other coaches continues to inspire her colleagues.

It's important people understand and appreciate that I followed my heart—and made a difference in the world. However, I have declined opportunities, as well as client work, because the values did not align with me. And it felt great to do so—to stick to my values regardless the cost or loss of opportunity.

However, in addition to helping others, I also make sure I take time for myself. This means getting regular, consistent sleep. I schedule time for physical activity, which is mostly walking, at least five times a week for twenty minutes. I also meditate occasionally to gain balance. For personal growth, I like to participate in the arts and spend time with family and friends.

No matter how busy you are, it is essential that you do one thing: Schedule, schedule, schedule. If it's not on the calendar, it rarely happens. Be sure you have *me* time no matter what, because it benefits everyone in your life.

I was once asked if a book was written about my life, what would the title be. My answer is: "She Gave Them Wings to Fly." This mantra serves me well in my coaching role when I support clients to empowerment and inspiration—and as a parent.

Aside from my professional life, I am an active volunteer, a mom and a grand-mom (my proudest titles). I have served as president of ICF Minnesota, the Eden Prairie AM Rotary club, and now I serve in a Rotary District 5950 leadership role designing and leading training events for sixty-two clubs. I co-facilitate and mentor women entrepreneurs for Women Entrepreneurs of Minnesota.

To me, to have success and be a top achiever, you must:
- Take time to know your purpose; only you can
- Know and follow your dreams, and take time to dream
- Respect and love yourself and others
- Focus on happiness—your own

- Be true to your values for veering from the course will leave you empty
- Know yourself because only you can
- Do what you love, and success will follow organically
- Treat others as you wish to be treated because you want that, too
- Nurture relationships that matter to you
- Share your gifts, and you will be gifted in return

*** PrismaLLC.com***
Irene.Kelly@PrismaLLC.com
612-240-0223

No matter how busy you are, it is essential that you do one thing: Schedule, schedule, schedule. If it's not on the calendar, it rarely happens. Be sure you have *me* time no matter what, because it benefits everyone in your life.

CHAPTER 34

Carving Out a Future ... the Old-Fashioned Way

It seems to me that our three basic needs, for food and security and love, are so mixed and mingled and entwined that we cannot straightly think of one without the others. So it happens that when I write of hunger, I am really writing about love and the hunger for it, and warmth and the love of it and the hunger for it ... and then the warmth and richness and fine reality of hunger satisfied ... and it is all one.

—M.F.K. Fisher, *The Art of Eating: 50th Anniversary Edition*

Kristin Tombers

This country was going to the dogs ... Americans didn't appear to be pro America anymore. It was sad to see so many people quit going to the mom-and-pop shops and, instead buying everything from soup to nuts and bolts from the big-box stores. Didn't they know they were choosing to support the economy of foreign countries over their own? Not only were small businesses collapsing, the small, independent farms were in danger of extinction.

This was in 2003 and the federal politics, especially around food and its production, were driving me crazy. That is when I took the bull by the horns and bought Linden Hills Meats and Deli, a small butcher shop in my neighborhood. I'd had a taste of running my own business, co-owning a construction and snowplowing company, but it was a far cry from becoming a butcher and selling steaks and chops.

The meat market had been a landmark in Minneapolis. Never in a million years would I have thought about buying it. I had been selling seafood for a local wholesaler and would call on different food markets and restaurants in town, including the owner of the butcher shop. He knew I had worked with many chefs and had built up a lot of trust with them. One day he said to me, "Find me one of the chefs in town who might want to buy this business and turn it into a little restaurant or something."

Then one day it dawned on me: "Maybe I could do this." I had a love of good food. I had an idea about the romantic side of butchery. I'd always fancied the way Europeans walked to the markets every day, finding the freshest and most tempting ingredients to prepare for dinner, instead of the American way of shopping once a week at a huge supermarket, loading up the SUV, and freezing most of the food. I may have been naïve, but it made sense to me, and the thought of being able to offer the consumer farm-raised meats was very appealing.

I think it took more guts than anything for me to say, "I can do this." There was never any consideration about running a male-dominated business; it was more about the politics of food for me. I was starting to identify the fact if our society didn't protect our food sources, we were going to be in trouble.

I had a degree in journalism from Marquette University, not exactly the perfect course of study for someone wanting to buy a butcher shop. I had worked in advertising for several years in Los Angeles. This experience turned out to be instrumental in developing an interest in food and expanding my palette from the Minnesota "pot roast mentality."

My Minnesota food experience also helped, since at a young age I was exposed to gardening and the joy of eating a splendid, ripe tomato right off the vine. Since my father was a flight surgeon for the army, we grew up living at Fort Snelling. One of my fondest memories of when we were little was my mom sending my two sisters and me off to a community garden with our little red wagon. But I was also the victim of the change from eating nothing but scratch cooking to consuming convenience foods, thanks to the introduction of "Hamburger Helper" and cake mix.

I had bounced around after graduating from college. I know my parents would have preferred I had become a doctor or a lawyer. At one point, I had considered Hospital Administration, but I didn't go any farther down the road to a particular career or profession.

A great part of my "education" came from living in the large, bustling cities of Los Angeles, New York, and Philadelphia. I'd spent nearly six years in Los Angeles working in advertising, and this experience sent me running in the opposite direction, never wanting to work in a corporate environment again. Then I tried New York and Philadelphia; they were not for me, either. But while in Philadelphia, I came up with the notion of opening up little mom-and-pop coffee shops. The huge coffee shop chains seemed to be taking over. So I got an idea to start a business called "Books and Brew." I had a high school friend whose dad had a house lined with books. His wife wanted the books out of the house, so we were going to do books on loan and not charge. People could come in and read. I thought it was a great idea. Even though "Books and Brew" didn't become a reality, it put me on the path to running my own business.

With no business acumen, and no clue about the level of work this undertaking would require, I plunged in and bought it. To get the business started, I was able to get a mortgage against my house. I'd never before heard of a woman butcher or a female-owned butcher shop. I'd never seen a steer ready to be butchered or had a clue about how a whole steer gets sorted out into the different cuts of meats I'd seen at the grocery store. Luckily, my good friend, Greg, a chef, started the business with me. Greg, at the time, was working as a chef at the Nicollet Island Inn; he became my first employee. He had had butchery courses, but we truly learned as we went along.

That was ten years ago. This entire undertaking simply was a "happy accident." I knew I had wanted to find something I could do, something I could work hard at, something I would love, and in so doing, make others happy. What I had set out to accomplish, creating a bounty of farm-raised, quality food into a retail market, was as true on day one as it is today.

In the beginning, I was behind the counter. My job was to build relationships, be the face of the business, and take on the whole picture of running the business. But my real love was standing up to the cutting table and working through those muscles. I've always liked working with my hands. Believe it or not, now my favorite thing is just doing the dishes.

We have been with the same five farmers for main supply animals since we opened. We are now working with over thirty farmers.[*] It has been extremely important to me to commit to these farmers that we would be buying whole animals from them. This is the kind of integrity we started with and continue to this day.

We only get one steer a week. It's six to nine hundred pounds, and comes in six pieces—each about one hundred pounds. We are also able to buy needed tenderloins, rib eye, and strip steak from supplemental brokers of grass-finished beef.

We get three lambs on Tuesday, three hogs on Thursday. Those are the animals where it's been a lot more difficult working out the logistics. What do we do with all the bones and fat from so many animals? We get very creative with sausage. We have a lot of lamb shoulders. Sometimes we get lucky and the *New York Times* will have a recipe, or the cover of the food magazines will come out and it might feature a recipe for "lamb shoulder stew." Then we sell all the lamb shoulders. We are constantly switching gears. It's interesting because when we think we can map out something and have a system in place, something is always changing.

This shop was named after my dog, Clancey. I learned so much from him, like how to slow down and better appreciate life. Before he came into my life, I was running and riding my bike or doing things in a hurry. Now I had my buddy, and we had such unconditional love for each other. Just seeing him, petting him, walking with him, talking with him, gave me a sense of peace and calm. Clancey allowed himself to become a friend to me. It was a great relationship. I had originally wanted to call the shop "The Commons," to give it the communal sense and feel in a place all about good food, but then a friend suggested I name it after Clancey—and I agreed.

We found out early on Linden Hills was a dog-friendly neighborhood. We'd let our customers bring their dogs into the shop, and we'd give them a little ground-beef snack. We noticed people were on their best behavior with their animals. Since then we've had doggy treats right at our entrance to welcome our four-legged friends.

I'll have to say, even with the all the fun, especially with the people and their pets, I was fearful for those first six or seven years. I didn't know if we'd be able to make it. We'd go two to three months, as far out as we could, before we paid our suppliers. I also heard a lot of people say, "Well, it's really never going to work." "You are going to have a hard time meeting your margins." "It's going to be a very difficult model to keep up." Then the joke, "How do you make a million dollars: you start with three and then open up a butcher shop." It was easy in the beginning to think, "My God, this is going to be like this forever; it's just always going to be hard work, and I'm never going to feel anything but fear."

Balance is always a challenge. It is difficult to keep up our inventory of beef, lamb, pork, poultry, and duck and then not have parts of the meat that we are throwing away. That is one of the most challenging aspects, but we are finding the balance of using all the other pieces and parts. I think we have surprised a lot of people that we've been able to make this system work.

I don't know if it was because we hit a plateau, where word of mouth saturated a little bit in the food world of Minneapolis. This was around the time that relationships were being cemented, and we started sensing abundance. We were becoming known as a "foodies' meat market." Enough people knew who we were, and once they would come and see what we had, whether it was the raw meat, seafood, scratch-made sandwiches, soups, salads, the stocks, seasonal and custom offerings, we had something here for everyone. So I think once people found out about us and came here, they ended up coming back.

We don't have a website, and we don't advertise much at all. So word of mouth has been huge in our development as a small business, which is the best as far as I'm concerned.

The success of this business truly has come from the relationships existing now. We have been involved in many people's lives on a lot of different levels. I love it when total strangers come into the shop and just start up conversations with one another.

If anyone would ask me about making a business successful, or just being successful in general, I would have to honestly say, "developing relationships." I believe it has truly helped us here. It's the main thing I care about. I am very open with the staff, which I think creates an environment where they have autonomy. I give them a lot of responsibility. Sometimes it can backfire, but for the most part, I think keeping open and honest dialogue and having very good, healthy relationships is huge in any business. I think it's what we've lost in general with the cell phones, the computers, and things happening at warp speed. We know we can't go back to the horse-and-buggy days, but I think we are losing out when we are moving away from one-on-one communication. I think it's something humanity needs.

In terms of growth and expansion of Clancey's Meats and Fish, whatever we do, I don't ever want to get it to where it's "out of hand." However, the ability to add on to our space to include seating and a communal table would be ideal.

When Clancey died three years ago, it was so amazing, because there was this outpouring of sympathy and love. So many people came into the shop, telling stories about the loss of their beloved pets.

Clancey's Meats & Fish's legacy continues. We have benefitted from the trend towards socially responsible, ethical consumerism. We are feeling the shift away from the country (or at least this neighborhood) from "going to the dogs." Clancey's has always been and will continue to be environmentally responsible and offer the freshest, finest local, sustainable, ethically-raised meats, seafood, house-made, grab-and-go specialty and seasonal items, all the while supporting our local farms and communities.

I consider these to be the keys to being successful:
- Passion about your mission
- Determination even in the face of fear
- Hard work
- Ignoring negative comments and remarks
- Developing relationships
- Open, honest communication
- Managing staff openly and creating an environment where each staff member has autonomy
- Holding true to your beliefs
- Being flexible; change is inevitable
- Maintaining integrity
- Handling challenges creatively
- Balance
- Employing the right accountant

* Clancey's Meats & Fish Sources are: Au Bon Canard, Burt's Hilltop Meats, Cedar Summit Farm, Craftmade Toffee, Dragsmith Farm, Fairview Farm, Fischer Family Farm, Garden Farme, Geneva Meats, Grass Run Farm, Great Ciao, Hidden Stream Farm, Hill & Vale Farm, Hope Creamery, Jane's Eggs, Larry Schultz, Ledebuhr Meats, Travis and Jen Peters, Philadelphia Community Farm, Rustica Bakery, Seed to Seed Farm, Silver Bison, Singer House Rabbits, Thousand Hills, Uecker Eggs, Venison America, Whitewater Garden, Wild Acres, Wild Idea Buffalo, William Yoder, and many more from S.E. MN that provide real food through networks of farmers working together.

CLANCEY'S MEATS & FISH
Located in downtown Linden Hills since 2004
4307 Upton Avenue South, Minneapolis
612-926-0222

Start to create an abundant, meaningful and productive life by living your life on your terms—finding your passion and living your dream.

CHAPTER 35

How Feng Shui Changed My Life

A journey of a thousand miles begins with a single step.
—Lao Tzu

Carol Seiler

When I was growing up, society viewed women as successful if they got married and had children—a path I didn't want to take. I knew at a young age I wanted a career, but had no idea what it would look like nor could I have imagined how it would unfold.

I always wanted to be an interior designer, but my family discouraged me, and I chose to listen to them. Since I wasn't trained and couldn't do the work for pay, I began a life-long journey of decorating for friends and myself. While enjoyable, it was clear I was being called to do something more.

I was introduced to Feng Shui in 2003 when I had a consultation in my home. I followed the consultant's suggestions and found it totally changed the way the space felt, and the process gave me clarity on what I wanted out of life. By making a few simple changes in furniture arrangement and putting intention into subtle changes, this transformed the space into the peaceful, tranquil home I had always desired.

You may be asking what is this strange thing called Feng Shui. It has been practiced in Eastern cultures for thousands of years and has been more widely embraced in the West over the past ten to fifteen years, but still many people are unfamiliar with the benefits. Simply stated, Feng Shui enhances your environment and minimizes challenges by making changes based on the principles of harmony and energy, giving you the potential to improve all aspects of your life (e.g., career, relationships, health, prosperity) which are in line with your life desires and goals. We remain true to the principles that have survived the tests of time, but utilize changes and enhancements with a Western approach.

In 2006, I was introduced to Fashion Feng Shui®. People sometimes ask if this is "Feng Shui for closets." The answer is a definite "no." Fashion Feng Shui® uses many of the principles of Feng Shui to honor your entire being—mind, body, and spirit. Your personal style is the ultimate outward expression of your entire being. Fashion Feng Shui® gives you tools to dress for the person you truly are, to attract what you want in your life and, as a result, flatters your physical, as well as emotional self. As with Feng Shui, the physical state of where you live and work influences the quality of your life experience, and what is a more intimate environment than the clothing you wear every day? Another way of looking at Fashion Feng Shui® is that it helps you arrange your outer world to enhance your inner world through the use of the Five Elements of nature: water, wood, fire, earth, and metal. These elements are used widely in Feng Shui, Chinese Medicine, and acupuncture and are expressed in what we wear through color, shape, substance or fabric texture.

I feel very fortunate to be able to help people create beauty and tranquility in their home and office environments, and through their clothing choices,

I've had many outstanding teachers and mentors over the years, and I have been blessed with remarkable friends who have been, and continue to be, supportive.

I have faced two obstacles. One I encounter in pursuing my passion is time. It would be ideal to quit my day job and devote time and attention to Feng Shui and Fashion Feng Shui®, but the realities of life don't make that possible. I continue to work in an unrelated job and steal a few hours here and there for my business. Secondly, many people are fearful about having someone come to their home for a Feng Shui consultation. It's like having to clean before the cleaning person arrives so he or she won't think you're messy. Many people have said, "I want you to come over for a consultation as soon as I clean up my clutter."

I don't know any Feng Shui professional who would be critical of a client or the space. The same is true for Fashion Feng Shui®. My mission is to help clients feel good about their space and the way they present themselves to the world. It's a gift to work with clients and watch them make positive changes in their lives.

I live my dream every time I do a consultation with an ideal client. Recently, I did a Feng Shui consultation at a natural health clinic. While I was working on the floor plan and preparing recommendations for the clinic, the time slipped away, and I was in my bliss. When I left the clinic after our last meeting, I was on cloud nine. I'd like to experience such joy and excitement every day whenever I work.

Success to me is:
- Have passion for what you're doing.
- Enjoy doing the work so much you'd do it without pay—but I would not recommend doing so.
- Do work that lifts your spirit and fills you with the certainty you're in the right place and doing the right thing
- Work hard.
- Do what you love.
- Serve others in some way.
- Support other women in their being successful.
- Be very clear about what you want to create in your life, and pursue it with all your heart.

Define success in your own terms; it doesn't matter how your mother, sister, husband, or anyone else defines it. There is no right path for all people, and every experience we have will some day be of benefit—even when it doesn't feel like it at the time.

And, last but not least, if you fall along the way, get up, dust yourself off, and move forward.

www.beyondtheclosetdoor.com
Carol Seiler, cjseiler@me.com

Be very clear about what you want to create in your life, and pursue it with all your heart.

CHAPTER 36

What I Was Born To Do

You are unlike anyone who has ever lived.
But that uniqueness isn't a virtue, it's a responsibility.
—Mark Batterson

Gloria Perez

If someone had told me when I was young that when I grew up, I would become the leader of an organization helping single mothers and their children—I wouldn't have been surprised. I grew up in a Latino community in San Antonio, Texas, surrounded by young women, some of whom were friends and family who became pregnant when they were still children. Even at my young age, I worried about what would happen to these young women and their children. I also felt compelled to get out of this environment, as soon as I was old enough, so my fate wouldn't be the same as so many in my community.

One could say I was born into poverty. My grandparents were migrant farm workers. They worked hard and didn't let their circumstances get them (or us) down. They taught us that education was the key to success, and being successful had nothing to do with money. What was important to them was being family-connected, contributing to their community, involved in neighborhood activities, and active in their church.

My father was a first-generation American. My grandparents raised him well. He was a very strong figure in our family, as well as our community. He graduated from St. Mary's University, a huge achievement for a first-generation Mexican-American born in 1929. I wanted to grow up and be just like him. He was a very beloved, generous and compassionate person. What a dear heart he was. Sadly, my father passed when I was only ten years old; it was achingly difficult.

As a vocation, my father was fittingly a social worker. He was all about helping others succeed. He worked for St. Vincent DePaul. For fun, he was a musician. Music had always been a big part of our lives, and I wanted to become a performer. I became an aspiring singer and took piano lessons, but was unable to continue after my father died. I took guitar lessons in high school, which led me to become part of musical and performance groups through the Catholic Diocese that traveled in Europe, performing in Romania, Yugoslavia, Bulgaria and Greece. Our mission was to try to promote peace in Eastern Europe. What amazing, eye-opening experiences.

When my father died, we had this fear about what *couldn't* happen; what would never happen, because we would never have the financial ability to follow our dreams. This was a heavy burden, and I wanted to get out from under it. I felt if I were able to leave San Antonio, a whole new world of possibilities would open for me. It was sad my first focus was on what I *couldn't* do, but I wasn't going to let that be my destiny.

My mother kept us enrolled in Catholic schools through high school. Since I had learned my whole life that education was the key to success, I investigated different colleges around the country. I applied for and was accepted at St. Catherine University, in St. Paul, Minnesota. It was quite a culture shock coming from Texas, and I truly felt like I didn't fit in. I had heard about Macalester College, located close by, and I learned they had a more diverse student body. I checked out Macalester and found it to be a school with a very accepting and nurturing spirit, so I made the switch.

Surprisingly I did not pursue a musical career. Instead, I majored in communications at Macalester. During college, and for a time after graduation, I had a part-time job in a restaurant waiting tables (I might as well have been the manager). One day the owner asked me if I would ever consider buying a franchise restaurant. It sounded intriguing, but I didn't want to jump at the opportunity without becoming fully knowledgeable about what it would entail. I took a class at Women Venture, where I received help writing a business plan, and decided I could probably earn as much as a new entrepreneur as I could as an underling at a communications firm. At twenty-two, I thought, "What do I have to lose, and who'd even care if I crashed and burned?" So, I purchased the Westside Café, a franchise of the Uptowner on Lexington and Grand Avenues.

In a flash, I became an entrepreneurial restaurateur. But the tug of wanting to follow in my father's footsteps kept haunting me. In addition to running the restaurant, I was volunteering in the Latino community related to domestic violence issues. I began working at the Harriet Tubman Center as an advocate for battered women who had ended up at Hennepin County Medical Center.

I was learning so much about the violence impacting families and children who witnessed violence. It felt so right for me to be helping these families.

My then-husband said, "If this seems to be an area of interest for you, and you are spending so much of your free time volunteering, perhaps you want to do that as your job, and then you will actually have some free time!" I was torn since I did like being a business owner. I eventually transitioned from being a restaurateur to being able to follow my true dream, helping others.

As I explored my options, I was given the opportunity to lead a domestic violence agency in St. Paul called Casa de Esperanza or House of Hope. I learned early on to deal with some horrendous situations. This government-funded agency gave families the opportunity to be safe in the moment. However, I often felt like we weren't making any progress for the families in the long run. Yes, it was a safe haven, but I wanted to do more, to be able to give them the resources to help them think about what the future could be beyond just being safe. I could feel positive about the immediate good we were doing, but I wished I could do more.

I had been at Casa de Esperanza for three years when a recruiter contacted me about a future project, the Jeremiah Program. This was to be a start-up, and even though I liked the mission of helping families of single mothers, I felt it was going to be a huge undertaking to get it off the ground. My main job would be to raise a lot of private dollars to get the program up and running, and up to this point in my career, I had not had such experience.

About nine months later, the same recruiter called again, saying, "We're nine months down the road, and we have raised all the capital. It's going to be opened in January, and we think you should lead it. They have the operating money and a wonderful group of volunteers who will teach you how to raise money. We think it would be a good fit." At the time, I felt I should at least interview for the position. If these people have raised five million dollars for such a great cause, then these are people I should meet.

By the end of the interview, I just knew I wanted to be in a relationship with those people. They were so passionate, dedicated, capable, and driven. They certainly understood the issues of poverty. They truly wanted to make a difference. I thought, "This is what I've been looking for; what I've been training for, *what I was born to do.*" So, once again, following in my father's footsteps, I took this giant leap into what was to become my life's work.

The person who brought the program to fruition was the Reverend Michael J. O'Connell. Community leaders in Minneapolis approached him to find a way to break the cycle of poverty for single mothers and their children. The scriptural passage of Jeremiah 29:7 provided the group's inspiration to move forward: "Seek the well-being of the city where I have sent you into exile and pray to the Lord on its behalf, for in its welfare you will find your own welfare."

Jeremiah resonated with me because of my own life experiences. My mother raised my two sisters and me in a very difficult environment. She struggled to provide for us. She also had drive and vision. Watching her struggle and successfully persevere has been my motivation. Her determination made me feel perhaps there would be some energy and vision I might be able to bring to this program. I know for women to get into the Jeremiah Program they have to be very motivated and, at the same time, clearly have had barriers in the way of their success for a long time.

My first experience with Jeremiah was to help build the building. At first, we had eighteen residential units, but no child development center. Since then, we have doubled our housing here in Minneapolis, added a child development center, built a campus in St. Paul, and have expanded nationally to Austin, Texas; Fargo, North Dakota/Moorhead, Minnesota; and we are also looking at opening a program in Boston, Massachusetts.

In the fifteen years since I have been at the helm of the Jeremiah Program, we have assisted more than 600 female-led families. What makes the program so special: it goes beyond just giving the families safe housing. It fosters an environment that teaches the women to trust in themselves; to learn, change, grow and develop life skills. It has education at the core as the key to success. Everyone who comes to Jeremiah must come with the expectation of attending and graduating from college.

We have SHERO celebrations [think HERO] to honor the women's courage and strength as they continue on their journey. These are the values Jeremiah represents:

    S – Stewardship
    H – Healthy Relationships
    E – Entrepreneurial Spirit
    R – Respect
    O – Outcomes (and how they are demonstrated)

We all need other people to help us along the way. Jeremiah gives single mothers and their children access to resources and encouragement they need for their success. Many people have helped me on my path. And I would say over and over again in my life, I have been truly blessed and surprised by how many people have offered to help me. I would also say my mother helped me the most. Even though she did not have it easy growing up, she had energy, vision and sought out opportunities, especially for my sisters and me. She strongly believed in me. I would be in a situation, and my mom would say, "My gosh, if anyone can do it, you can." She'd also say, "I don't know how you'll get through such and such, but if anyone can do it, you can." She never had the financial resources to significantly help me, but emotionally she could say, "You can do this." Such support is not to be underestimated.

I think people need to understand we create our own futures. We constantly ask the women at Jeremiah, "Where do you want to be in five or ten years from now?" "What are you doing now to get there?" So the choices you make should be in alignment with your vision. The degree to which we can do that, the more successful we will be. Education is the key to success, and secondly, it is self-determination. One of the bedrock ideas of the program is to teach women to trust in themselves and also recognize they are capable human beings. They may not know how to do a lot of things when they get to Jeremiah, but they have the capacity to learn and grow—we simply give them the access to resources and encouragement.

People need to understand we create our own future. Where do you want to be in five or ten years? What are you doing now to get there?"

CHAPTER 37

Making My Mark

Whatever you give your energy and attention to will come back to you. If you are focused upon lack and negativity, then that is what will be attracted into your life.
—Jack Canfield

Kathy Heiland

When I was a high school senior, I got the "burning desire" to make my mark by writing. It was New Year's Day. I trudged out in the snow and from the back of my parents' garage, I announced my New Year's Resolution to the world: "I'm going to write a book!"

Three decades later, the first eBook I self-published at Amazon Kindle is entitled: "Say What You Mean: Because You'll Have What You Say." In this book, I share my personal experiences with the power of words. Have you ever noticed how what you think can become the words that come out of your mouth? I have. Furthermore, the words you speak aloud can bring forth the very thing you say. Yes, your words actually attract what you say. Jack Canfield says it so eloquently in his quote. He has been teaching on the Law of Attraction for over thirty years.

Because I spent a decade listening to the way people around me were talking, I discovered many people were not aware their own words were having an effect on their lives. I wondered, before writing the book, whether a renewed knowledge of the power words have, would affect the way people spoke. Some of the people who have read my book have changed the way they speak. This doesn't build me up; rather, it blesses me because some people are starting to take notice of what they say and are giving some thought to whether or not they truly want to receive what they say.

Another important idea concerning words is that visualization affects life's outcomes. I've listened to the stories of Olympic champions who have said they spent plenty of time seeing themselves winning before they even stepped out onto the field of competition. Repeatedly, winners see themselves crossing the finish line first. What is noteworthy is that visualization applies not only to every sport, but also to victories in general. Many business people use visualization to achieve success in their jobs, their promotions, and their negotiations. I worked with an avid golfer who told me that the night before his foursome played the next morning, he would lie there, in bed, and see himself putting or chipping into specific troublesome holes until he got the shot "right." Sure enough, the next day, he would take the perfect shot he saw himself performing the night before.

Speaking of business people and success, there are also personal stories of popular and successful people like Mary Kay Ash, Eleanor Roosevelt, Mahatma Gandhi, and Henry Ford—people whose words made a big and noticeable difference not only in their own lives, but also in the lives of many others.

In another chapter, we take a look at how the human brain processes words and thoughts through the research performed by Dr. Caroline Leaf, who claims "87–95 percent of mental and physical illness today comes from our 'thought lives.'"

Especially interesting is a thought-provoking chapter on the "Water Crystal Experiment" performed by Dr. Masaru Emoto. Dr. Emoto started photographing frozen water crystals. He then began to "speak" to the water crystals, and what he discovered in the photographs is simply amazing. He discovered water reacts to the spoken word. Not only that, but water responds to "good" words by producing beautifully formed crystals, whereas "bad" words caused the water to create fragmented and malformed crystals.

Even though my "burning desire" to write took thirty years to unfold, a combination of my life experiences and desire to help others got me started. Two things resonated deep within me. One is I never give up. I will stand and fight for what is right to the very end. Number two is my personal philosophy that whenever I overcome a problem and achieve success, I can be certain of one thing: If I am willing to look over my shoulder, there is going to be someone who is struggling to overcome a problem similar to the battle I just won. It is my duty and my desire to reach out and encourage that struggling man or woman. Thus I have created a series of books to help those struggling. I also share (with permission) the success stories of those people I know personally, in order to help others overcome the variety of life's difficulties many of us deal with on a day-to-day basis.

A good example of not giving up is found in the way my first eBook became available. This book required over two dozen major re-writes, which is no surprise to anyone who wishes to write professionally. I thought I hit pay dirt when I found a small, new, but growing publisher out on the East Coast, who was actually willing to talk to me via email. This was family-owned, where the father was the sole editor and publisher. I was asked to submit my manuscript, which I did. However, my manuscript had become lost in the shuffle when the publisher moved from Virginia to Texas. Because I didn't want to become a bother to the new business, I didn't find this out until many months later. After about a year, I followed up on some hints and suggestions. Since this publisher was small, they asked me to figure out what I needed to do to get my book noticed by others. I spent six months examining marketing books and materials before submitting my plan, only to find out the publisher had finally connected with a certain experienced author, on whom they spent their advertising dollars promoting his words and helping him to make his mark. I was politely told that I would have to resubmit and pay a fee to get anyone to look further at my work.

I then turned to the assistant pastors at my local church. Unfortunately, they did not have the expertise or time to help me either.

I did manage to get the attention of a local parish nun who told me her sister was a retired English teacher, and she may be able to help. Two hundred dollars later, all I had to show for my money was less than two-dozen punctuation markups. After more revisions of my own, my husband agreed to help me with the editing process—*for free*. As it turns out, my husband has a wonderful gift for editing my manuscripts. He checks for grammar, balance, flow and a whole list of other items. After his editing process, I had a sound, readable book.

One night at meeting I attended, one of the women suggested I should go to a community center nearby to attend a class on how to self-publish an eBook. After a little research on my own, I downloaded some information that helped me to self-publish my eBooks on Amazon Kindle.

Yes, many times along the way I wondered if I should just give the writing up, but it was, and still is, something I love to do. I just can't give up when I believe in something, and I believe in my ability to weave a story and make a mark in a reader's life. This is especially true when I know my books are encouraging, inspirational, and motivational. Everyone needs a shoulder to lean on and a good dose of encouragement—and that's what my "Kat's Recipes for Life" series does for its readers.

My five eBooks on Amazon Kindle are:
1. Say What You Mean: Because You'll Have What You Say
2. Love Never Fails If We Never Give Up
3. 5 Things Women Do In Relationships That Drive Men Crazy
4. Defeat Divorce In Your Marriage
5. Menopause: What Your Mama Didn't Tell You

Because I realize not everyone likes to read non-fiction inspirational titles, I am currently working on my first fiction eBook. It will be part of a new series that will accomplish my goal of looking over my shoulder to encourage someone who is struggling to make sense of life's daily difficulties. I have been blessed with a vivacious imagination, so I know the toughest part of this fiction series journey will be to learn to write good fiction. And as I said earlier, I *will not* give up. So look forward to some knee-jerking, belly-laughing goodness to come from Kat Heil soon. Until then, remember what one of my favorite leadership mentors, John C. Maxwell, likes to say: "People don't care how much you know until they know how much you care." So go out and show people you care and success is sure to follow you.

Here are my suggestions for success and following your dreams:
- Faith and belief. Believe that nothing is impossible for God. After all, He made you.
- Be persistent and willing to wait your turn. Spend your waiting time helping others.
- Do something you are absolutely passionate about and let it benefit someone else.
- Predetermine to never take a step upward if it means you have to step on somebody else to get there.
- Forgive. Always. You'll find forgiveness liberating and life-giving.
- Take risks; educated risks.
- Gain knowledge. It's surprising how many people forget teachers and professors teach from books.
- If you don't give up—you succeed.
- Have a good business plan. Revise and update as necessary.
- Solve problems. Quit waiting for someone else to do it.
- "Every time you think you have it bad, look around and you'll see someone who has it worse."

www.KatHeilBooks.com

Faith and belief. Know you know you can do it. Do what you do to bring benefit and blessing to others, and in time, your rewards will come. Be persistent. Do something you are absolutely passionate about and show it.

CHAPTER 38

Overcoming Personal Challenges to Help Children in Need

Do not grieve over the past, for it is gone and comes not back again. Nor should you fear the future, for it has not yet come. Live in the present, and make it so beautiful it will be worth remembering.
—Jane Crosby, (1820–1915), English author and hymn writer.

ANDREA MILLER

When I was a year old, I was diagnosed with a severe and deadly type of brain cancer, called medulloblastoma. Doctors said I would not live; never walk if I did live, and never pass a third-grade learning level.

I had no hair on the back of my head, and I was teased throughout elementary school. In seventh grade, my parents decided to move me from a public to a private school in Deephaven, Minnesota. I was scared to death, fearful that even in this new environment I would make no friends.

Nuns from India taught in the classrooms, which was new for me. We all wore uniforms except on certain Fridays when we had "dress-down" days, and could pay five dollars to wear what we liked. My religion teacher, Sister Teresa Jose, explained to us that the money we raised went to India to help a group of orphaned girls who lived close to her hometown.

After hearing this many times, I began to wonder if there was something *I* could do to help these orphans, perhaps writing a letter to family and friends to see if they would be willing to donate some money. So I did, and within a very short time I raised $500, which I gave to Sister Teresa Jose to take to the orphans in her village.

Seeing how successful my first attempt was, I decided to keep going, and with my parents, developed a non-profit, charitable foundation to raise money for orphans throughout the world. We named it the Andrea Miller Foundation. When Hurricane Katrina hit New Orleans, I thought we could also help children in the area. We expanded the foundation's mission to include all needy children, not just orphans.

Knowing children around the world were hurting much more than I was, motivated me to start this journey. I jumped on the opportunity to do what I could to help. I love children; I admire the way they think, and it is always such a pleasure to see them smile. It was a joy for me to know I could help even one of them.

With my parents' support, we have made the Andrea Miller Foundation what it is today. They've helped me every step of the way, spreading the word about the foundation. They even encouraged me to write a book of poetry I could then sell and raise more money to help my cause. The book, *Andrea and the Children of Karunalayan*, was illustrated by a friend of ours—the renowned artist T. White. With this book and stationery/notecards we created, I have been able to raise significant funds to support the foundation, and thus the children.

One day, Sister Teresa asked me if I would share my story with the school and speak about where I'd come from and what plans I had for the future. The truth is I didn't know the answer to either of those questions; all I knew was that somehow I had made it through a severe type of brain cancer and a tremendous amount of teasing in elementary school. So I talked about those experiences, and I was surprised to find I was quite a good speaker. My parents and I began to look for opportunities for me to talk publicly about my foundation. These speaking events attracted attention to my mission and increased the number and participation of our donors.

As I learned more about the girls in India, I focused less on myself and more on those I could help. As I learned more about God in our religious studies each day, I began to think that maybe there was a reason I was saved from my cancer—perhaps God's purpose for me was learning about the little orphaned girls in India, and then starting the Andrea Miller Foundation.

There were certainly innumerable challenges and obstacles along the way, including this surgery when I was a year old. Radiation treatments after the cancerous tumor was removed left me nearly blind in my right eye, and almost deaf, which made learning in school tremendously difficult. I probably asked more questions than anyone else, and sat in the front row so I had a better chance to see what the teachers wrote on the board.

The summer following eleventh grade, I began to "see things in my mind," as I told my parents. After numerous tests, I was diagnosed with epilepsy and Complex Seizure Disorder—which was frightening. How could I continue pursuing my dream? What if I had a seizure while I spoke? How could I go on writing? However, with the support of my parents and relatives, with the proper medication to get my seizures under control, I was able to continue pursuing my dream.

Most of my life had been focused on trying to be accepted by my classmates and others—and the public at large. That was my dream, nothing else. Easter Sunday 2010 I felt the Holy Spirit speak to my heart, telling me living for the foundation and raising money to help children in need around the world was indeed my dream—and God's purpose for my life. It felt strange at first, but it was a feeling of relief I had finally found what I wanted to do with my life, what God wanted me to do.

Success to me:
- It is not about how much money you make, or what title or position you have.
- Taking a hard look at who you truly are, at what your special gifts are, what brings a smile to your face, and a smile to God's, and how you can use your gifts and passions to contribute in this world. That is what's important.
- Don't just follow the crowd or do what everyone else says you should do.
- Listen to your heart, live your dream and find your purpose.
- You can't make everyone happy. Make yourself happy by living your dream—and make others happy by changing the world, if only in small ways.

www.AndreaMillerFoundation.org

Take a hard look at who you truly are, at what are your special gifts, and how you can use your gifts and passions to contribute in this world.

CHAPTER 39

Nike Has the Answer: Just Do It!

When you know better you do better.
—Maya Angelou

Diane Keyes

It's important to look at success not as the end, but as a step on the journey. Even though you may attain success in one area, there are infinite avenues in life to pursue—more to do, more to explore, more heights to reach—no matter what your age. I eagerly look forward to my senior years because the elderly can begin any new venture, and it's considered an achievement and success from the get-go. Although not every endeavor may be a success in the classic sense of the word, I've made it a practice to never look back in regret. The takeaway: everything I learn brings me closer to my next success.

I have gone about finding my way in a very haphazard fashion. By nature, I am not a planner. A friend of mine wrote his thesis about the unscheduled way I live my life. When Tom and I married, it was a year before I decided which side of the bed I would sleep on, and I still sit don't sit in a certain chair at the dining table. Undoubtedly, this quality made my journey more convoluted but, in the end, it suited me. I studied English and social science in college; returned to college to study theology and ministry for three more years, and finally I spent another three years studying spirituality with the Franciscan sisters in La Crosse, Wisconsin.

My approach might seem haphazard, but a pattern of sorts did develop. As an English major, I learned to express myself, my social science gave me insight into relationship, and my spirituality studies provided a compassionate context and equipped me with an ability to listen.

Those skills are paramount in my work as a home stager. One of the first home stagers in the country, I created my niche over twenty-five years ago, before the word "staging" even existed. I've watched countless stagers move into, and quickly out of, the business because they think their job is about decorating. Long ago, I learned staging is about psychology and listening. The

HGTV approach doesn't work very well in real life—with decorators taking every opportunity to criticize and pass judgment on the homeowner's taste. The real answer lies in building bridges and enhancing the home's value—not just accessorizing. And this has never been more important than it is in today's housing market. Previous generations approached home-buying as an investment. But the last several years contradict that theory, so today's homebuyers do not look at the potential value of the home, only its current value. I educate sellers so they understand the perceived value is the *real* value, as far as the buyer is concerned.

Not long ago, I met a man at his deceased parents' home, which had been for sale for almost a year. As the seller reached out to shake my hand, he said, "Just so you know, *I'm not* going to paint a single room." The whole interior was in desperate need of a fresh coat of paint. By the time I left, he had decided to paint, and by the end of the following week, he had painted every room in the house. Results: He received a full-price offer, plus two offers above the list price.

What made the difference? I listened while he expressed his grief and started to shed his anxiety about spending time in his old home. After I listen to my clients' stories they are more easily able to accept my recommendations because they trust me to suggest *only* what is best for them. Without question, staging a home is best for sellers. Homes prepared for the real estate market sell in half the time, and for a significantly higher price than their competitors. My approach differs because it costs a tenth of what most stagers charge and is just as effective, if not more so. I've been able to simplify the staging process enough that I've written an award-winning book on the subject called *This Sold House* that my home-sellers and real estate agents find very helpful.

Sellers need reassurance and encouragement. After all, most people are not moving from a home for fun. A change of residence is one of life's top stressors, and often another stressor, such as job loss, divorce, or death accompanies the move. If I can help my client see their move as the *beginning* of something—rather than the end, they are more able to let go of their home and move on.

Many people have given me sound advice, I've had many wonderful mentors and, of course, I've learned a lot from Oprah's TV shows. But one specific piece of advice has shaped my life more than any other. After finishing the manuscript for my first book, *Spirit of the Snowpeople*, I sent it off to a local publisher. They had published a book I admire very much, which has a message similar to my own book. A few weeks later, I got a letter from the publisher telling me how much they liked my book, but they would not be able to publish it because their docket was already full for the next three years—and they did not wish to tie up my work for so long.

I was excited about receiving a personal letter, but disappointed I'd come close—but not close enough. After meditating about it for a week, I got up the nerve to call and ask what I could do to change the book so they would publish it. The publisher gave me the best piece of advice I have ever gotten. He said, "This is a business decision, it is not personal. Your book is perfect. Do not change a single word. Lots of books in print are not nearly as good as yours. If it doesn't get published, it's your own d***n fault. If you're not willing to fight for your book and market it, quit right now. Because being an author today is about more than writing. It's about putting yourself out there and doing the work."

This was the best piece of advice I could have ever been given to christen my work as a writer—or anything else, for that matter.

My husband and children have always made me feel free to pursue whatever presented itself. Tom has been such a positive influence—always encouraging me, but knowing I don't respond well to demands, he doesn't insist. Very shy, I had never raised my hand to volunteer to ask or answer questions during my first sixteen years of school.

It wasn't until after we attended a Marriage Encounter weekend that I made up my mind to overcome my shyness. I desperately wanted to be part of their leadership team—believing I had a lot to offer on making marriage work. Tom held my hand through every part of the training and held my head while I threw up before I gave my first stomach-turning presentation as a leader. If he hadn't supported me, I would have given up. But he did, and I didn't.

Do not, under any circumstances, make decisions based on fear. Fear rules and ruins so many lives. If I had not faced my shyness and fear of public speaking, I would never have been able to market my books at book signings and other public places, or be strong and confident enough to stage clients' homes, expressing my opinion and reacting to their feedback. The worst thing about fear is that it's futile. Most of the time, we spend our time worrying about things that never materialize. Instead, we are blindsided by events we rarely see coming. Being afraid is a waste of time, so think of FEAR this way: *False Evidence Appearing Real*. Discover what you fear, and like Nike says, just do it. Your action will conquer and obliterate it. Fear is the only thing holding you back.

No question, my husband nudged me out of the nest to follow my dreams. In addition, eleven years ago a staging client invited me to join a writers' group, and these women have taught me to fly. Amazingly talented, diverse, and universally supportive, they have helped me grow my wings, and my roots. Always looking for ways to help, encourage, and cajole me into action, I owe each of them a debt of gratitude I will gladly pay forward for the rest of my life. Thank you WOW (Women of Words) women.

I am most proud of my marriage. Tom and I have watched so many of our friends get divorced, and we feel so fortunate we stumbled across what, for us, is the secret of our happy marriage. We tell each other daily how blessed we are to be together. We have had our share of financial, relationship, and health problems but, somehow we have always been able to separate the circumstances from our relationship. These days this is an uncommon gift, and we are both very grateful for it.

Professionally, I am most proud that my illustrated children's book, *Spirit of the Snowpeople*, was published. Every word of the text "came to me" at a stoplight, settling into my consciousness between the red and green light. Knowing I hadn't actually written *Snowpeople*—but it had come *to me and through me*, I felt God was asking me to get it into print.

It is the story of a small village of north woods folks who brighten the long, gloomy days of winter by building detailed and lifelike snow sculptures for their children. Soon visitors come to see the snowpeople and find themselves touched by the villagers' gentle goodwill and simple hospitality. But when warm spring winds melt the snowpeople, the villagers teach their new friends how to keep the spirit of the snowpeople alive in their hearts all year.

Although it took time to find an agent and a publisher, nearly twelve years later the book was released with the largest presale orders in the company's sixty-year history, and it sold out within three weeks of its release. Considering only three out of 10,000 children's manuscripts are published, and only 3 percent of those published ever go into a second printing, I feel very pleased the book has done so well. It was even performed by the prestigious children's theatre group in Maine less than a year after its publication.

A school librarian told me it is the only book she has read to her students in twenty years that consistently gets applause every time she reads it—no matter the grade level.

Although children see *Snowpeople* as fun-filled and entertaining, it is able to touch adult readers on a spiritual level as well. Its deeper message reminds readers how much easier life is when we surrender to the passing of each *season* and find ease in its natural rhythm. Its gentle theme of birth, death, and resurrection has struck a cord with people all over the world.

I am especially gratified so many people are consoled by its message. A widow in Michigan told me reading *Snowpeople* was the first time she'd felt hope in the seven years since her husband's death. When my illustrator, Helen

Stevens, read *Snowpeople* to a third-grade class, little Natalie told her she loves the book, always carries it with her, and reads it every day. When Natalie went back to her desk, the teacher told Helen the child's parents had both been killed in a car accident, and without Natalie knowing why, the book is helping her through this difficult time. I have other inspiring stories confirming the value of the message I received at the stoplight years ago. I am grateful to be part of bringing a book to the world that comforts Natalie.

I may not have written *Spirit of the Snowpeople*, but I was faithful to it—and I am proud of getting it published, in large part due to the advice given me earlier by the local publisher. However, I believe my success with *Snowpeople* is incomplete. Several children's oncologists have told me they think it would be helpful to children who are dealing with serious illness or death-related issues, either their own, or like Natalie, a family member. I won't consider my job done until I get the book widely distributed in those circles.

I've discovered there are plenty of smart people out there. The folks who have become well-known experts in their fields, whether their specialty is relationship, finance, finding your bliss, or living a happy life, have made it for a reason. Don't waste your time recreating the wheel when books and networking events hold the key. I'm not saying to take everything at face value. What I am saying, though, is to attend networking events where you can associate with your people in your field or area of interest. Discover their strategies and tips. Read some books on your chosen topic, and own the material, extrapolating what works for you, and toss the rest. You can amass a great deal of wisdom in a short time and cut your learning curve dramatically, allowing you to achieve your dreams much faster.

Truth is: I wish I'd taken the advice offered above much sooner.

I have been very slow to embrace the art of play. I grew up with the old saying, "Idle hands are the devil's workshop." And while the saying may be true in a sense, "Be still and know I am God" is also true. Four years ago I discovered qigong and began practicing it daily. Qigong meditation has given me a peace of mind I've never before experienced. Although it is not play, it has opened me up to the value of non-work and self-care, which in turn has resulted in more play, more joy, more peace, and more abundance.

Recently, I have written a book about my life. It's called *To Wendy's With Love,* and will be released next fall. It chronicles how a brain hemorrhage at the age of eight left me with painful memories and lots of unanswered questions. It was only after I began having lunch with my mother every week at Wendy's fast-food restaurant that I began to find answers and the gifts for my healing. What happened along the way has changed my life, as well as those who join Mom and me around the Wendy's table—for twenty years and counting.

I've had challenges and obstacles, and still do. But don't we all. The question is not how many times we fall, fail, or trip, but to realize the only thing important is that we rise again.

For years I would see men and women sitting at bus stops and envy them because they had a place to go, to feel productive and useful. When I was offered a nine-to-five desk job, I turned it down because I realized my gifts do not include a scheduled workday. I would have done my employer a great disservice and been unhappy in the bargain. Most of the time, I'm at peace with my decision because I understand more about who I am and what I'm on the planet to do. It took me some time to get over feeling guilty about absolving myself from a lifestyle most people force themselves to accept, whether they like it or not.

When I think of "top achievers," I find these following quotations say it so well:

"Go confidently in the direction of your dreams. Live the life you have imagined." – *Henry David Thoreau*

"Never, never, never give up." – *Winston Churchill*

"Follow your bliss and the universe will open doors for you where there were only walls." – *Joseph Campbell*

"Failure is success if we learn from it." – *Malcolm Forbes*

"Luck is what happens when preparation meets opportunity." – *Seneca*

The world is full of many inspiring pieces of wisdom on this topic going back to the first century. They are lasting and popular because they are all true. And what has always been true is still true. If you walk your chosen path, continuing on in spite of challenges, failure and, seemingly insurmountable obstacles, you will achieve. The only secret—proceed with diligence, patience and faithfulness.

Success to me is:
- Never give up. Continue in spite of challenges, failures and obstacles.
- Do not let fear rule your life.
- Read books about your area of interest and learn from others' expertise.
- Network with successful people in your field to jumpstart your success.
- Remain faithful and committed to your path.

Joan Kennedy

"The question is not how many times we fall, fail, or trip, but to realize the only thing that matters is we rise again."

CHAPTER 40

The Past Is Not Your Future

Journey into self is not the most important journey, it is the only journey.
—William Butler Yeats

JOAN KENNEDY

In 1927, when I was five years old, our family moved from a small farming community in Sheboygan, Wisconsin, to Minneapolis, Minnesota. My father had a small farm, and he also worked for a textile mill. When the company moved to Minnesota, they brought our family with them.

After a few years, the company moved the mill to St. Paul's West Side. At the time, this area was a poor section of St. Paul. It didn't matter to my dad because he could walk to work. The move affected my mother the hardest. After three moves away from friends, and having to leave one lovely neighborhood, my mother had a nervous breakdown.

Aunt Mary came to live with us for a short time. Before she returned home to Villard, Minnesota, she and my dad made arrangements for us four children—brother, Eddy, my sisters Dolly and Marie and me—to go to an orphanage until things at home had changed, and my mother was back with us. Mother was hospitalized, and once released, went to live with a friend because she was not able to care for us. She finally divorced my dad and moved into an apartment. I don't know what happened between them because I was young and not very discerning.

I don't remember the day or the month we were taken to St. Joseph's Orphanage. I was ten years old at the time. All I remember is my dad had trouble finding the place. When we finally arrived, it was after dark. The orphanage was a large five-story, red stone building with huge concrete steps. My dad drove up the circular driveway; then, the four of us followed our tired father up the steps to a large imposing front door. When he rang the bell, a nun came to the door and let us in. After we said good-bye to him,

Dad walked away. I don't remember if I was sad or frightened, or both. When I think back, I can't imagine what my dad must have been feeling as he left all his children there, and went home alone. Those were different times, and I suppose he had few choices if no relative was able and willing to help him keep his children.

The next morning, as I woke up in a dormitory full of girls, I realized it was now time for me to get used to a whole new life and routine. Little did I know then my stay there would last for the next five years. The day started with morning mass. All the girls wore black veils and sat on one side of the chapel. The boys sat on the opposite side. The nuns sat in the back pews. The girls and boys were always segregated in the building, sleeping on different floors, or playing in separate playground areas, working at their chores apart, and even eating at different ends of the dining hall. I rarely had an opportunity to talk to my brother with the exception of visiting hours with our parents. It was difficult for us kids during visiting hours because both parents came—because they were *not* speaking to each other.

Our parents were able to visit us twice a month on Sundays, and this was the only time we were all together. The other Sundays were the loneliest days. If we had money in our bank accounts, we might be able to buy a candy bar. I didn't always have money, and those who didn't, received a chocolate. I never popped the whole chocolate into my mouth; I would sit on the fire escape and scoop out the cream in the center with a bobby pin. The kids always laughed at me, but I didn't care. My chocolate lasted a lot longer than theirs.

When I turned twelve, I was old enough to work in the kitchen. The first morning, Sister Lena, who was the cook in charge, said to me, "Go into the pantry and get me a colander." I had no idea what a colander was, so I started to pray to God to show me a colander. Sister Lena was not a patient woman, and she came into the pantry and grabbed it herself before my prayer could be answered.

Working in the kitchen for the next three years didn't ensure I would be a good cook. Later on in life, my husband would tell our friends, or anyone who'd listen, our stove had two temperatures—off and burn.

Turning twelve opened up a whole new way of life. I not only worked in the kitchen, I was also old enough to work in the laundry, located in a separate building. It had huge laundry tubs, drying racks, ironing boards, and a large black coal stove in the middle of the room with ledges around it to heat the irons. We took the irons off the stove with hot pads. When the irons cooled down, we put them back on the stove and took another hot iron and continued ironing. As I recall, there were a lot of scorched clothes and burned knuckles.

There's an old saying, I'm just sure the nuns at St. Joseph's coined, "Busy hands are happy hands." In addition to schooling, the nuns taught us how to work and how to worship ... and they taught us discipline. Strange as it may seem, I enjoyed the years I spent at the orphanage because in truth, I felt safe.

When I was fifteen, my brother Eddy and I graduated from the eighth grade, which meant we could leave the orphanage. My mother was still living away from home. Because there would be only Dad and my brother in my house, I was placed in a foster home where I stayed for about eight months. Then Dad married a woman named Lena (Sister Lena had been already in my life).

We four children all moved back home. After she married my dad, the one thing Lena brought with her was a sofa. It was the first sofa we ever had. Lena stayed only a short time. She was a kind woman, and I liked her. I'm certain four kids were too much of a handful. However, when she left, she took the sofa.

In time, we all ran away from home. My brother Eddy was the first one to run away to be with our mother. Next my sisters, Dolly and Marie, ran away to join them. I was the last one to leave because I felt sorry for Dad. He married again, but she was not a very friendly woman. I finally had it. I missed my mother and my sisters and brother. My mother wasn't prepared for the four of us. She worked hard, cleaning houses for other people. She didn't make much money, so we were on relief, which is called welfare today. Each month we received the staples—flour, sugar, salt, potatoes, etc. We ate a lot of potato pancakes during those lean years.

One day when we went to pick up food, I was also given a brown corduroy shirtwaist dress with brown buttons down the front. I was excited to have a new dress. I wore it to school the next day, and quickly discovered about nine or ten other girls had on the same brown corduroy shirtwaist dresses with brown buttons down the front. Much to our chagrin, now we all knew who was poor—and on relief. Undaunted, I went home, cut off all the buttons, and found enough pink buttons in my mother's sewing box to replace the brown ones. When I went back to school the next day, I was the only girl in a brown corduroy shirtwaist dress with pink buttons down the front. Being a girl, I always liked pretty things. When I was nine years old, I painted my Buster Brown laced-up shoes pink. I'm not crazy about the color pink, but at the time, it was the only color I could find in buttons and paint.

The years in high school were happy times while living with my mother, sisters, and brother. After high school, I went to work to help support the family. When I was twenty, I got married. It was during the Second World War. My husband, Ray, and I lived together as newlyweds for only five weeks before he was transferred overseas. I went back to live with my mother, and had a son eight months later. My mother took care of baby Bobby, and I continued to work. My husband never came back home. He wasn't killed in action—he just never came back home to me.

I worked for 3M, which in the forties was called Minnesota Mining & Manufacturing Company. I worked three different shifts in the tape department. Each week the shifts would change. One week I worked 7:00 to 3:00; the next week, I would work 3:00 to 7:00. The following week I worked 7:00 to 11:00. It was a difficult time. I didn't own a car; thus the streetcar was my only form of transportation. I remember after one of my night shifts I fell asleep and woke up at the end of the line, which was at Fort Snelling. After several years, I finally decided to leave Minnesota Mining, and I applied for a job at Buckbee & Mears. During the war, they made gun sights. I was on an assembly line, and one of the benefits was it was a day job. I can't recall any other benefits, except perhaps a paycheck. At the time, life seemed extremely bleak and tiring.

I soon felt as though I had to make some changes, but what? I had heard about a school in Minneapolis called the McConnell School of Modeling and Self-improvement. I signed up. I knew I needed help to look and feel more confident. The fee was $35 for the six-week self-improvement course.

When I finished the class, I borrowed a beautiful coat from my friend Denise. I don't know where I found the nerve, but I went down to Rosen & Engleson's in St. Paul where I applied for a job as a receptionist and model. They hired me on the spot. Life was looking up for me. After working there for one year, I asked for a raise, which was denied.

I knew Field Schlick, a high-end fashion store in downtown St. Paul, hired models for one year. I applied and was hired. I worked in the fashion office, and I was their store model. After this position, I became a free-lance model in the Twin Cities. I did runway shows for stores, women's groups and country clubs.

Today, I shudder at the thought of working in those factories. My dissatisfaction and sheer determination lifted me out of those difficult and depressing situations. My mother was my greatest help, with encouragement and support. I couldn't have done it without her.

Joan Kennedy

About five years later, I remarried and had three more children, all girls. For eighteen years, I was a stay-at-home mom. During those years, my married life fluctuated between feelings of frustration and contentment. When I felt frustrated, I took down walls, moved furniture, and changed my kitchen curtains. When I was content, I enjoyed vacuuming, dusting, and baking. I remember telling my friends I was contented during one of our coffee times together. My friend, Irene, turned to me and said, "Joan, only cows are content."

During the years I was married and raising our children, I realized I was forever busy. The decorating, remodeling and all the other busy work were an escape. I was avoiding the real conflicts within my life—and myself. My marriage was crumbling. I was forty-five years old, with three children still at home, minimal work experience, and no money of my own.

Through the years, I never prepared myself for a job either mentally or emotionally. I saw no need for any further planning. I had achieved my major goal in life, the role of wife, mother and homemaker. I didn't want to make any drastic changes. A feeling of panic would set in each time I considered giving up my familiar ways. The thought of undertaking anything as monumental as getting a job was frightening.

If I had known what was taking place in my life, I would have realized the urgency for finding my talent and developing it. Why did I feel I had to braid my own rugs, make my own quilts and constantly change the color of the walls? Today, my rugs are worn out, and my quilts have disintegrated from the sun's rays. The only thing remaining is the result of the thoughts I entertained as I braided, quilted and painted. Those thoughts became my present.

After many financial setbacks, I finally reached the decision to find a job. With my sketchy working experiences, the thoughts that kept surfacing were, "What can I possibly do?" and "Who wants me?"

At the suggestion of a friend, I applied for a job at the University of Minnesota. Along with my application, I was told I had to take a Civil Service test. After having filled in all the required questions, I started the second phase of the test, which consisted of some math problems, word association and other tests I have blocked from my consciousness in the ensuing years.

When I finally completed the tests, they told me to wait in the corridor for the results. The personnel manager started calling people into his office for their interviews. When he finally called my name, I jumped up with great anticipation and headed for his office when he stopped me in the corridor. "Mrs. Kennedy, you passed your tests, but you don't know how to do anything."

Well, I knew that when I left home in the morning, and now he knows it—and everyone within earshot heard I don't know how to do anything. I don't remember the answer I gave, if any. All I remember is the embarrassment I felt. My first thought was, "How can I tell my family I didn't get the job because I don't know how to do anything?" Then he said, "We do have a part-time job at Nicholson Hall Bookstore." Although it was only for two weeks out of every quarter, I jumped at the opportunity. I was excited because I finally had a job. My enthusiasm soon diminished when I realized it would not provide an adequate income. Later they told me because it was part-time, the job didn't require a Civil Service Test. To work at Nicholson Hall Bookstore, I just had to be ambulatory.

I still had to figure out how to make more money. There was only one other alternative. I turned to my friends, and said, in all honesty, "I need to make more money. You have the work you never get around to doing, and I have the energy. I'll work for you." They thought it was a great idea.

For the next year, I painted walls, refinished furniture, mended Oriental rugs, helped sand and paint a sailboat, washed and ironed clothes, and cleaned a friend's house. Yet, in time, the work became extremely dissatisfying, especially working in my friend's basement ironing her clothes. At the time, I had such a desire to get out of the situation I was in, but I didn't know how to do it ... so I just kept on going.

I clearly remember the day I came home after one of my jobs. Tired, I sat for a few minutes and started reading our monthly community newspaper. I always read the book review first, and today Phyllis Olmen, our librarian, had written a review on the book, *Psycho-Cybernetics*, by Dr. Maxwell Maltz. Although I didn't have a clue as to what Psycho-Cybernetics meant, I continued to read. One line caught my eye. It said simply, "Chances are, if life has passed you by, it's because you yourself have not unlocked your success door." Well, I knew immediately I had to read Maltz's book.

The next day, I went to the library and picked up the book and started reading. Dr. Maltz's theories started to make sense. One of the things he said especially hit home: "We all have within us a mental picture of the kind of person we think we are." So it isn't who we are, it's who we think we are that sets the boundaries of our accomplishments.

As I began to read, I knew this philosophy made sense to me. I was aware of a feeling of knowing I was finally on to something which would make a difference in my life. I read and reread, and found I was discovering another self, a part of me that had always been there, and another self encased in a hard shell of a low self-image.

As a result of the months studying Psycho Cybernetics, I finally realized I could become the independent and confident woman I always wanted to be. I also realized no one else could take the gamble out of my life for me. I had set up limitations in my mind, and in my mind I began to change those limitations and reshape my life. I developed a feeling of security for the first time. The security came from the knowledge I had the ability to deal with life and not depend on a promise from someone else.

Months later, after re-reading the book several times, and following the techniques laid out in the book, I asked myself again, "What can I do?" This time, when my endeavor to return to work in fashion re-surfaced, instead of thinking, "Who'd want me?" I realized something had changed. I felt differently about myself. I could truthfully say, "Why not me?" I knew I had the talent and the ability, even though I was now forty-seven, it didn't seem ridiculous to try to get back into the fashion business. For the first time, I knew in my heart I could do it.

I called to schedule an interview at one of the leading department stores, and scheduled an appointment for an interview the following month. Starting then, until the day of my appointment, I visualized the interview.

Dr. Maxwell Malts writes about the power of our imagination. "The nervous system cannot tell the difference between a real or an imaginary happening. One imagined vividly."

To me this information was the solution to my problem. I now had a way of getting out of my situation. I became (and still am) a believer, and besides, what did I have to lose?

Each night when I got into bed, I would completely relax my body, and I'd rehearse the interview in my mind. Every night, as I pictured the interview, the fashion director would say, "You're hired."

One month later, armed with a feeling of great expectation, a good self-image, and a feeling of confidence, I headed for my interview. We were not far into the interview when the fashion director said she was losing her fashion coordinator, who was pregnant. She then said she had made up her mind the next fashion coordinator would have to be a mature woman—a woman who wasn't going to get pregnant. I thought, "Here I am … in living color!" At 2:30 in the afternoon of the same day, I received a phone call from the personnel director who said, "You're hired."

The first thing I did was quit all my jobs. My friends were happy and excited for me. No more cleaning, mending, or furniture refinishing. I was now a fashion coordinator—and a most happy woman.

I had just one drawback when I started as a fashion coordinator: a fear of public speaking. At the fashion shows I had coordinated, the fashion director would stand up and take over for me and give the commentary. I was content to stay backstage and help the models get ready for the show.

For years I said, "It makes me nervous to stand up and speak," or I'd say, "I'm afraid to stand up and speak." After I started working as a fashion coordinator, I went to a seminar called Executive Dynamic. There I found out about affirmations. I stopped saying, "It makes me nervous to stand up and speak." Instead, I said the affirmation, "I'm an excellent speaker, well prepared, logical and completely at ease before any group." I said this affirmation five times every morning and five times every night. Gradually I got over the fear of public speaking, I was finally able to stand up before an audience and not panic.

Two years later, at age fifty, I became a professional speaker. In the years following, I regularly traveled around the country. I spoke at conventions, conferences, sales meetings, women's groups and organizations on the importance of having a good self-image, confidence, and of setting goals. Since then, I have written three books and created a workshop called "The Confident Way."

Success to me is:
- Always keeping in mind we have abilities we don't realize we have.
- Acknowledging we can do things we never dreamed we could do.
- Relating positively to the forces causing us to rise to the occasion/situation.
- Realizing *you* are your own power source.
- Knowing you can make changes in your life and circumstances.
- Look at opportunities for what they are or can offer.
- Try new things; you never know what might fit you perfectly.
- You're never too old to learn something new or find a new path.

Anyone wanting to make changes in her life needs to keep in mind the potential for achievement exists within you. To achieve your goals, find the success you desire, you have to believe you are your own power source. These three points will help you in the pursuit of your dreams:

1. Know and have confidence in your own talents and abilities.
2. Dare to attempt the seemingly impossible.
3. Persist courageously in the face of all obstacles.

Take the time now to decide what you want your life to be, in the next year, or five years from now.

Ask yourself: "What can I change within myself and within my world now to make the dream possible.

Thomas Edison reminds us, "If we did all the things we are capable of doing, we would literally astound ourselves."

Jvkennedy1@aol.com
www.JoanKennedy.com

In order to make changes in yourself and in your life, you will have to deal with your self-image, it is this inner-self that creates the limitations, and sets the boundaries of your accomplishments.

Additional Tips and Strategies

Feel the Fear and Do It Anyway

Successful people see an opportunity and seize upon it. Perhaps the thought that they could fail might occur to them, but it does not influence their decision to proceed. They see the opportunity and know how to harness resources to help them achieve the best results.

Many others see the opportunity and wish they could take advantage of it. But they are fearful their abilities or their money may not be equal to the task. While they hesitate, others who have the self-confidence achieve what could have been theirs.

Two things to keep in mind:
1. The only way to get rid of fear of doing something is to go out and do it.
2. Not only are you going to experience fear whenever you are in unfamiliar territory—but so is everyone else.

The Motivating Force Within

One of the prime factors in achievement is motivation. No matter how intelligent or talented you are, or how many opportunities come your way, if you are not motivated, you will accomplish very little.

Millions of people work all their lives with no stronger motivation than acquiring the necessities of life, such as a roof over their heads, food on the table, and clothes on their backs.

Without a strong desire for more, nothing happens. Desire is the motivating force within you. Decide on the changes you want to make, and then have a strong desire about making these changes.

Take Charge of Your Life

You have only one life to live. So while there is still time, don't waste it making excuses, or thinking you don't have what it takes. If you see yourself as in charge and in control of your life, you will feel strong, capable and confident.

There is always a risk in trying something new. Once you decide to change some area of your life, do something. Action strengthens your confidence. Without action, your thoughts become worrisome, and your confidence is undermined. Make the decision, "This is what I want." Decide, choose and be positive.

Just Do It!

In every major decision, you may be in conflict with yourself whether or not to act. If you are not aware of this, indecision can become habitual and prevent you from taking constructive steps. You can do several things to avoid the tendency to wait until conditions are just right before you act:

Accept the possibility you may encounter future obstacles and difficulties.

Don't waste time beforehand worrying about those possibilities.

When you have a problem, you always have two options: worry about it, or solve it.

Do something, no matter how simple, that shows action. Send an e-mail, make a phone call asking for information—something.

Don't harbor doubts about the decision once you've made it.

Start each day with the conviction that many new ideas will come to you, and they will provide unusual opportunities.

The Power of Your Imagination

If you can picture the way you really want your life to be, you greatly improve your chances of achieving your goals. Imagine the things you would like to see in your life. Forget about the negative things that have happened to you. In place of them, mentally create the conditions you would like to see in your life now. Create positive images of yourself and make room for new things in your life.

Albert Einstein said, "Your imagination is your preview to life's coming attractions." All the things that are now your reality were once simply ideas in your consciousness. You hold the power to manifest different circumstances for your life. If you desire to manifest a new reality for yourself, you need to consciously focus your imagination on what you want—not on what you don't have.

BE THERE ... NOW

Success comes from feelings you are successful in the present moment. It is not something you will be *someday* when you've reached a goal, or have received something you've wanted. You are successful when you identify yourself with the reality of success.

Acknowledge all the successful things you are doing right now. Appreciate where you are at this moment. Rather than focusing on how far you have to go, savor how far you've come. Take a moment to tell yourself you are already a success.

Think of all the reasons why you are closer to getting what you want than you have ever been. And while you are at it, use the power of affirmation and say, "I am a success, and I allow myself to feel successful now."

IT TAKES COURAGE

When the dominating influence is fear, rather than confidence, sometimes staying in an uncomfortable rut is preferable to change. Nearly all of us can look back to a time in our lives and say, "If I had only taken that chance, I would be much better off now."

No philosophy will help people to succeed when they doubt their abilities to do so. No matter how hard you work for success, if your thoughts are saturated with the fear of failure, it will destroy your efforts.

One of the secrets of success is to vividly imagine the achievement of your goal in your mind, then you literally exude success. You feel successful, you look successful, and the result is, before long, you are successful. Shakespeare expresses the same thought in another way, "Assume a virtue if you have it not, or 'Act as If.'"

A STATE OF BECOMINGNESS

One of the most common statements of defeat the majority of us make is, "I can't picture myself doing that." If we are not able to picture success, we will rarely achieve it. We all use our imagination unconsciously, when we worry about tomorrow, we are imagining, projecting something about an occurrence that has not yet taken place. People say, "I'm afraid I won't get the job." "I don't think I can pass the test." "I'm sure I won't find what I want." These are all the instances of negatively imagining something that hasn't yet taken place.

Take some time out during the day and get away by yourself. Sit in a comfortable chair and relax. Start seeing yourself as the successful person you would like to become. Feel excited by the picture. Make the affirmation, "I am successful in all I do."

A mental image provides the basis for everything we want. Through our imagination, and affirmation, we can create a different environment, better our conditions and achieve a definite goal.

It's About Time

The things we will regret most of all in our lives will be the things we put off, the dreams we let slip away, relationships we failed to nurture, and projects we started but never finished. Keep in mind no one is promised tomorrow.

It's important to have a philosophy of life that will help you to relate to what time really is. Author Edna Ferber summed it up when she said, "Life is a fine thing. It's the finest thing in the world. Though hazardous, it's a unique thing it only happens once in a lifetime."

Life is too short, time too precious—and to waste your time is to waste your life.

More About Our Successful Women

Connie Anderson is a writer, editor and resource for authors, helping them find the right person to design their cover, format their book, or create an e-Book. In 2012, she edited almost 20 books of various genres. After editing hundreds of books, in spring of 2013 she produced her own gift book, *In My Next Life, I Want to be My Dog*. In December 2013, she launched *When Polio Came Home: How Ordinary People Overcame Extraordinary Challenges*, which is a collection of stories from people who had polio in 1940s and '50s. She is currently collecting stories from people who had polio in the 1940s and 50s. *When Polio Came Home: Minnesotans Tell Their Story* will be launched December 2013. As a consummate "idea person," she is already planning her next book geared to young women. Read her authors' testimonial about working with her.

Connie@WordsandDeedsInc.com
www.WordsandDeedsInc.com

Kristen Brown is a renowned speaker, certified coach, widow mom, award-winning entrepreneur, and bestselling author of *The Best Worst Thing, The Happy Hour Effect, Beat the Blues,* and the forthcoming, *The Entrepreneur Promise*. She is the founder of Happy Hour Effect, LLC, a company that helps people ignite their work and life. She is a professional speaker, brand ambassador, Huffington Post blogger, and media personality who has been featured on TV, radio, print and online including *Live with Kelly & Michael, Inc., Psychology Today* and HLN. Named one of the top three finalists in Ali Brown's "Entrepreneur to Watch 2013" contest, she trains teams, entrepreneurs and authors to create a low-stress, high-success game plan to achieve their professional and personal goals.

www.HappyHourEffect.com
kristen@happyhoureffect.com

Nancy Chakrin Entrepreneur, Healthcare Advocate, A Creative, Business Mentor, and Visionary. A native of Minneapolis, Nancy graduated from the University of Minnesota with a Bachelors Degree in Art Education. She also studied at the Minneapolis Institute of Art; The Pennsylvania Academy of Fine Arts, Philadelphia, Pennsylvania; and the Cambridge Technical School in Cambridge, England. Over the past five decades, Nancy has developed three award-winning careers: photography, graphic design and landscape painting. Her recently published gold medal book, *FRIENDSHIP The Art of the Practice*, co-authored with yogini Laurie Ellis-Young, represents a unique combination of these talents. Her artwork is collected internationally and is focused in two unique but complementary themes: "Art as a Healing Therapy" and "Women Who Help Transform the Lives of Others."

Nancy@NancyChakrin.com
www.NancyChakrin.com

Meg Blaine Corrigan's memoir, *Then I Am Strong: Moving From My Mother's Daughter to God's Child*, is available in print and electronic form through Amazon.com. With a Master's Degree in Counseling from the University of New Mexico, Corrigan has thirty-plus years of experience working with mental health issues. Meg now speaks to various groups about her faith in God and her resilience following the traumatic events of her life. She is a speaker and trainer at colleges, churches, book clubs, mental health and juvenile facilities, law enforcement agencies and on several radio interviews. Meg recently returned to the location of her sexual assault and spoke with the current law enforcement staff there. Her story was featured in the Minnesota Women's Press in 2013.

www.MegCorrigan.com
MegCorrigan@comcast.net
O: 651-295-7099

Michelle Dustin From a very young age, she was a frequent thrift shopper. With extensive retail experience and years of avid secondhand shopping, she has developed an impressive knack for shopping and styling on a thrift-store budget. In 2011, she approached the team at Arc Value Village Thrift Stores with the innovative idea to offer the same personal shopping services found in high-end department stores at Arc Value Village stores—and customers responded enthusiastically. To date, Michelle has shopped with thousands of Value Village customers, and regularly sees happy returning clients.

PersonalShopper@theArcgtc.org

JoAnne Funch has been an entrepreneur since 1994, dedicating most of those years to marketing and promotion. Since 1996, her company GIR-Graphics &Innovative Resources has assisted hundreds of businesses in marketing strategies, promotion, and developing consistent branding messages. Her business has evolved to include website development, social media strategies and training. Her current passion is to teach people in her age group who didn't grow up with technology to gain exposure in a digital world. JoAnne is a writer, consistently blogs about business as well as other personal interests such as grief and has written a book called, *I Don't Know What to Say: Thoughtful Steps to Support Anyone Who is Grieving a Loss.*

www.girpromotions.com
www.marketingdish.com

Nadia Giordana is an author, mentor, and motivator. She not only transformed her personal appearance when she lost 80 plus pounds at the age of 60, she went on to conquer a paralyzing fear of public speaking. She now inspires and motivates other women to live their second act ... to reactivate their sidelined dreams, and reinvent new chapters in their lives. Her books, *New Chapters in Your Life at any Age* and *Thinking Skinny,* are available Amazon.com.

iinadia@msn.com
EmbodyYourVision.com

Linda Hachfeld is an author, editor, publisher, small business owner, and a registered dietitian. Her book is *Cooking Ala Heart.* She has served the profession of dietetics in clinical, administrative, community, public policy, and research capacities. Recognized by the Minnesota Academy of Nutrition & Dietetics (RYDY Award) and regional publishing industry (MBA Distinguished Service Award), Linda also received the Secretary's Award for Excellence in Public Health (US DHHS), a Governor's Certificate of Commendation for Community Health Promotion (MN), and the Small Business Advocate of the Year Award for Women in Business (US SBA). She has been honored as the Outstanding Alumna from FCS Dept. at MSU-Mankato, the Distinguished Woman Leader from the YWCA–Mankato and the 2011 Yellow Rose Award recipient from three women's civic organizations (BPW, ZONTA and WEB).

lindah@hickory.net
www.AppletreePress.com

Kathy Heiland is an author of eBooks that are designed to encourage and motivate readers to never give up. She received her B.S. in Accounting from Metropolitan State University. After eleven years in accounting and eight years in pharmacy customer service, Kat is now pursuing her life's dream by making her mark as an inspirational and family matters author. When victory is achieved over one of life's difficulties, Kat writes about it in an easy-to-read format to help readers. Kat has written five books in her series entitled "Kat's Recipes For Life": *Say What You Mean: Because You'll Have What You Say, Love Never Fails If We Never Give Up, 5 Things Women Do In Relationships That Drive Men Crazy, Defeat Divorce In Your Marriage, Menopause: What Your Mama Didn't Tell You.* Kat has a fiction series coming soon. She lives in Minneapolis with her husband Dan.

KatHeilBooks@comcast.net
www.KatHeilBooks.com

Becky Henry, CPCC, is an author and speaker, as well as a coach who provides coaching to families impacted by eating disorders. As a mom of someone with an eating disorder, she educates health sciences students about eating disorders in general, and also the impact on families. Her national award-winning book, *"Just Tell Her To Stop: Family Stories of Eating Disorders"* shines light on the realities of these often-misunderstood brain illnesses.

Coachbeckyhenry@gmail.com
www.EatingDisorderFamilySuppport.com
952-451-5663

Devie Hagen started in the hospitality industry back in the seventies. She was a meeting planner at Medtronic for thirteen years. When she accepted a position at the United Way as a loaned executive, she decided to make the career change and go into hospitality sales. She spent twenty-two years at national hotel/resort companies (such as Hilton International and Madden's Resort) moving to vice president/general manager after consistently exceeding revenue targets. During this timeframe, she was honored to receive such industry awards as: Volunteer of the Year 2011, Mentor of the year 2009 and 2010, Lifetime Achievement, Best Supporting Company, and Hilton International Salesperson of the year. Devie has moved into a new career in hospitality as an agent for speakers and presenters.

www.ElanSpeakersAgency.com

Patty Hall is co-founder of H2O for Life, a nonprofit with a mission to engage educate and inspire youth to study the global water crisis while taking local and global actions. Through service learning, youth learn that their actions have impact and can make a difference. Her story has been featured in *Reader's Digest*, the "The Today Show" and "Good Morning America." She was honored as one of six "Inspiring Women" by CNN. Patty was an educator for twenty years, and today is a full-time volunteer for H2O for Life. H2O for Life has provided educational outreach to more than 200,000 U.S. youth, and has funded water, sanitation and hygiene education projects (WASH in Schools) for more than 500 schools around the world.

www.h2oforlifeschools.org

JacLynn Herron is a retired teacher. She received her BS degree in Home Economics Education from Concordia College in Moorhead, Minnesota, and taught at high schools in Fridley and New Brighton, Minnesota. She is a member of the Loft Literary Center in Minneapolis and is active in P.E.O., a philanthropic, educational organization for women. She is a mother of two adult daughters and thoroughly enjoys her newest role as grandmother. Author of *Singing Solo: In Search of a Voice for MOM*, she lives in New Brighton, Minnesota, with her husband Tom.

www.JacLynnHerron.com

Barb Hunn went to work with her then-business partner Beverly Oien in 1973 to open the first Keys Restaurant on Raymond Avenue in St. Paul. After refining and improving their most-successful formula, she opened the second Keys in New Brighton in 1983, as the sole owner. Now that this is a family business, with her children owning and managing most of the stores, Keys Café has expanded to nine locations in the Twin Cities. They have been recognized nationally for their fine food.

www.keyscafe.com

Jill Johnson is president of Johnson Consulting Services and an award-winning management consultant who has impacted nearly $3 billion worth of business decisions. Jill has worked with entrepreneurs, corporations and non-profits located across the United States, as well as in Europe and Asia. She is an expert at evaluating critical decisions and assessing the impact of market forces on strategic and business planning efforts, both at the board and operating level. She has been a member of the board of directors of numerous business and non-profit organizations. She has served on two federal boards for three presidents representing both political parties. Jill is one of the first women ever inducted into the Minnesota Women Business Owner Hall of Fame. She was honored for a career dedicated to business leadership and mentorship, as well as her advocacy on behalf of Minnesota businesswomen.

www.jcs-usa.com
Jill@jcs-usa.com
Facebook: www.facebook.com/Jill.Johnson.USA
Twitter: @JillJohnsonUSA
Linkedin: www.linkedin.com/in/johnsonconsultingservices

Julie Kay is an accomplished interior decorator who loves to empower her clients and bring serenity to their spaces. Her "less is more" attitude helps clients de-clutter and allows them to focus on the important parts of the space they are working on. Her passion is to get the "spaceless," which enables her clients to create amazing rooms at discount prices. Julie's outgoing personality, enthusiasm, kind spirit and sense of humor make it a pleasure to work with her.

Irene M. Kelly, NCOC, CVI CC, is a Life, Leadership & Academic Coach, has a diverse background in sales, business ownership, and organizational leadership. She serves clients to examine beliefs that interfere with their dreams and goals. Her strengths are grounded in her ability to create safe, trusting environments that open pathways to new possibilities. Irene is a critical thinker with extensive experience creating new programs and leading innovative projects. Much of her work is in the educational arena working with educators, students and parents—both individuals and groups.

www.PrismaLLC.com

Joan Kennedy

Diane Keyes has owned a successful staging business for more than twenty years. She also has an extensive and eclectic background working as a book reviewer, editor, retreat director, grief group facilitator, and commercial floral designer, as well as speaking often at real estate functions and making appearances on local TV and radio programs. Diane's *Spirit of the Snowpeople*, sold out its first printing three weeks after publication. Her second book, *This Sold House*, received two Best Book Awards, in the business and how-to categories, from the Midwest (twelve state region) Independent Publishers' Association and is endorsed by Joan Steffend, host of HGTV's, Decorating Cents.

www.thissoldhouse.biz
www.spiritofthesnowpeople.com
www.ifbhomesale.com

Ellajane Knott has been a columnist reporter for Sun Newspaper for some twenty-six years, public relations director for Hotel Nicollet and *Minnesota Calls* magazine. She also worked as a PR assistant for American Heart Association. During her husband's thirteen-year battle with Alzheimer's, she authored a book, *The Last Flight: A Marine Pilot's Slow Decent in the Void of Alzheimer's*.

Victoria Kriz is a positive outgoing wife, mother, and business owner. She opened a hair salon in her home after her first daughter was born. Her favorite part of her job is making people not only look good on the outside, but also feel good on the inside. She is most passionate about people receiving healing and complete balance and joyfulness in their life. Her business has become her ministry, and every day is a new adventure.

Pat Lindquist has reported on and supported the arts, hospitality and communication fields in Minnesota since 1970. She has been a columnist with local publications from *Skyway/Freeway News* and the *Sun News* as well as well *Restaurant Hospitality Magazine* and *Food Service News*. In addition to freelancing writing and photography, she was an Art Director and Marketing Director for retail department stores, the Minneapolis Institute of Art and CG Rein Galleries. In 1984, she opened her own marketing and PR agency, Pat Lindquist & Associates.

Julie Lother has a Bachelors Degree in Exercise Science, is a yoga instructor, inspiring personal trainer and business entrepreneur. She has over fifteen years experience in the fitness and wellness industries. Julie lives her business name: Fit 2b Well. She uniquely blends her knowledge and exercise to create programs, classes and workshops that truly do bring mind and body together for positive change, inspiring people to live their most authentic life. She incorporates new ways of thinking into classes and programs on positive living, manifesting and changing subconscious beliefs.

Julie@fit-2b-well.com
651-235-5546

Deborah Lysholm is an accomplished dancer whose professional career spans more than four decades—from performing, choreographing, and teaching thousands of students, to building Heartbeat Performing Arts Center, in Apple Valley, Minnesota. Reaching out to the world dance community, her journey has taken her around the U.S. and to Europe and Asia, and to Cuba where she established travel study and cultural exchange programs—and many friendships. She has written her autobiography, *Dancing to My Heartbeat*.

www.heartbeat-studios.com

Melissa (Carpenter) McGath applied her creativity and passion for drawing and designing in both corporate and agency environments. Her diverse skills allowed her to start her career as an illustrator at a card company before moving on as a graphic designer at a Twin Cities hospital and then to other positions in marketing. Melissa illustrated a series of children's books that were published by Picture Window Books in 2003.

http://www.linkedin.com/in/mjmcgath

Zhenya Melnick grew up on an island in the Russian Far East during the Soviet era, She left her life in Russia for the United States at the age of sixteen to pursue her education and dreams of a career in business. Fifteen years later, she has achieved a Master's degree in Business Administration and is successfully managing a business intelligence team for a medical technology company. Zhenya has been married for the last eight years and now, has a son, opening a new chapter in her life.

Andrea Rose Miller was born on January 4, 1988. At age one, Andrea was diagnosed with medulloblastoma, a very rare type of brain cancer. Doctors gave her a ten percent chance of survival. Andrea battled the cancer for two years, through two operations, radiation, and a year of chemotherapy—and she beat the odds. Andrea's survival did not come without consequences: she has no hair on the back of her head, she has balance and motor skill difficulties, as well as lack of good hand-eye coordination, slight deafness, and weak eyesight. Andrea learned of the plight of seventy-five orphaned girls in India and decided to do something to help them. She established the Andrea Miller Foundation, a non-profit, charitable organization that provides support and services to orphans/needy children throughout the world. Andrea paints, writes books and is an inspirational speaker. She uses these talents to raise money to benefit the orphans and less-fortunate children and continues to develop new ways to raise money for her cause.

www.AndreaMillerFoundation.org

Janice Novak developed her unique posture program over twenty years of working with individual clients and teaching thousands of workshops. She has a Master's Degree in Health and Physical Education. She is an internationally acclaimed author, speaker and wellness consultant who teaches workshops and seminars for hospitals, corporations and professional organizations, plus community education classes. Janice regularly presents health segments on television and radio, including a guest spot on the Oprah Winfrey Show discussing her book, *Posture, Get It Straight! Look Ten Years Younger, Ten Pounds Thinner and Feel Better Than Ever.*

www.ImproveYourPosture.com

Tara O'Brien is a licensed Realtor in the state of Minnesota with ReMax Advantage Plus and has been since licensed 2001. She has a Bachelor of Science degree from the University of Minnesota in Mortuary Science. She enjoys being self-employed and being her own boss. Helping people to buy and sell homes is very rewarding. She was married in October 2013, and her husband and she live with his daughter and her nephew, of whom she has full custody.

www.TaraOBrien.com

Mary Treacy O'Keefe, MA, is the award-winning co-founder and President of Well Within, a nonprofit holistic wellness resource center in Woodbury, Minnesota. Her presentations have been enthusiastically received by religious groups, healthcare and hospice organizations, women's groups, wellness expos, associations and various other public and private organizations. Mary's heartwarming stories are included in several books, including three *Chicken Soup for the Soul* books, plus in *Women's Day, Catholic Digest*, and other publications. Her first book, *Thin Places: Where Faith is Affirmed and Hope Dwells*, received Honorable Mention from national Independent Publishers Book Awards. Her second book, *Meant to Be: Do Things Really Happen for a Reason?* will be published in 2014.

www.marytreacyokeefe.com.

Gloria Perez joined Jeremiah Program in 1998. As president and CEO, she has become one of the country's leading experts in two-generational strategies to reducing poverty. She has led the organization from its first capital campaign to the nationally recognized and expanding organization of today. Gloria recently was named a Fellow in the prestigious Ascend Program of the Aspen Institute where she is working with twenty other leaders from across the county who are driving innovative ideas and proven strategies to help families achieve education success and economic security. A Latina and native of San Antonio, Texas, Gloria infuses her rich cultural background into her professional involvement with women, families, and people of color. A graduate of Macalester College, she is a recipient of the Ellis Island Medal of Honor, Women of Distinction Award from the Girl Scouts Council of Minnesota and Wisconsin River Valleys, and Citizen of the Year Award from the Minneapolis University Rotary Club.

www.JeremiahProgram.org

Carol Seiler, MA, PHR, WWC, was certified by the Wind and Water School of Feng Shui as a Black Sect Tradition professional in 2007, as a Fashion Feng Shui facilitator by Fashion Feng Shui International in 2008, and in Traditional Compass Feng Shui through the New York School of Feng Shui in 2010. In addition, she has a Master of Arts degree in Leadership, Professional Human Resource certification and has held various positions in human resources and benefits for over thirty years.

www.beyondtheclosetdoor.com

Marilyn Sellars has a soul-stirring voice, the megawatt smile, and the affable personality. An award-winning entertainer, her talent, engaging presence and quick wit have charmed audiences ever since she was little. From country to pop and Broadway to gospel, Marilyn performs it all with captivating style. She displays a special gift for bringing a sense of hope and comfort to audiences the world over. Musical versatility makes Marilyn a sought-after performer in a diverse array of settings: corporate shows, charitable events, celebrity golf tournaments, county and state fairs, telethons, political conventions, sporting events, dinner theatres, churches and senior centers. Time for her family always comes first, but along with her love of reading, cooking and golf, she continues to perform and record with her distinctive blend of effervescence and grace.

www.MarilynSellars.com

Susan St. James is President/CEO of LABRADOR LifeScience, founded November 1998. She has twenty-five years of recruiting experience, but now focuses in life-sciences field. Among her numerous community involvements is being a past member of Washburn Center for Children. She was past chair for Hennepin County Workforce Investment Board. In the past, she volunteered for The Jeremiah Program for Women and Children. Susan's efforts have been recognized by various honors:

- 2008 "Top Most Enterprising Women in Business" recognition
- Past president of National Association of Business Women (NAWBO)
- Finalist in 2010 "Most Ethical Business in Minnesota"
- Listed as one of the Top Diversity Businesses in 2012 by *Diversity Magazine*
- Finalist in Better Business Bureau's "Integrity Award," 2011
- Listed as one of Inc Magazine's "Fastest Growing Companies in America" in 2012

www.LabradorTalent.com

Colleen Szot is the owner and president of Colleen Szot Wonderful Writer, Inc., a highly successful freelance writing company within the infomercial industry. She is the first and only (to date) infomercial writer to be awarded the coveted Clio, the advertising industry's Oscar. She also has several Tellys (recognizing achievement in television advertising), ERA Awards (Electronic Retailing Association) and Addys (the world's largest and most competitive advertising competition) to her credit. Colleen's claim to fame was cemented when she changed the ever-popular line of "Operators standing by" to "If lines are busy, please call again." That one line has been chronicled in numerous publications around the world and been cited by Apple guru, Guy Kawasaki, and Robert B. Cialdini, an expert in social influence. She has also been called "The most successful DRTV writer in the world" by no less than the *Harvard Business Review*. In 1987, She wrote the bestselling book, *Christian Wives: The Women Behind the Evangelists*. Her book broke the infamous Jim Bakker scandal. She was interviewed on Good Morning America and CNN. Her book was written under her maiden name Colleen Todd.

www.wonderfulwriter.com

Sharon Wagner was born in St. Cloud, Minnesota in 1956, ten minutes after her twin sister Karen. She has been married for thirty-seven years to her high-school sweetheart. She worked as a cook for the Anoka Hennepin School District for seventeen years, now is an artist with her own mural and art business.

Molly Cox Ziton is a speaker, humorist, and award-winning film producer and the co-author of the book *Improvise This! How to Think on Your Feet So You Don't Fall on Your Face*. She has contributed to four books, has created several comedic short films and is a member of the National Speakers Association and the National Speakers Association, Minnesota. Some days she's quite successful, while others, not so much.

www.mollyspeaks.com

Gloria VanDemmeltraadt is an energetic grandmother who has survived a number of lifestyle extremes. Her first book, *Musing and Munching*, is both a memoir and detailed cookbook, and is a collection of her own life stories as they relate to food and travel. Her 2013 book, *Memories of Lake Elmo,* is the history of a small town as told in personal stories.

govand@comcast.net

Roxanne Zoet is a retired Senior Master Sergeant from the United States Air Force. She served for twenty-six years before retiring in 2010. While on active duty, Roxanne has traveled the world and deployed in support of several wars. She earned several awards and commendations for her lengthy, honorable service. Since retiring, she has pursued her passion and has become an elementary school teacher. An important aspect of her life is her family, husband, three sons and one daughter.

About Joan Kennedy

Co-Editor and Story Collector

Joan Kennedy is a strong and insightful speaker whose content is rich with personal experiences, optimism, and humor. She continues to draw rave reviews from audiences of all ages, delivering a powerful message that life is for living now, and "The goal for all of us is a life of good health, productivity, fun, and laughter."

Living life and defying the myths of aging, Joan has spent a lifetime battling life's adversities with humor, grit, and joy. Joan published three books. The third book, *What's Age Got to do With It?*, is a quick and inspirational read for anyone eager to change. She also produced several booklets and a CD for babies called Lull-a-Baby, which is a collection of lullabies filled with positive and loving messages.

Joan has spread her philosophy through books and speaking engagements across the country. She has worked with major corporations, health care organizations, conventions and conferences, and groups of all sizes and ages.

Three major factors in living the good life with energy and productivity are simply: Protect your health, at all cost. Have a positive attitude. Keep your dreams alive and set goals for your future.

Joan has spent over 35 years striding across stages with energy and enthusiasm, proudly billing herself as the "oldest female motivational speaker in the country."

For further information about Joan's books and workshops, or to schedule her for a presentation, contact Joan at:

jvkennedy1@aol.com
www.JoanKennedy.com

Made in the USA
Charleston, SC
03 March 2015